Rev. 11/23

# Project Management

## FOR DUMMIES®

### 2ND EDITION

# by Stanley E. Portny

## Certified Project Management Professional (PMP)

BICENTENNIAL
1807
WILEY
2007
BICENTENNIAL

Wiley Publishing, Inc.

**Project Management For Dummies**®, **2nd Edition**

Published by

**Wiley Publishing, Inc.**

111 River St.

Hoboken, NJ 07030-5774

www.wiley.com

**LIMIT OF LIABILITY/DISCLAIMER OF WARRANTY: THE PUBLISHER AND THE AUTHOR MAKE NO REPRESENTATIONS OR WARRANTIES WITH RESPECT TO THE ACCURACY OR COMPLETENESS OF THE CONTENTS OF THIS WORK AND SPECIFICALLY DISCLAIM ALL WARRANTIES, INCLUDING WITHOUT LIMITATION WARRANTIES OF FITNESS FOR A PARTICULAR PURPOSE. NO WARRANTY MAY BE CREATED OR EXTENDED BY SALES OR PROMOTIONAL MATERIALS. THE ADVICE AND STRATEGIES CONTAINED HEREIN MAY NOT BE SUITABLE FOR EVERY SITUATION. THIS WORK IS SOLD WITH THE UNDERSTANDING THAT THE PUBLISHER IS NOT ENGAGED IN RENDERING LEGAL, ACCOUNTING, OR OTHER PROFESSIONAL SERVICES. IF PROFESSIONAL ASSISTANCE IS REQUIRED, THE SERVICES OF A COMPETENT PROFESSIONAL PERSON SHOULD BE SOUGHT. NEITHER THE PUBLISHER NOR THE AUTHOR SHALL BE LIABLE FOR DAMAGES ARISING HEREFROM. THE FACT THAT AN ORGANIZATION OR WEBSITE IS REFERRED TO IN THIS WORK AS A CITATION AND/OR A POTENTIAL SOURCE OF FURTHER INFORMATION DOES NOT MEAN THAT THE AUTHOR OR THE PUBLISHER ENDORSES THE INFORMATION THE ORGANIZATION OR WEBSITE MAY PROVIDE OR RECOMMENDATIONS IT MAY MAKE. FURTHER, READERS SHOULD BE AWARE THAT INTERNET WEBSITES LISTED IN THIS WORK MAY HAVE CHANGED OR DISAPPEARED BETWEEN WHEN THIS WORK WAS WRITTEN AND WHEN IT IS READ.**

WILEY

# About the Author

 **Stanley E. Portny,** president of Stanley E. Portny and Associates, LLC, is an internationally recognized expert in project management and project leadership. During the past 30 years, he's provided training and consultation to more than 120 public and private organizations in fields such as finance, consumer products, insurance, pharmaceuticals, information technology, telecommunications, defense, and health care. He has developed and conducted training programs for more than 30,000 management and staff personnel in engineering, sales and marketing, research and development, information systems, manufacturing, operations and support areas.

Stan combines an analyst's eye with an innate sense of order and balance and a deep respect for personal potential. He helps people understand how to control chaotic environments and produce dramatic results while still achieving personal and professional satisfaction. Widely acclaimed for his dynamic presentations and unusual ability to establish a close rapport with seminar participants, Stan specializes in tailoring his training programs to meet the unique needs of individual organizations. His clients have included ADP, ADT, American International Group, Burlington Northern Railroad, Hewlett Packard, Nabisco, Novartis Pharmaceuticals, Pitney Bowes, UPS, Vanguard Investment Companies, and the United States Navy and Air Force.

A Project Management Institute–certified Project Management Professional (PMP), Stan received his bachelor's degree in electrical engineering from the Polytechnic Institute of Brooklyn. He holds a master's degree in electrical engineering and the degree of electrical engineer from the Massachusetts Institute of Technology. Stan has also studied at the Alfred P. Sloan School of Management and the George Washington University National Law Center.

Stan provides on-site training in all aspects of project management, project team-building and project leadership. He can work with you to assess your organization's current project-management practices, develop planning- and control-systems and procedures, and review the progress of ongoing projects. In addition, Stan can serve as the keynote speaker at your organization's or professional association's meetings.

To discuss this book or understand how Stan can work with you to enhance your organization's project-management skills and practices, please contact him at Stanley E. Portny and Associates, LLC, 20 Helene Drive, Randolph, New Jersey 07869; phone 973-366-8500; fax 973-366-0077; e-mail Stan@StanPortny.com; Web site www.StanPortny.com.

# Dedication

To my wife, Donna, and my sons, Jonathan and Brian. May we continue to share life's joys together.

# Author's Acknowledgments

Writing and publishing this book was a team effort, and I would like to thank the many people who helped to make this possible. First, I want to thank Tracy Boggier, my acquisitions editor, who first contacted me to discuss the possibility of my writing this second edition of my book. Thanks to her for that phone call, for helping me prepare the proposal, for helping to get the project off to a smooth and timely start, for coordinating the publicity and sales, and for helping to bring all the pieces to a successful conclusion.

Thanks to Chad Sievers, my project editor, and Pam Ruble, my copy editor, for their guidance, support, and the many hours they spent polishing the text into a smooth, finished product.

Finally, thanks to my family for their continued help and inspiration. Thanks to Donna, who never doubted that this book would become a reality and who shared personal and stylistic comments as she reviewed the text countless times while always making it seem that she found it enjoyable and enlightening. Thanks to Jonathan and Brian, whose interest and excitement helped to motivate me to see this book through to its completion.

## Publisher's Acknowledgments

We're proud of this book; please send us your comments through our Dummies online registration form located at `www.dummies.com/register/`.

Some of the people who helped bring this book to market include the following:

*Acquisitions, Editorial, and Media Development*

**Project Editor:** Chad R. Sievers

*(Previous Edition: Tere Drenth)*

**Acquisitions Editor:** Tracy Boggier

*(Previous Edition: Holly McGuire)*

**Copy Editor:** Pam Ruble

**Technical Editor:** Jeffrey K. Pinto, PhD

**Editorial Manager:** Michelle Hacker

**Editorial Assistants:** Erin Calligan, Joe Niesen, David Lutton

**Cartoons:** Rich Tennant (`www.the5thwave.com`)

*Composition Services*

**Project Coordinator:** Patrick Redmond and Heather Kolter

**Layout and Graphics:** Carl Byers, Lavonne Cook, Barry Offringa, Lynsey Osborn, Alicia B. South

**Anniversary Logo Design:** Richard Pacifico

**Proofreaders:** Techbooks, John Greenough, Brian H. Walls

**Indexer:** Techbooks

---

**Publishing and Editorial for Consumer Dummies**

> **Diane Graves Steele,** Vice President and Publisher, Consumer Dummies
>
> **Joyce Pepple,** Acquisitions Director, Consumer Dummies
>
> **Kristin A. Cocks,** Product Development Director, Consumer Dummies
>
> **Michael Spring,** Vice President and Publisher, Travel
>
> **Kelly Regan,** Editorial Director, Travel

**Publishing for Technology Dummies**

> **Andy Cummings,** Vice President and Publisher, Dummies Technology/General User

**Composition Services**

> **Gerry Fahey,** Vice President of Production Services
>
> **Debbie Stailey,** Director of Composition Services

# Contents at a Glance

# Table of Contents

# Introduction

· · · · · · · · · · · · · · · · · · · · · · · · · · · · · · · · · · · · · · · · ·

*P*rojects have been around since ancient times. Noah building the ark, Leonardo da Vinci painting the *Mona Lisa,* Edward Gibbon writing *The Decline and Fall of the Roman Empire,* Jonas Salk developing the polio vaccine — all projects. And, as you know, these have been masterful successes. (Well, the products were a spectacular success, even if schedules and resource budgets were drastically overrun!)

Why, then, is the topic of project management of such great interest today? The answer is simple: The audience has changed and the stakes are higher.

Historically, projects were large, complex undertakings. The first project to use modern project-management techniques — the Polaris weapons system in the early 1950s — was a technical and administrative nightmare. Teams of specialists planned and tracked the myriad of research, development, and production activities. And they produced mountains of paper to document the intricate work. As a result, people started to view project management as a highly technical discipline with confusing charts and graphs; they saw it as inordinately time-consuming, specialist-driven, and definitely off-limits for the common man or woman!

Because the world has a growing array of huge, complex, and technically challenging projects, people are still needed who want to devote their careers to planning and managing them. But over the past 15 to 20 years, the number of projects in the regular workplace has skyrocketed. Projects of all types and sizes are now *the* way that organizations accomplish their work.

At the same time, a new breed of project manager has emerged. These people may not have set career goals to become project managers — many don't even consider themselves to be project managers. But they do know they must successfully manage projects in order to move ahead in their careers. In other words, project management has become a critical skill, not a career choice.

Even though these people are realizing they need special tools, techniques, and knowledge to handle their new types of assignments, they may not be able or willing to devote large amounts of time to acquiring them. I devote this book to that silent majority of project managers.

# About This Book

This book helps you recognize that the basic tenets of successful project management are simple. The most *complex* analytical technique takes less than ten minutes to master! In this book, I introduce information that's necessary to plan and manage projects, and I provide important guidelines for developing and using this information. You discover that the real challenge to a successful project is dealing with the multitude of people whom a project may affect or need for support. I present plenty of tips, hints, and guidelines for identifying key players and then involving them.

But knowledge alone won't make you a successful project manager — you need to apply it. This book's theme is that project-management skills and techniques aren't burdensome tasks you perform because some process requires it. Rather, they're a way of thinking, communicating, and behaving. They're an integral part of how we approach all aspects of our work every day.

So I've written the book to be direct and (relatively) easy to understand. But don't be misled — the simple text still navigates all the critical tools and techniques you'll need to support your project planning, scheduling, budgeting, organizing, and controlling. So buckle up!

I present this information in a logical and modular progression. Examples and illustrations are plentiful — so are the tips and hints. And I inject humor from time to time to keep it all doable. My goal is that you finish this book feeling that good project management is a necessity and that you're determined to practice it!

# Conventions Used in This Book

To help you navigate through this book, I use the following conventions to help you find your way:

- Every time I introduce a new word, I *italicize* it and then define it.
- I use **bold** text to indicate keywords in bulleted lists or to highlight action parts in numbered lists.
- I put all Web sites in `monofont`.

# What You're Not to Read

Of course, I want you to read every single word, but I understand your life is busy and you may only have time to read what's relevant to your experience.

In that case, feel free to skip the sidebars. Although the sidebars offer interesting and real-life stories of my own experiences, they're not vital to grasping the concepts. If you do have the time though, read them for some interesting anecdotes.

# Foolish Assumptions

When writing this book, I've assumed a widely diverse group of people will read it, including the following:

- ✔ Senior managers and junior assistants (the senior managers of tomorrow)
- ✔ Experienced project managers and people who've never been on a project team
- ✔ People who've had significant project-management training and people who've had none
- ✔ People who've had years of real-world business and government experience and people who've just entered the workforce

I assume that you have a desire to take control of your environment. After reading this book, I hope you wonder (and rightfully so) why all projects aren't well managed — because you'll think these techniques are so logical, straightforward, and easy to use. But I also assume you recognize there's a big difference between *knowing* what to do and *doing* it. And I assume you realize you'll have to work hard to overcome the forces that conspire to prevent you from using these tools and techniques.

Finally, I assume you'll realize that you can read this book repeatedly and learn something new and different each time, thinking of this book as a friend or a comfortable resource that has more to share, as you read between the lines and experience new situations.

# How This Book Is Organized

Like every other *For Dummies* book, each chapter is self-contained, so you can read the chapters first that interest you the most. The book is divided into the following six parts.

# Part I: Understanding Expectations (The Who, What, and Why of Your Project)

In this part, I discuss the unique characteristics of projects and key issues that you may encounter in a project-oriented organization. I also show you how to clearly define your project's proposed results, how to identify the people who will play a role, and how to determine your project's work.

# Part II: Determining When and How Much

In this part, I cover how to develop the project schedule and estimate the resources you need. I also show you how to identify and manage project risks.

# Part III: Putting Your Team Together

I show you how to identify, organize, and deal with people who play a part in your project's success. I explain how to define team members' roles and get your project off to a positive start.

# Part IV: Steering the Ship: Managing Your Project to Success

In this part, I explain how to monitor, track, analyze, and report on your project's activities. Then I discuss how to bring your project to a successful closure.

# Part V: Taking Your Project Management to the Next Level

I discuss how to deal with a multiple-project environment, use available technology to help you plan, organize and control your project, and introduce your new project-management skills and knowledge into your environment. I also discuss a technique for evaluating activity performance and resource expenditures on larger projects.

## Part VI: The Part of Tens

Every *For Dummies* book has this fun part that gives you tidbits of information in an easy-to-chew format. In this part, I share tips on how to plan a project and how to be a better project manager. This part also has two additional nuggets of information: Appendix A is a comprehensive list of the most common project-management terms and definitions, and Appendix B is an illustration of the steps for planning your project and for using the essential controls that I discuss throughout the book.

# Icons Used in This Book

I include small icons in the left margins of the book to alert you to special information in the text. Here's what they mean:

This icon highlights techniques or approaches to improve your project-management practices.

I use this icon to point out project-management terms or issues that are a bit more technical.

This icon leads into real-world and hypothetical situations illustrating techniques and issues.

This icon highlights potential pitfalls and danger spots.

I use this icon to show important information to keep in mind as you apply the techniques and approaches.

# Where to Go from Here

You can read this book in many ways, depending on your own project-management knowledge and experience and your current needs. However, I suggest you first take a minute to scan the Table of Contents and thumb through the sections of the book to get a feeling for the topics I address.

If you're new to project management and are just beginning to form a plan for a project, first read Parts I and II, which explain how to plan outcomes, activities, schedules, and resources. If you want to find out how to identify and organize your project's team and other key people, start with Chapter 4 and Part III. If you're ready to begin work or you're already in the midst of your project, you may want to start with Part IV. Or, feel free to jump back and forth, hitting the chapters with topics that interest you the most.

The most widely recognized reference of project-management best practices is *A Guide to the Project Management Body of Knowledge (PMBOK),* published by the Project Management Institute (PMI). The Project Management Professional (PMP) certification — the most recognized project-management credential throughout the world — includes an examination (administered by PMI) with questions based on PMBOK.

Because I base my book on best practices for project-management activities, the tools and techniques I offer are in accordance with the most recent version of PMBOK. However, if you're preparing to take the PMP examination, use my book as a companion to PMBOK, not as a substitute for it.

The two books have some significant differences.

- ✔ First and foremost, PMBOK identifies *what* best practices are but doesn't address in detail *how* to perform them or deal with difficulties you may encounter as you try to perform them. In contrast, my book focuses heavily on *how* to perform the project-management techniques and processes.

- ✔ Second, PMBOK often contains highly technical language and detailed processes, which people mistakenly dismiss as requirements for larger projects. My book, however, deliberately frames terms and discussions to be user-friendly. As a result, people who work on projects of all sizes can understand how to apply the tools and techniques presented.

In any case, plan on reading all the chapters more than once — the more you read a chapter, the more sense its approaches and techniques will make. And who knows? A change in your job responsibilities may create a need for certain techniques you've never used before. Have fun and good luck!

# Part I

# Understanding Expectations (The Who, What, and Why of Your Project)

## In this part . . .

The most difficult part of a new project often is deciding where to begin. Expectations are high, while time and resources are frequently low.

In this part, I identify how a project differs from other activities you perform in your organization, and I present a snapshot of the steps you take to plan, organize, and control your project. I offer you specific techniques and approaches to clearly define what you want your project to accomplish and who needs to be involved. Finally, I show you how to determine the work you'll have to do to meet the expectations for your project.

# Chapter 1

# Project Management: The Key to Achieving Results

● ● ● ● ● ● ● ● ● ● ● ● ● ● ● ● ● ● ● ● ● ● ● ● ● ● ● ● ● ● ● ● ● ● ● ● ● ● ● ● ● ● ● ● ● ● ● ● ●

*In This Chapter*

▶ Distinguishing projects

▶ Breaking down project management

▶ Coming to grips with the project manager's role

▶ Cycling through the phases of a project

▶ Eyeing potential problems with your project

▶ Examining the requirements for project success

● ● ● ● ● ● ● ● ● ● ● ● ● ● ● ● ● ● ● ● ● ● ● ● ● ● ● ● ● ● ● ● ● ● ● ● ● ● ● ● ● ● ● ● ● ● ● ● ●

**S**uccessful organizations create projects that produce desired results in established time frames with assigned resources. As a result, businesses are increasingly driven to find individuals who can excel in this project-oriented environment.

Because you're reading this book, chances are good that you've been asked to manage a project. So, hang on tight — you're going to need a new set of skills and techniques to steer that project to successful completion. But not to worry! This chapter gets you off to a smooth start by showing you what projects and project management really are and helping you separate projects from nonproject assignments. The chapter also offers the rationale for why projects succeed or fail and gets you into the project-management mindset.

## What Exactly Is a Project?

No matter what your job, you handle a myriad of assignments every day: prepare a memo, hold a meeting, design a sales campaign, or move to new offices. Or maybe your day sounds more like this: make the information systems more user-friendly, develop a research compound in the laboratory, or improve the organization's public image. Not all of these assignments are projects. How can you tell which ones are? This section can help.

Large or small, a project always has the following ingredients:

✔ **Specific outcomes:** Products or results (check out Chapter 2 for more on describing desired results)

✔ **Definite start and end dates:** Projects don't go on forever (refer to Chapter 5 for developing a schedule for your project)

✔ **Established budgets:** Required amounts of people (see Chapter 6), funds (see Chapter 7), equipment (see Chapter 7), facilities (see Chapter 7), and information (see Chapter 7)

Each ingredient affects the other two. Expanding specific outcomes may require more time (a later end date) or more resources. Moving up the end date may necessitate paring down the results or increasing project expenditures (exceeding the established budgets) by paying overtime to project staff. Within this three-part project definition, you perform work to achieve your desired results.

Projects come in a wide assortment of shapes and sizes:

✔ **Large or small**

- Installing a new subway system, which may cost more than $1 billion and take 10 to 15 years to complete, is a project

- Preparing a report of monthly sales figures, which may take you one day to complete, is a project

✔ **Involving many people or just you**

- Training all 10,000 of your organization's staff in a new affirmative-action policy is a project

- Rearranging the furniture and equipment in your office is a project

✔ **Defined by a legal contract or an informal agreement**

- A signed contract between you and a customer that requires you to build a house defines a project

- An informal promise you make to install a new software package on your colleague's computer defines a project

✔ **Business-related or personal**

- Conducting your organization's annual blood drive is a project

- Having a dinner party for 15 people is a project

No matter what the individual characteristics of your project are, you define it by the same three ingredients: outcomes, start and end dates, and resources. The information you need to plan and manage your project is the same, although the ease and the time to develop it may differ. The more thoroughly you plan and manage your projects, the more likely you are to succeed.

PROJECT PARLANCE

## A project by any other name — just isn't a project

People often confuse two other terms with *project:*

✔ A *process* is a series of routine steps to perform a particular function, such as a procurement process or a budget process. A process isn't a one-time activity that achieves a specific result; instead it defines *how* a particular function is to be done every time. Processes like the activities to buy materials are often parts of projects.

✔ A *program* can describe two different situations. First, it's a set of goals that gives rise to specific projects but it can never be completely accomplished. A health-awareness program and an employee-morale program are examples. These programs never completely achieve their goal (for example, the public will never be totally aware of all health issues as a result of a health-awareness program), but one or more projects may accomplish specific results related to the program's goal (such as a workshop on minimizing the risk of heart disease). Second, a program sometimes refers to a group of specified projects that achieve a common goal.

# Defining Project Management

*Project management* is the process of guiding a project from its beginning through its performance to its closure. Project management includes three basic operations:

✔ **Planning:** Specifying the desired results, determining the schedules, and estimating the resources

✔ **Organizing:** Defining people's roles and responsibilities

✔ **Controlling:** Reconfirming people's expected performances, monitoring actions and results, addressing problems, and sharing information with interested people

Successfully performing these activities requires:

✔ **Information:** Accurate, timely, and complete data for the planning, performance monitoring, and final assessment

✔ **Communication:** Clear, open, and timely sharing of information with appropriate individuals and groups

✔ **Commitment:** Team members' personal promises to produce the agreed-upon results on time and within budget

Projects are temporary, created to achieve particular results. So when the results are achieved, the project should end. But this transitory nature of projects may create some challenges such as the following:

- **Additional assignments:** Project managers may be asked to accept a new project in addition to — not in lieu of — existing assignments. And they may not be asked how the new work may affect their existing projects. (Higher management may just assume the project manager can handle it all.) When conflicts arise over a person's time, the guidelines or procedures to resolve those conflicts may not exist or may be inadequate.

- **New people on new teams:** On small projects, project managers often seek the help of other people. But on larger efforts, people who haven't worked together before may be formally assigned to a project team. In fact, some people may not even know each other. These unfamiliar relationships may slow the project down because team members may

  - Have different operating and communicating styles.

  - Use different procedures for performing the same type of activity.

  - Not have had the time to develop mutual respect and trust.

- **No direct authority:** For most projects, the project manager and team members have no direct authority over each other. Therefore, the rewards that usually encourage top performance (such as salary increases, superior performance appraisals, and job promotions) aren't available. In addition, conflicts over time commitments or technical direction may require input from a number of sources. As a result, they can't be settled with one, unilateral decision.

# Knowing the Project Manager's Role

The project manager's job is challenging. She often coordinates technically specialized professionals — who may have limited experience working together — to achieve a common goal. The project manager's own work experience is often technical in nature, yet her success requires a keen ability to identify and resolve sensitive organizational and interpersonal issues.

## Looking at the project manager's tasks

Historically, the performance rules in traditional organizations were simple: Your boss made assignments; you carried them out. Questioning your assignments was a sign of insubordination or incompetence.

But these rules have changed. Today, your boss may generate ideas, but you assess how to implement them. You confirm that a project meets his real need and then determine the necessary work, schedules, and resources.

It doesn't make sense to handle a project any other way. The project manager must be involved in developing the plans because she needs the opportunity to clarify expectations and proposed approaches and then raise any questions.

The key to project success is to be proactive. Instead of waiting for others to tell you what to do,

- ✔ Seek out information because you know you need it.
- ✔ Follow the plan because you believe it's the best way.
- ✔ Involve people who you know are important for the project.
- ✔ Raise issues and risks, analyze them, and elicit support to address them.
- ✔ Share information with the people you know should have it.
- ✔ Put all important information in writing.
- ✔ Commit to your project's success; ask and expect other people to do the same.

## *Staving off potential excuses*

Be prepared for other people to fight your attempts to be proactive. And trust me, you'll have to be prepared for everything! This short section provides a few examples of excuses that you may encounter as a project manager and the appropriate responses you can give to keep the project on track.

- ✔ **Excuse:** Our projects are all crises; we have no time to plan.

  **Response:** Unfortunately, this logic is illogical! In a crisis, you can't afford not to plan. Why? Because you have a critical situation that you have to address with limited time and resources. You can't afford to make mistakes. And acting under pressure and emotion (the two characteristics of crises) practically guarantees that mistakes will occur.

- ✔ **Excuse:** Structured project management is only for large projects.

  **Response:** No matter what size the project, the information you need to perform it is the same. What are you to produce? What work has to be done? Who's going to do it? When will it end? Have you met expectations?

  Large projects may require many weeks or months to develop satisfactory answers to these questions. Small projects that last a few days or less may take 15 minutes. But you still have to answer the questions.

✔ **Excuse:** These projects require creativity and new development. They can't be predicted with any certainty.

**Response:** Some projects are more predictable than others. However, people awaiting the outcomes still have expectations for what they'll get and when. Therefore, a project with many uncertainties needs a manager to develop and share initial plans and then assess and communicate the effects of unexpected occurrences.

You may never encounter these specific excuses or you may encounter them on a regular basis. No matter. Adapt these response examples to address your own situations.

# Considering the Life and Times of Your Project

Do you have a good grasp of what a project manager does and what makes a good project manager? If so, you're ready for the basics of a project. Every project, whether large or small, entails five distinct types of work:

✔ **Conceive:** Coming up with the idea

✔ **Define:** Developing a plan

✔ **Start:** Forming a team

✔ **Perform:** Doing the work

✔ **Close:** Ending the project

For small projects, this entire process can take a few days. Larger projects may take many years! No matter how simple or complex the project, however, the process is the same. (Check out Figure 1-1.)

**Figure 1-1:**
Guide your
project
through the
five phases
of its life.

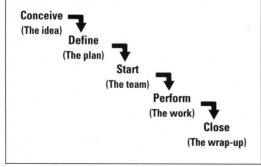

Conceive
(The idea)

Define
(The plan)

Start
(The team)

Perform
(The work)

Close
(The wrap-up)

# The conceive phase: In the beginning . . .

All projects begin with an idea. Perhaps your organization's client identifies a need, or maybe your boss thinks of a new market to explore, or maybe you think of a way to refine your organization's procurement process. When an idea forms, your project has entered the conceive phase.

Sometimes this phase is informal. For a small project it may just consist of a discussion and a verbal agreement. In other instances, especially for larger projects, a project requires a formal review and decision.

Decision-makers consider the following two questions when deciding whether to move ahead with a project:

- ✔ **Should we do it?** Are the benefits we expect to achieve worth the costs we'll have to pay?

- ✔ **Can we do it?** Is the project technically feasible? Are the required resources available?

If the answer to both questions is "Yes," the project can proceed to the define phase (see the following section) where a project plan is developed. If the answer to either question is a definite, iron-clad "No!" then under no circumstances should the project go any farther. If nothing can be done to make it feasible and desirable, it should be cancelled now. Doing anything else guarantees wasted resources, lost opportunities, and a frustrated staff.

Suppose you're in charge of the publications department in your organization. You've just received a request to have a 20,000-page document printed in ten minutes, which requires equipment that can reproduce at the rate of 2,000 pages per minute.

You check with your staff and confirm that your document-reproducing equipment has a top speed of 500 pages per minute. You check with your suppliers and find out that the fastest document-reproducing equipment available today has a top speed of 1,000 pages per minute. Would you agree to plan and perform this project when you can't possibly meet the request? Of course not.

Rather than promising something you know you can't achieve, consider asking your customer whether she can change the request. For example, can she accept the document in 20 minutes? Can you reproduce certain parts of the document in the first 10 minutes and the rest later?

Sometimes you're convinced that you can't meet a request or that the benefits aren't worth the cost. Be sure to check with the people who developed or approved the request. They may have information that you don't, or you may have additional information that they weren't aware of.

# Performing a benefit-cost analysis

A *benefit-cost analysis* is a comparative assessment of all benefits you anticipate from your project with all the costs to introduce the project, perform it, and support the changes resulting from it. Benefit-cost analyses help you to

✔ Decide whether to undertake a project or decide which of several projects to undertake

✔ Frame appropriate project objectives

✔ Develop appropriate *before* and *after* measures of project success

You can express some anticipated benefits in monetary equivalents (such as reduced operating costs or increased revenue). For other benefits, numerical measures can approximate some, but not all, aspects. If your project is to improve staff morale, for example, you may consider associated benefits to include reduced turnover, increased productivity, fewer absences, and fewer formal grievances. But, whenever possible, express benefits and costs in monetary terms to facilitate the assessment of a project's net value.

Consider costs for all phases of the project. Such costs may be nonrecurring (such as labor, capital investment, and certain operations and services) or recurring (such as changes in personnel, supplies, and materials or maintenance and repair). In addition, consider:

✔ The potential costs of not doing the project

✔ The potential costs if the project fails

✔ Opportunity costs (the potential benefits if you had spent your funds successfully performing a different project)

The farther into the future you look when performing your analysis, the more important it is to convert your estimates of benefits over costs into today's dollars. Unfortunately, the farther you look, the less confident you can be of your estimates. For example, you may expect to reap benefits for years from a new computer system, but changing technology may make your new system obsolete after one year.

Therefore, two key factors influence the results of a benefit-cost analysis:

✔ How far into the future you look to identify benefits

✔ The assumptions on which you base your analysis

Although you may not want to go out and design a cost-benefit analysis by yourself, you definitely want to see whether your project already has one and, if so, what the specific results were.

The excess of a project's expected benefits over its estimated costs in today's dollars is its *net present value (NPV)*. The net present value is based on two premises:

✔ **Inflation:** The purchasing power of a dollar will be less one year from now that it is today. If the rate of inflation is 3 percent for the next 12 months, a dollar today will be worth $.97 12 months from today. In other words, 12 months from now, you'll pay $1 to buy what you paid $.97 for today.

✔ **Lost return on investment:** The amount you can earn if you invest your money conservatively today. For example, if you put $1 in a bank and received simple interest at the rate of 3 percent compounded annually, 12 months from today you'll have $1.03 (assuming 0 percent inflation).

To address these considerations when determining net present value, you specify the following numbers:

> ✔ **Discount rate:** The factor that reflects the future value of $1 in today's dollars, considering the effects of both inflation and lost return on investment.
>
> ✔ **Allowable payback period:** The length of time for anticipated benefits and estimated costs.
>
> In addition to determining the NPV for different discount rates and payback periods, figure the project's *internal rate of return* (the value of discount rate that would yield an NPV of 0) for each payback period.

Beware of assumptions that you or other people make when assessing your project's potential value, cost, and feasibility. For example, just because your requests for overtime have been turned down in the past doesn't guarantee they'll be turned down again this time.

## The define phase: Establish the plan

When you know what you hope to accomplish and you believe it's possible, you need a detailed plan to describe how you and your team will make it happen.

Include the following in your project plan:

✔ An overview of the reasons for your project (Chapter 2 tells you what to include)

✔ A detailed description of results (Chapter 2 explains how to describe desired results)

✔ A list of all work (Chapter 4 illustrates how to identify all required project work)

✔ The roles you and your team members will play (Chapter 10 explains how to describe roles and responsibilities)

✔ A detailed project schedule (Chapter 5 explains how to develop your schedule)

✔ Budgets for required personnel, funds, equipment, facilities, and information (Chapter 6 illustrates how to estimate resource needs)

✔ Assumptions (Chapter 2 discusses how to frame assumptions)

In addition, be sure to identify and describe how you plan to manage any significant risks and uncertainties. (Chapter 8 explains how to identify and plan for risks.)

Always put your plans in writing; it helps you to clarify details and reduces the chances that you'll forget something. Plans for large projects can take hundreds of pages, although a plan for a small project can take a few lines on a piece of paper (or a tablecloth!).

The success of your project depends on the clarity and accuracy of your plan and whether people believe they can achieve it. Whenever you consider past experience, your plan is more realistic; and whenever you involve people in the plan's development, you encourage their commitment to achieving it.

Often the pressure to get fast results encourages people to skip the planning and get right to the tasks. This strategy can create a lot of immediate activity, but it also creates significant chances for waste and mistakes.

Be sure your project's drivers and supporters review and approve the plan in writing (see Chapter 3) before you begin your project. For a small project, you may only need a brief e-mail or someone's initials on the plans.

## The start phase: Get ready, get set

Preparing project work requires the following (see Chapter 11 for details):

- **Assigning people to all project roles:** Identify the individuals who'll perform the project work and negotiate agreements to assure they'll be available to work on the project team.

- **Giving and explaining tasks to all team members:** Describe to each team member the work that he or she is to produce and how the team members will coordinate their efforts.

- **Defining how the team will perform the necessary tasks:** Decide how the team will handle routine communications, make different project decisions, and resolve conflicts.

- **Setting up necessary tracking systems:** Decide which system(s) and accounts you'll use to track schedules, work effort, and expenditures.

- **Announcing the project to the organization:** Let the necessary people know that your project exists, what it will produce, and when it will begin and end.

Suppose you don't join your project team until the start phase. Your first task is to understand how people decided (during the conceive phase) that the project was possible and desirable. If people have overlooked important issues, you need to raise them now. When searching for the project's history, check minutes from meetings, memos, letters, e-mails, and technical reports. Then consult with all of the people involved in the decision.

## The perform phase: Go!

Finally you get to perform the project work! This phase entails the following (see Chapters 12, 13, and 14 for more details):

- **Doing the tasks:** Perform the work that's in your plan.
- **Continually comparing performance with plans:** Collect information on outcomes, schedule achievements, and resource expenditures; identify deviations from your plan; and develop corrective actions.
- **Fixing problems that arise:** Change tasks, schedules, or resources to bring project performance back on track with the existing plan, or negotiate agreed-upon changes to the plan itself.
- **Keeping everyone informed:** Tell people about the team's achievements, project problems, and necessary revisions to the established plan.

## The close phase: Stop!

Finishing your assigned tasks is only part of bringing your project to a close. In addition, you must do the following (see Chapter 15 for discussions on each of these points):

- Get your clients' approvals of the final results.
- Close all project accounts (if you've been charging time and money to special project accounts).
- Help people move on to their next assignments.
- Hold a postproject evaluation to recognize project achievements and to discuss lessons you can apply to the next project. (At the very least, make informal notes about these lessons and how you'll use them in the future.) See Chapter 15 for how to prepare, design, and conduct a postproject evaluation.

# Anticipating the Most Common Mistakes

The short-term pressures of your job may encourage you to act today in ways that cause you to pay a price tomorrow. Especially with smaller, less formal projects, you may feel no need for organized planning and control.

Don't be seduced into the following, seemingly-easier shortcuts:

- ✔ **Jumping directly from the conceive phase to the perform phase:** You have an idea and your project's on a short schedule. Why not just start doing the work? Sounds good, but you haven't defined the activities! Other variations on this shortcut include the following:

  - • "Our project's been done many times before, so why do I have to plan it out again?"

    Even though projects can be similar to past ones, some elements are always different. Perhaps you're working with some new people, using a new piece of equipment, and so on. Take a moment now to be sure your plan addresses the current situation.

  - • "Our project's different from before, so what good is trying to plan?"

    This is like saying you're traveling in an unknown area, so why try to lay out your route on a road map? Planning for a new project is important because no one's taken this particular path before. Although your initial plan may have to be revised during the project, you and your team need to have a clear statement of your intended plan.

- ✔ **Omitting the start phase completely:** Time pressure is often the culprit here. People don't appreciate the need to define procedures and relationships before jumping into the actual project work. See Chapter 11 for a discussion of why this phase is so important — and get tips on how to complete it.

- ✔ **Jumping into the work when you join the project during the start phase:** The plan has already been developed, so why go back and revisit the conceive and define phases? Actually, you do this for two reasons:

  - • To identify any issues that the developers may have overlooked

  - • To understand the reasoning behind the plan and decide whether you feel the plan is achievable

- ✔ **Only partially completing the close phase:** At the end of one project, you often move right on to the next. Scarce resources and short deadlines encourage this, and a new project is always more challenging than wrapping up an old one.

However, you never really know how successful your project is if you don't take the time to ensure that all tasks are complete and that you've satisfied your clients. And if you don't take positive steps to apply the lessons this project's taught you, you're likely to make the same mistakes again or fail to repeat this project's successful approaches.

# Do I Have What It Takes to Be an Effective Project Manager?

You're reading this book because you want to be a better project manager. However, before you really jump in, I suggest you do a quick self-evaluation to see what your strengths and weaknesses are. By answering these ten questions, you'll get an idea of what subjects to spend more time on so you can be as effective as possible. Good luck.

## Questions

1. Are you more concerned about being everyone's friend or getting a job done right?

2. Do you prefer to do technical work or manage other people doing technical work?

3. Do you think the best way to get a tough task done is to do it yourself?

4. Do you prefer your work to be predictable or constantly changing?

5. Do you prefer to spend your time developing ideas instead of explaining those ideas to other people?

6. Do you handle crises well?

7. Do you prefer to work by yourself or with others?

8. Do you think you shouldn't have to monitor people after they've promised to do a task for you?

9. Do you believe people should be self-motivated to perform their jobs?

10. Are you comfortable dealing with people at all organizational levels?

## Answers

1. Although maintaining good working relations is important, the project manager often must make decisions for the good of the project that some people don't agree with.

2. Most project managers achieved their position because of their strong performance on technical tasks. However, after you become a project manager, your job is to encourage other people to produce high-quality technical work rather than to do it all yourself.

3. Believing in yourself is important. However, the project manager's task is to help other people develop to the point where they can perform tasks with the highest quality.

4. The project manager tries to minimize unexpected problems and situations through responsive planning and timely control. However, when problems do occur, the project manager must deal with them promptly to minimize their impact on the project.

5. Though coming up with ideas can help your project, the project manager's main responsibility is to ensure everyone correctly understands all ideas that are developed.

6. The project manager's job is to provide a cool head to size up the situation, choose the best action, and encourage all members to do their parts in implementing the solution.

7. Self-reliance and self-motivation are important characteristics for a project manager. However, the key to her success is to facilitate interaction among a diverse group of technical specialists.

8. Although you may feel that honoring one's commitments is a fundamental element of professional behavior, the project manager should ensure that people maintain their focus and should model how to cooperatively work with others.

9. They should be, but the project manager should encourage them to remain motivated by their job assignments and related opportunities.

10. The project manager deals with people at all levels, from upper management to support staff, who perform project-related activities.

# Chapter 2

# Clarifying What You're Trying to Accomplish — and Why

. . . . . . . . . . . . . . . . . . . . . . . . . . . . . . . . . . . . . . . . . . . .

## In This Chapter

▶ Understanding your project's Statement of Work (SOW)

▶ Clarifying the need for the project

▶ Handling the unknowns

▶ Forming your own Statement of Work

. . . . . . . . . . . . . . . . . . . . . . . . . . . . . . . . . . . . . . . . . . . .

All projects are created for a reason. Someone identifies a need and devises a project to address that need. How well the project ultimately addresses that need defines the project's success or failure.

This chapter helps you develop a mutual agreement between the project's requesters and the project team about your project's goals. It also helps you establish the conditions necessary to perform the project work.

## Defining Your Project with a Statement of Work

A *Statement of Work* (SOW) is a written confirmation of what your project will produce and the terms and conditions under which you will perform your work. Both the people who requested the project and the project team should agree to all terms in the SOW before actual project work begins.

# Kissing cousins: Documents closely related to a Statement of Work

Your organization may use a number of other documents that address issues similar to those in the Statement of Work (SOW). If you use these as sources of information to prepare or describe your project plan, be careful to note how they differ from your SOW.

✔ **Market requirements document:** A formal request to develop or modify a product. This document (typically a member of your organization's sales and marketing group prepares it) may lead to the creation of a project. However, in its original form, this document only reflects the *desires* of the person who wrote it. It doesn't reflect an assessment of whether it's possible or in the company's best interest to meet the request, nor is it a commitment to meet it.

✔ **Business requirements document:** A description of the business needs that a requested product, service, or system must address.

✔ **Project request:** A written request for a project by a group within the organization. The project request indicates a desire for a project rather than a mutual agreement and commitment to perform it.

✔ **Project charter:** A document issued by upper management that formally establishes a project and authorizes the project manager to use organizational resources to perform project activities.

✔ **Project profile:** Highlights of key information about a project. Sometimes this is also called a *project summary* or a *project abstract.*

✔ **Work order:** A written description of work that people or groups within your organization will perform in support of your project. The signed work order focuses on work performance rather than overall project outcomes.

✔ **Contract:** A legal agreement for goods or services from an external vendor or contractor. On occasion, the term *Statement of Work* refers to the part of a contract that describes these goods and services.

Your SOW includes the following information:

✔ **Purpose:** How and why your project came to be, the scope of your project, and its general approach

✔ **Objectives:** Specific outcomes you'll produce

✔ **Constraints:** Restrictions that will limit what you achieve, how and when you can achieve it, and their cost

✔ **Assumptions:** Statements about how you will address uncertain information as you conceive, plan, and perform your project

Think of your SOW as a binding agreement.

- ✔ You and your team commit to producing certain results.

  Your project's requesters commit that they'll consider your project 100 percent successful if you produce these results.

- ✔ You and your team identify all restrictions regarding your approach to the work and what you need to support your work.

  Your project's requesters agree there are no restrictions other than the ones you have identified and that they'll provide you the support you declare you need.

- ✔ You and your team identify all assumptions you made when agreeing to the terms of your SOW.

Of course, predicting the future is impossible. In fact, the farther into the future you try to look, the less certain your predictions can be. However, your SOW represents your project commitments based on what you know today and expect to be true in the future. If and when situations change, you'll assess the effect of the changes on your SOW and propose the necessary corresponding changes to your project. Your project's requesters always have the option of accepting your proposed changes (allowing the project to continue) or canceling your project.

# *Looking at the Big Picture: How Your Project Fits In*

Understanding the situation and thought processes that led to your project helps ensure that your project successfully meets people's expectations. Your project's *purpose statement* should include the following information:

- ✔ **Background:** Why people authorized your project
- ✔ **Scope:** What work will be performed
- ✔ **Strategy:** How you'll approach the major work of this project

This section helps you identify all the people who may use your project's results and their specific expectations, needs, and interests. The section also helps you clarify the extent of the project's work and describe your strategies for accomplishing major project activities.

# Figuring out why you're doing this project

When you take on a project, *why* you're doing it may seem obvious — because your boss told you to. The real question, though, is not why you choose to accept the assignment but why the project must be done in the first place.

The following sections help you identify people who may benefit from your project so you can then determine their specific expectations and needs regarding the project.

## Identifying the initiator

As your first task, determine who had the original idea that led to your project. Project success requires that, at a minimum, you meet this person's needs and expectations.

Identifying your project's initiator is easy when he directly assigns it to you. More likely, however, the person who assigns the project is passing along an assignment he received from someone else. If your project has passed through several people before it reaches you, you may have difficulty determining who really had the initial idea. Further, the original intent may have become blurred if every person in the chain purposely or inadvertently changed the assignment a little as he passed it on.

Take the following steps to determine who came up with the original idea for your project.

1. **Ask the person who assigns you the project whether she originated the idea.**

2. **If that person's didn't initiate the idea, ask:**

   Who gave her the assignment?

   Who else, if anyone, was involved in passing the assignment to her?

   Who had the original idea for the project?

3. **Check with any other people you identified in Step 2 and ask them the same questions.**

4. **Check the following written records that may confirm who originally had the idea:**

   Minutes from division-, department-, and organization-wide planning and budget sessions

   Correspondence and e-mail referring to the project

   Reports of planning or feasibility studies

A *feasibility study* is a formal investigation to determine the likely success of performing certain work or achieving certain results.

In addition to helping you identify the people who initiated your project, these sources may shed light on what these people hope to get from it.

5. **Consult with people who may be affected by or need to support your project; they may know who originated the idea.**

Identify your project initiator by name and position description. In other words, don't write "The sales department requested promotional literature for product Alpha," but write "Mary Smith, the sales representative for the northeast region, requested promotional literature for product Alpha."

Distinguish between drivers and supporters as you seek to find your project initiator. (See Chapter 3 for more information about drivers and supporters.)

✔ *Drivers* have some say when defining the results of the project. They tell you what you *should* do.

✔ *Supporters* help you perform your project. They tell you what you *can* do.

For example, suppose the vice president of finance requests a project to upgrade the organization's financial information systems — she's a project driver. The manager of the computer center must provide staff and resources to upgrade the organization's information systems — he's a project supporter.

Sometimes supporters claim to be drivers. For example, when the manager of the computer center is asked, he may say he initiated the project. In reality, the manager authorized the people and funds to perform the project, but the vice president of finance initiated it.

## *Recognizing other people who may benefit from your project*

Although they may not have initiated the idea, other people may benefit from your completed project. They may be people who work with, support, or are clients of your project's drivers, or they may have performed similar projects. They may have expressed interests or needs in areas addressed by your project in meetings, correspondence, or informal conversations.

Identify these people as soon as possible to determine their particular needs and interests and how you can appropriately address them. These additional audiences may include people who

✔ Know the project exists and have expressed an interest in it.

✔ Know it exists but don't realize it can benefit them.

✔ Are unaware of your project.

Identify these additional audiences by

- ✔ Reviewing all written materials related to your project.
- ✔ Consulting with your project's drivers and supporters.
- ✔ Encouraging everyone that you speak to about the project to identify others they think may benefit from it.

As you identify people who can benefit from your project, also identify people who strongly oppose it. Figure out why they oppose your project and whether you can address their concerns. Take the time to determine whether they may be able to derive any benefits from your project and, if so, explain these benefits to them. If they continue to oppose your project, make note in your risk-management plan of their opposition and how you plan to deal with it (see Chapter 8 for how to analyze and plan for project risks and uncertainties).

### Distinguishing the project champion

A *project champion* is a person in a high position in the organization who strongly supports your project; advocates for your project in disputes, planning meetings, and review sessions; and takes necessary actions to help ensure that your project is successful. (See Chapter 3 for more discussion about a project champion.)

Sometimes the best champion is one whose support you never have to use. Just knowing that this person supports your project helps other people appreciate its importance and encourages them to work diligently to ensure its success.

Check with your project's drivers and supporters to find out whether your project already has a champion. If it doesn't, work hard to recruit one by looking for people who can reap benefits from your project and who have sufficient power and influence to encourage serious, ongoing organizational commitment to your project. Explain to these people why the success of your project is in their best interest and how you may need their specific help as your project progresses. Assess how interested they are in your project and how much help they're willing to provide.

### Considering people who'll implement the results of your project

Most projects create a product or service to achieve a desired result. Often, however, the person who asks you to create the product or service isn't the one who'll actually use it.

Suppose your organization's director of sales and marketing wants to increase annual sales by 10 percent in the next fiscal year. She decides that developing and introducing a new product, XYZ, will allow her to achieve this goal. However, she won't actually go to all of your organization's customers and sell them XYZ; her sales staff will. Even though they didn't come up with the idea to develop XYZ, the sales staff may have strong opinions about the characteristics XYZ should have — and so will the customers who ultimately buy (or don't buy!) the product.

To identify the users of project products and services, try to

- ✔ Clarify the products and services that you anticipate producing.
- ✔ Identify exactly who will use these products and services and how they'll use them.

After you identify these people, consult with them to determine any additional interests or needs they may have that your project should also address.

### Determining your project drivers' real expectations and needs

The needs that your project addresses may not always be obvious. Suppose, for example, that your organization decides to sponsor a blood drive. Does this project address the shortage of blood in the local hospital or does it improve your organization's image in the local community?

When you clearly understand the needs your project must satisfy, you can

- ✔ Choose project activities that enable you to accomplish the true desired results (see Chapter 4 for information on identifying project activities).
- ✔ Monitor performance during and at the end of the project to ensure that you're meeting the real needs (see Chapter 12 for more information on how to track a project during performance).
- ✔ Realize when the project isn't meeting the real needs and suggest modifying or canceling it.

You hope that you're told what the project should produce and the needs it should address when you're initially assigned the project. However, usually you're told what to produce (the outcomes), and you have to figure out the needs yourself. Check out the sidebar "Know your project's true measure of success" in this chapter for an example.

Consider the following questions as you work to define the needs:

- ✔ **What needs do people want your project to address?** Don't worry at this point whether your project actually can address these needs or whether it's the best way to address the needs. You're just trying to identify the hopes and expectations that led up to this project.
- ✔ **How do you know that the needs you identify are the real hopes and expectations that people have for your project?** Determining people's real thoughts and feelings can be difficult. Sometimes they don't want to share them; sometimes they don't know how to express them clearly.

When speaking with people to determine the needs your project should address, try the following suggestions:

- ✔ Encourage them to speak at length about their needs and expectations.
- ✔ Listen carefully for any contradictions
- ✔ Encourage them to clarify vague ideas.
- ✔ Try to confirm your information from two or more sources.

See whether your organization performed a formal benefit-cost analysis for your project. A *benefit-cost analysis* (see Chapter 1 for further details) is a formal identification and assessment of

- ✔ The benefits anticipated from your project
- ✔ The costs for

    • Performing your project

    • Using and supporting the products or services produced by your project

The benefit-cost analysis documents the results that people were counting on when they decided to proceed with your project. Therefore, the analysis is an important source for the real needs that your project should address.

---

## Know your project's true measure of success

A friend of mine received an assignment to develop a new product from his boss, who had just returned from an upper-management retreat. Max knew that company sales had been dipping and that the purpose of the retreat was to discuss possible approaches for reversing the trend. He also knew that the company's highly skilled market-research department had been investigating new product ideas for the past six months. Max assumed, therefore, that upper management had established this project to increase sales in the coming year, based on recommendations from the market research department.

Max's conclusion was reasonable but completely wrong. In reality, right before the retreat, the company president had received a call from a friend who asked whether the company marketed a product like XYZ. Instead of admitting that his company wasn't state-of-the-art, the president promised to provide the product. In fact, no one had any idea whether anyone other than the president's friend would ever buy the product! When Max found out the truth, he realized that this project's true measure of success was the president's friend's reaction to XYZ — not the sales increase as a result of introducing XYZ into the company's product line.

### Assuring that your project addresses people's needs

Although needs may be thoroughly documented, you may have difficulty determining whether your project can successfully address those needs. On occasion, companies fund formal feasibility studies to determine whether a project can successfully address a particular need.

Other times, however, your project may be the result of a brainstorming session or someone's creative vision. In this case, you may have less confidence that your project can accomplish expected results. Don't automatically reject a project at this point but aggressively determine the chances for success and how you can increase these chances. If you can't find sufficient information to support your analysis, consider asking for a formal feasibility study.

If you feel the risk of project failure is too great, share your concerns with the key decision makers and explain why you recommend not proceeding. See the discussion of risk management in Chapter 8 for more information.

### Uncovering other activities that relate to your project

Your project doesn't exist in a vacuum. It may require results from other projects, it may generate products that other projects will use, and it may address needs that other projects also address. You should identify projects related to yours as soon as possible so you can coordinate the use of shared personnel and resources and minimize unintended overlap in project activities and results.

### Emphasizing the importance of your project to the organization

How much importance the organization places on your project directly influences the chances for your project's success. When conflicting demands for scarce resources arise, resources usually go to those projects that can produce the greatest benefits for the organization.

Your project's perceived value depends on its intended benefits and people's awareness of those benefits. Take the following steps to help people understand how your project will support the organization's priorities:

✔ **Look for existing statements that confirm your project's support of organization's priorities.** Consult the following sources to find out more about your organization's priorities:

- **Long-range plan:** A formal report that identifies your organization's overall direction, specific performance targets, and individual initiatives for the next one to five years

- **Annual budget:** The detailed list of categories and individual initiatives that require organization funds during the year

- **Capital appropriations plan:** The itemized list of all planned expenditures (over an established minimum amount) for facilities and equipment purchases, renovations, and repairs during the year

- **Your organization's Key Performance Indicators (KPIs):** Performance measures that describe your organization's progress towards its goals

When you review these documents, note whether your project or its intended outcome is specifically mentioned.

In addition, determine whether your organization has made specific commitments to external customers or upper management related to your project's completion.

✔ **Describe in the Background portion of your purpose statement how your project relates to the organization's priorities.** Include existing discussions of your project from the information sources mentioned previously. If your project isn't specifically referenced in these sources, prepare a written explanation of how your project and its results will impact the organization's priorities.

Occasionally you may find it difficult to identify specific results that people expect your project to generate. Perhaps the person who initiated the project has assumed different responsibilities and no longer has any interest in it, or maybe the original need the project was designed to address has changed. If people have trouble telling you how your project will help your organization, ask them what would happen if you didn't perform your project. If everyone concludes that it wouldn't make a difference, ask them how your project can be modified to benefit the organization. If they feel it can't be changed to produce useful results, consider suggesting that the project be cancelled.

Organizations are consistently overworked and understaffed. Spending precious time and resources on a project that everyone agrees will make no difference is the last thing the organization needs or wants.

More likely, people do realize that your project can have a positive impact on the organization. Your job, then, is to help these people consistently focus on these valuable results.

### Being exhaustive in your search for information

You're seeking information that's sensitive, sometimes contradictory, and often verbal (not in writing). Getting the information isn't always easy, but these tips can help:

✔ **Try to find several sources for the same piece of information.** The greater the number of independent sources that contain the same information, the more likely the information is correct.

✔ **Whenever possible, get information from primary sources.** A *primary source* contains the original information. A *secondary source* is someone else's report of the information from the primary source.

Suppose you need information from a recently completed study. You can get the information from the primary source (which is the actual report of the study by the scientists who performed it), or you can get it from secondary sources (such as articles in magazines or scientific journals by authors who paraphrased and summarized the original information).

The farther your source is from the primary source, the more likely the secondary information differs from the real information.

✔ **Written sources are the best.** Check relevant minutes from meetings, correspondence, e-mail, reports from other projects, long-range plans, budgets, capital improvement plans, market-requirement documents, and benefit-cost analyses.

✔ **Speak to two or more people from the same area to confirm information.** Different people have different styles of communication as well as different perceptions of the same situation. Speak with more than one person and compare their messages to determine any contradictions.

If you get different stories, speak with the people again to verify their initial information. Determine whether the people you consulted are primary or secondary sources (primary sources tend to be more accurate than secondary ones). Ask the people you consulted to explain or reconcile any remaining differences.

✔ **When speaking with people about important information, arrange to have at least one other person present.** Doing so allows two different people to interpret what they heard from the same individual.

✔ **Write down all information you obtain from personal meetings.** Share your written notes and summaries with other people who were present at the meeting to ensure that your interpretation was correct and to serve as a reminder of agreements.

✔ **Plan to meet at least two times with key audiences.** Your first meeting starts them thinking about issues. Allow some time for them to think over your initial discussions and to think of new ideas related to those issues. A second meeting also gives you a chance to clarify any ambiguities or inconsistencies from the first session. (See Chapter 3 for more information on project audiences.)

✔ **Wherever possible, confirm what you heard in personal meetings with written sources.** When you talk with people, they share their perceptions and opinions. Compare those perceptions and opinions with written, factual data (from primary sources, if possible). Discuss any discrepancies with those same people.

## Drawing the line: Where your project starts and stops

Sometimes your project stands alone, but more often it's one part of related efforts to achieve a common result. You want to avoid duplicating the work of these other projects, and, where appropriate, you want to coordinate your work with theirs.

Your project's statement of scope should clearly describe where your project starts and where it ends. Suppose your project develops a new product for your organization. You may describe your project's scope as follows:

> This project entails designing, developing, and testing a new product.

If you feel your statement is in any way ambiguous, you may clarify your scope further by stating what you will not do:

> This project won't include finalizing the market requirements or launching the new product.

To make sure your scope description is clear,

- **Check for hidden inferences.** Suppose your boss has asked you to design and develop a new product. Check to be sure she doesn't assume you'll also perform the market research to determine the new product's characteristics.

- **Use words that clearly describe intended activities.** Suppose your project includes *the implementation of a new information system.* Are you sure that everyone defines *implementation* in the same way? For instance, do people expect it to include installing the new software, training people to use it, evaluating its performance, fixing problems with it, or something else?

- **Confirm your understanding of your project's scope with your project's drivers and supporters.**

A colleague of mine had an assignment to prepare for the competitive acquisition of certain equipment. She developed a plan to include the selection of the vendor, award of the contract, and production and delivery of the equipment. Her boss was stunned with my colleague's project estimate of six months and $500,000. He thought it would take less than two months and cost less than $25,000.

After a brief discussion with her boss, my colleague realized she was only to select the potential vendor, not actually place the order and have the equipment delivered. Although she clarified her misunderstanding, she still wondered aloud, "But why would we select a vendor if we didn't want to actually buy the equipment?"

Of course, she missed the point. The question wasn't whether the company planned to buy the equipment. (Certainly the intention to buy the equipment was the reason for her project.) The real question was whether her project or a different project in the future would purchase the equipment.

# Designing your approach to project work

Your *project strategy* is the general approach you plan to take to perform the work in your project scope. Examples of a project strategy include the following:

✔ We'll buy the needed supplies from an outside vendor.

✔ We'll conduct our training in instructor-led sessions.

Your project strategy can help determine whether you're able to meet the demands and expectations of your audiences. As early as possible, find out whether any of your audiences has preconceived ideas about how to — or how not to — approach the project. If you feel your client's approaches will work, consider using them. If you feel they won't, explain why to your client and explain the strategies you will use.

When selecting a strategy,

✔ **Consider your organization's usual approaches for handling similar projects.** Chances of a mistake are smaller if you ask people to use processes or procedures they've used before.

✔ **Where possible, choose a strategy with the fewest risks, uncertainties, and uncontrollables.** You don't want a strategy that *may* work; you want one with the greatest chance that it *will* work.

✔ **For riskier projects, consider developing backup strategies in case your primary strategy runs into problems.** A different strategy may be the simple answer for meeting an unachievable expectation.

A strategy isn't a detailed list of activities. You derive activity lists from your project Work Breakdown Structure, which Chapter 4 describes in detail. If you haven't chosen a strategy before you prepare your SOW, make a note in the SOW that the strategy is *to be determined* (TBD). This note can remind you that you're actually going to do it at some future point!

## Facing challenging expectations

When you plan to perform an activity that you've successfully done before, you often use the same strategy that worked in the past. That strategy is fine if it allows you to meet your current project's requirements and expectations. If it doesn't, however, you must explore different approaches. When you have challenging expectations, try the following:

✔ **Be careful not to assume a particular approach just because you've always used it in the past.** A client of mine was criticized for buying a piece of equipment from a vendor that charged 20 percent more for the item than other vendors. When asked why he hadn't checked out the other vendors, he replied that the organization had used this vendor for years and no one had complained before.

✔ **Be careful not to prejudge other people's willingness to use different approaches.** Years ago I had to get a proposal out the door by the end of the week, and I needed a full day of secretarial support to meet my deadline. However, the company's secretaries were all tied up with other assignments. When I told my boss we couldn't get the proposal out on time, he asked me why. I explained that all the secretaries were busy and the company had always turned down requests for temporary secretarial help. He stunned me by saying that, if the choice was between hiring a temp and missing the due date, I should hire a temp!

## *Specifying your project's objectives*

*Objectives* are outcomes your project will produce. These outcomes may be products or services you develop or the results of using these products and services. The more clearly you define your project's objectives, the more likely you'll achieve them.

Include the following elements to make your objectives clear and specific:

✔ **Statement:** A brief narrative description of what you want to achieve

✔ **Measures:** Indicators you'll use to assess your achievement

✔ **Performance targets:** The value of each measure that defines success

Suppose you take on a project to reformat a report that summarizes monthly sales activity. You may frame your project's objective as shown in Table 2-1.

| Table 2-1 | An Illustration of a Project Objective | |
|---|---|---|
| *Statement* | *Measures* | *Performance Targets* |
| Create a revised report that summarizes monthly sales activity | Content | Report must include the following data for each product line:<br><br>Total number of items sold<br><br>Total sales revenue<br><br>Total returns |
| | Schedule | Report must be operational by August 31 |
| | Budget | Development expenditures are not to exceed $40,000 |
| | Approvals | New report format must be approved by<br><br>Vice president of sales<br><br>Regional sales manager<br><br>District sales manager<br><br>Sales representatives |

Sometimes people try to avoid setting a specific target by only establishing a range. But a range just avoids the issue.

Suppose you're a sales representative and your boss says you'll be successful if you achieve $20 million to $25 million in sales for the year. As far as you're concerned, you'll be 100 percent successful as soon as you reach $20 million. Most likely, however, your boss will consider you 100 percent successful only when you reach $25 million. Although you and your boss appeared to reach agreement, you didn't.

### Making your objectives clear and specific

You need to be crystal clear when stating your project's objectives. The more specific your project objectives, the greater your chances are of achieving them. Here are some tips for developing clear objectives:

- ✔ **Be brief when describing an objective.** If you take an entire page to describe a single objective, most people won't read it. Even if they do read it, your objective probably won't be clear and may have multiple interpretations.

✔ **Don't use technical jargon.** Each industry (such as pharmaceuticals, telecommunications, finance, and insurance) has its own vocabulary and so does each company within that industry. Within companies, different departments (such as accounting, legal, and information services) also have their own jargon. The same three-letter acronym (TLA) can have two or more meanings in the same organization!

✔ **Make your objectives SMART, as follows:**

- **S**pecific: Define your objective clearly, in detail, with no room for misinterpretation.

- **M**easurable: Specify the measures or indicators you'll use to determine whether you've met your objective.

- **A**ggressive: Set challenging objectives that encourage people to stretch beyond their comfort zones.

- **R**ealistic: Set objectives the project team believes it can achieve.

- **T**ime-sensitive: Include the date by which you'll achieve the objective.

✔ **Make your objectives controllable.** Make sure that you and your team believe you can influence the success of each objective. If you don't believe you can, you may not commit to achieve it (and most likely you won't even try). In that case, it becomes a wish, not an objective.

✔ **Identify all objectives.** Time and resources are always scarce, so if you don't specify an objective, you won't (and shouldn't) work to achieve it.

✔ **Be sure drivers and supporters agree on your project's objectives.** When drivers buy into your objectives, you feel confident that achieving the objectives constitutes true project success. And when supporters buy into your objectives, you have the greatest chance that people will work their hardest to achieve them.

If drivers don't agree with your objectives, revise them until they do agree. After all, your drivers' needs are the whole reason for your project! If supporters don't buy into your objectives, work with them to identify their concerns and develop approaches they think can work.

### Probing for all types of objectives

When you start a project, the person who makes the request often tells you the major results he wants to achieve. However, he may want the project to address other items that he forgot to mention. And other (as yet unidentified) people may also want your project to accomplish certain results.

You need to identify all project objectives as early as possible so you can plan for and devote the necessary time and resources to accomplish each one. When you probe to identify all possible objectives, consider that projects may have objectives in the following three categories:

- ✔ A physical product or service
- ✔ The effect of a product or service
- ✔ A general organizational benefit that wasn't the original reason for the project

Consider that your Information Technology (IT) department is about to purchase and install a new software package for searching and analyzing information in the company's parts-inventory database. The following are examples of objectives this project may have in each category:

- ✔ **Product or service:** The completed installation and integration of the new software package with the parts-inventory database
- ✔ **An effect of the product or service:** Reduced inventory storage-costs due to timelier ordering with the new software
- ✔ **A general organizational benefit:** Use of the new software with other company databases.

An objective is different from a *serendipity* (a chance occurrence or coincidence). In the previous example of the new software package, consider that one project driver won't be completely satisfied unless the software for the parts-inventory database is also installed and integrated with the company's product-inventory database. In this case, installing the system on the company's product-inventory database must be an objective of your project so you must devote specific time and resources to accomplish it. On the other hand, if your audience will be happy whether you do or don't install the software on the second database, then being able to use the software on that database is a serendipity — so you shouldn't devote any time or resources specifically to accomplishing it.

Determining all project objectives requires you to identify all drivers who may have specific expectations for your project. See Chapter 3 for a discussion of the different types of audiences and how to identify them all.

### Anticipating resistance to clearly defined objectives

Some people are uncomfortable committing to specific objectives because they're concerned they may not achieve them. Unfortunately, no matter what the reason, not having specific objectives makes it more difficult to know whether you're addressing your drivers' true expectations and whether you're meeting those expectations. In other words, when you have no specific objectives, you increase the chances that your project won't succeed.

Here are some excuses people give for not being too specific along with suggestions for addressing those excuses.

✔ **Excuse 1: Too much specificity stifles creativity.**

**The response: Creativity should be encouraged — the question is where and when.** You want your project's drivers to be clear and precise when stating their objectives; you want your project's supporters to be creative when figuring ways to meet these objectives. You want to understand what people *do* expect from your project, not what they *may* expect. The more clearly you can describe their actual objectives, the easier it is to determine whether (and how) you can meet them.

✔ **Excuse 2: Your project entails research and new development, and you can't tell today what you'll be able to accomplish.**

**The response: Objectives are targets, not guarantees.** Certain projects have more risks than others. When you haven't done a task before, you don't know whether it's possible. And, if it is possible, you don't know how long it'll take and how much it'll cost. But you must state at the outset exactly what you want to achieve and what you think is possible, even though you may have to change your objectives as the project progresses.

✔ **Excuse 3: What if interests or needs change?**

**The response: Objectives are targets based on what you know and expect today.** If conditions change in the future, you may have to revisit one or more objectives to see whether they're still relevant and feasible or whether they, too, must change.

✔ **Excuse 4: The requestor doesn't know what he specifically wants his project to achieve.**

**The response: Ask him to come back when he does.** If you begin working on his project now, you have a greater chance of wasting time and resources to produce results that he later decides he doesn't want.

✔ **Excuse 5: Even though specific objectives help determine when you've succeeded, they also make it easier to determine when you haven't.**

**The response: Yep. That's true.**

# Marking the Boundaries

You want to operate in a world where everything is possible — that is, where you can do anything necessary to achieve your desired results. Your clients and your organization, on the other hand, want to believe that you can achieve everything with minimal or no cost to them. Of course, neither situation is true.

Defining the restrictions on your approach introduces reality to your plans and helps clarifies expectations. Think in terms of the following:

- **Limitations:** Restrictions that other people place on the results you have to achieve, the time frames you have to meet, the resources you can use, and the way you can approach your tasks

- **Needs:** Requirements that you specify to achieve project success

This section helps you determine your project's limitations and needs.

## Working within limitations

Project limitations may influence how you perform your project and may even determine whether to proceed with your project. Consult with your project's drivers and supporters to identify limitations as early as possible so you can design your plan to accommodate them.

### Understanding the types of limitations

Project limitations typically fall into several categories. By recognizing these categories, you can focus your investigations and thereby increase the chances that you'll discover any limitations. Your project's drivers and supporters may have preset expectations or requirements regarding

- **Results:** The products and effect of your project. For example, the new item must cost no more than $300 per item to manufacture or the book must be less than 384 pages in length.

- **Time frames:** When you must produce certain results. For example, your project must be done by June 30. You don't know whether it's possible to finish by June 30; you just know that someone expects the product then.

- **Resources:** The type, amount, and availability of resources to perform your project work. Resources can include people, funds, equipment, raw materials, facilities, information, and so on. Examples are: You have a budget of $100,000; you can have two people full time for three months; or you can't use the test laboratory during the first week in June.

- **Activity performance:** The strategies for performing different tasks. For example, you understand that you must use your organization's printing department to reproduce the new user's manuals for the system you're developing. You don't know what the manual will look like, how many pages it'll be, the number of copies you'll need, or when you'll need them. Therefore, you can't know whether your organization's printing department is up to the task. But at this point, you do know that someone expects you to have the printing department do the work.

Be careful of a vague limitation; it provides poor guidance for what you can or can't do, and it can demoralize people who have to deal with it. Here are some examples:

✔ **Schedule limitation:**

- **Vague:** "Finish this project as soon as possible." This statement tells you nothing. With this limitation, your audience may suddenly demand your project's final results — with no advance warning.

- **Specific:** "Finish this project by close of business June 30."

✔ **Resource limitation:**

- **Vague:** "You can have an analyst part-time in May." How heavily can you count on this analyst? From the analyst's point of view, how can she juggle all of her assignments in that period if she has no idea how long each one will take?

    When people aren't specific about a constraint, you can't be sure whether you can honor their request. The longer people wait to be specific, the less likely you can adhere to the limitation and successfully complete your project.

- **Specific:** "You can have an analyst four hours per day for the first two weeks in May."

### *Looking for project limitations*

Determining limitations is a fact-finding mission, so your job is to identify and examine all possible sources of information. You don't want to miss anything and you want to clarify any conflicting information. After you know what people expect, you can determine how (or whether) you can meet those expectations. Try the following approaches:

✔ **Consult your audiences.** Check with drivers about limitations regarding desired outcomes; check with supporters about limitations concerning work approach and resources.

✔ **Review relevant written materials.** These materials may include long-range plans, annual budgets and capital-appropriations plans, benefit-cost analyses, feasibility studies, reports of related projects, minutes of meetings, and individuals' performance objectives.

✔ **When you identify a limitation, be sure to note its source.** Confirming a limitation from different sources increases your confidence in its accuracy. Resolve conflicting opinions about a limitation as soon as possible.

### Addressing limitations in your plan

List all project limitations in your SOW. If you have to explore ways to modify your project plan in the future, the list can help define alternatives that you can and cannot consider.

You can reflect limitations in your project in two ways. First, you can incorporate them directly into your plan. For example, if a key driver says you have to finish your project by September 30, you may choose to set September 30 as your project's completion date. Of course, because September 30 is the outside limit, you may choose to set a completion date of August 31. In this case, the limitation influences your target but isn't equivalent to it.

Second, you can identify any project risks that result from a limitation. For example, if you feel the target completion date is unusually aggressive, the risk of missing that date may be significant. You'll want to develop plans to minimize and manage that risk throughout your project. (See Chapter 8 for more information on how to assess and plan for risks and uncertainties.)

## Dealing with needs

As soon as possible, consider the situations or conditions necessary for your project's success. Most of these needs relate to project resources. The following are examples:

- ✔ **Personnel:** "I need a technical editor for a total of 40 hours in August."

- ✔ **Budget:** "I need a budget of $10,000 for computer peripherals."

- ✔ **Other resources:** "I need access to the test laboratory during June."

Be as clear as possible when describing your project's needs. The more specific you are, the more likely other people will understand and meet those needs.

Sometimes you can identify needs very early. More often, however, particular needs surface as you create a plan that addresses the drivers' expectations. Your list of needs grows as you continue to plan your project.

## Facing the Unknowns When Planning

As you proceed through your planning process, you can identify issues or questions that may affect your project's performance. Unfortunately, just identifying these issues or questions doesn't help you address them.

For every issue you identify, make assumptions regarding unknowns associated with it. Then use these assumptions as you plan your project. Consider the following examples:

✔ **Issue:** How much money will you get to perform your project?

**Approach:** *Assume* you'll get $50,000 for your project. *Plan* for your project to spend up to, but no more than, $50,000. Develop detailed information to demonstrate why your project budget must be $50,000 and share that information with key decision makers.

✔ **Issue:** When will you get authorization to start work on your project?

**Approach:** *Assume* you'll receive authorization to start work on August 1. *Plan* your project work so that no activities start before August 1. Explain to key people why your project must start on August 1 and work with them to facilitate your project's approval by that date.

Consider all project assumptions when you develop your project's risk management plan. See Chapter 8 for more info.

# Chapter 3

# Knowing Your Project's Audience: Involving the Right People

*In This Chapter*

▶ Figuring out your project's diverse audiences

▶ Naming the drivers, supporters, and observers

▶ Determining who has authority in your project

$O$ften a project is like an iceberg: Nine-tenths of it lurks below the surface. You receive an assignment and you think you know what it entails and who needs to be involved. Then, as the project unfolds, new people emerge — one by one — people who will affect your goals and your approach to the project.

You run two risks when you don't involve key people or groups in your project in a timely manner. First, you may miss important information that can affect the project's performance and ultimate success. Second, and sometimes more painful, you may insult someone. And you can be sure that, when someone feels slighted or insulted, he'll take steps to make sure you don't do it again!

As soon as you begin to think about your project, start to identify people who may play a role. This chapter shows you how to identify these candidates; how to decide whether, when, and how to involve them; and how to determine who has the authority to make critical decisions.

## Understanding Your Project's Audiences

A *project audience* is any person or group that supports, is affected by, or is interested in your project. Your project audiences can be inside or outside your organization. Knowing your project's audiences helps you to

✔ Plan whether, when, and how to involve them.

✔ Determine whether the scope of the project is bigger or smaller than you originally anticipated.

You may hear other terms used in the business world for project audiences, but each term addresses only some of the people from your complete project audience list. Here are some examples:

✔ A *stakeholder* list identifies people and groups who'll support or be affected by your project. The stakeholder list doesn't usually include people who are merely interested in your project.

✔ A *distribution* list identifies people who receive copies of written project communications, and the lists are often out of date. Some people are on the list simply because no one removes them; other people are on the list because no one wants to run the risk of insulting them by removing them. In either case, their name on this list doesn't ensure that they actually support, are affected by, or are interested in your project.

✔ *Team members* are people whom the project manager directs. All team members are stakeholders and, as such, they're part of the project audience, but the audience list includes more than just the team members.

As you identify the different audiences for your project, write them in an audience list. Check out the next section for more information on how to prepare this list.

# Developing an Audience List

A project audience list is a living document. Start to develop your list as soon as you begin to think about your project. Write down any names that occur to you; when you discuss your project with other people, ask them who they think may be affected or interested. Then select a small group of people and conduct a formal brainstorming session. Continue to add and subtract names until the list is complete. To increase your chances of identifying all appropriate people, develop your audience list in categories. For example, you're less likely to overlook people if you consider them department by department or group by group instead of trying to identify all of the people from the entire organization at the same time.

Start your audience list by developing a hierarchical grouping of categories that covers the universe of people who may be affected by, needed for their support, or interested in your project. I often use the following list:

## Categorize, categorize, categorize

A client of mine asked me to review an audience list he had prepared for a multiyear project that would touch every aspect of his organization. His list included more than 300 names, organized alphabetically, and he asked me whether I thought anyone was missing. The problem was that I had no way of knowing whether anyone was missing. Because the list had 300 uncategorized names, I had no idea why the people were on the list or what areas they represented.

If the names in the list were categorized by department or group, I could have easily checked to see whether the areas of the company that I thought should be involved were represented. I could also tell when one person represented two or more different areas. Unfortunately, the list's format made it impossible to tell whether audiences had been overlooked or whether people on the list really didn't belong there.

✔ **Internal:** People and groups inside your organization

> **Upper management:** Executive-level management responsible for the general oversight of all organization operations

> **Requester:** The person who came up with the idea for your project and all people through whom the request passed before you received it

> **Project manager:** The person with overall responsibility for successfully completing the project

> **Team members:** People whose work the project manager directs

> **Groups normally involved:** Groups typically involved in most projects in the organization, such as human resources, finance, contracts, and the legal department

> **Groups needed just for this project:** Groups or people with special knowledge related to this project

✔ **External:** People and groups outside your organization

> **Clients or customers:** People or groups that buy or use your organization's products and services

> **Collaborators:** Groups or organizations with whom you may pursue joint ventures related to your project

> **Vendors, suppliers, and contractors:** Organizations that provide human, physical, or financial resources to help you perform your project's work

> **Regulators:** Government agencies that establish regulations and guidelines that govern some aspect of your project work

**Professional societies:** Groups of professionals that may influence or be interested in your project

**The public:** The local, national, and international community of people who may be affected by or interested in your project

Continue to develop your audience list by subdividing these categories further until you arrive at position descriptions and the names of the people who occupy them.

As you develop your audience list, be sure not to overlook the following potential audiences:

- ✔ **All support groups:** These people don't tell you what you should do; instead, they help you accomplish the project's goals. If support groups know about your project early, they can fit you into their work schedules more readily. They can also tell you information about their capabilities and processes that may influence what your project can accomplish and by when. Such groups include

  - Facilities

  - Finance

  - Human resources

  - Information services

  - Legal services

  - Procurement or contracting

  - Quality

  - Security

- ✔ **End-users of your project's products:** In some cases, you may omit end-users on your audience list because you don't know who they are. In other situations, you may think you have taken them into account through *liaisons* — people who represent the interests of the end-users. (Check out the nearby sidebar "Discovering the real end users" for a costly example.)

- ✔ **People who will maintain or support the final product:** People who will service your project's products affect the continuing success of these products. Involving these people throughout your project gives them a chance to make your project's products easier to maintain and support. Their involvement also allows them to become familiar with the products and effectively build their maintenance into existing procedures.

## Dealing with reality rather than ignoring it

A number of years ago, I ran into a woman who had attended one of my project-management training sessions. Although she felt the session had been very helpful and she had already put several techniques into practice, she said the audience list seemed to be useless.

She then explained what had happened. Her boss had assigned her a project that she had to finish in two months. She immediately developed an audience list, but, much to her horror, the list included more than 150 names! How, she wondered, was she supposed to involve more than 150 people in a two-month project? She concluded that the audience list was clearly useless.

In fact, her audience list had fulfilled its purpose perfectly. Apparently she initially felt that each

of the people on her list would affect the success of her project. Identifying them at the start of her project gave her three options:

- ✔ She could plan how and when to involve each person during the project.

- ✔ She could assess the potential consequences of not involving one or more of her audiences.

- ✔ She could discuss extending the project deadline or reducing its scope with her boss if she felt she couldn't ignore any of the audiences.

The audience list itself doesn't decide who you should involve in your project. Instead, it specifies the people to consider involving by weighing the benefits and the costs.

## Discovering the real end-users

A major international bank had spent millions of dollars revising and upgrading its information system. The people in charge of the project had worked closely with special liaisons in Europe who represented the interests of the local bank personnel — the people who would enter and retrieve data from the system. When the system became operable, they discovered a fatal problem: More than 90 percent of the local bank personnel in Europe were non-English speaking, but the system documentation was in English. The entire system was unusable!

The system designers had spent substantial time and money working with the liaisons to identify and address the interests and needs of the users. However, the liaisons had identified issues from their own experience instead of identifying and sharing the needs and concerns of the local bank personnel. Because English was the primary language of all the liaisons, the issue of language never came up. Putting both the liaisons and the local bank personnel on the audience list would have reminded the project staff to consider the concerns of the local bank personnel.

Suppose you're asked to coordinate your organization's annual blood drive. Table 3-1 illustrates some of the groups and people you may include in your project's audience list.

| Table 3-1 | A Portion of an Audience List | |
|---|---|---|
| *Category* | *Subcategory* | *Audiences* |
| Internal | Upper management | Executive oversight committee, vice president of sales and marketing, vice president of operations, vice president of administration |
| | Team members | Customer service representative, community relations representative, administrative assistant |
| | Groups normally included | Finance, facilities, legal department |
| | Groups or people with special knowledge or interest | Project manager and team from last year's blood drive, public relations |
| External | Clients, customers | Donors from prior years, potential donors |
| | Regulatory agencies | Local Board of Health |
| | Vendors, contractors | Nurses in attendance, food-service provider, landlord of the facility |
| | Professional societies | American Medical Association, American Association of Blood Banks |
| | Public | Local community, local newspapers, local television and radio stations |

# Ensuring your audience list is complete and up-to-date

A wide range of people influences the success of your project. Knowing who these people are allows you to plan to involve them at the appropriate times during your project. Therefore, identifying all project audiences as soon as possible and reflecting any changes as soon as they occur are important steps.

To ensure your audience list is complete, consider the following guidelines:

- ✔ **Eventually identify each audience by position description and name.** You may, for example, initially identify people from *sales and marketing* as an audience. Eventually, however, you want to specify the particular people from that group, such as *brand manager for XYZ product, Sharon Wilson.*

- ✔ **Speak with a wide range of people.** Check with people in different organizational units, from different disciplines, and with different tenures in the organization. Ask every person whether he can think of anyone else that you should speak with. The more people you speak with, the less likely you are to overlook someone important.

- ✔ **Allow sufficient time to develop your audience list.** Start to develop your list as soon as you become project manager. The longer you think about your project, the more potential audiences you can identify. Throughout the project, continue to check with people about additional audiences.

- ✔ **Include audiences who may play a role at any time during your project.** Your only job at this stage is to identify names so you don't forget them. At a later point, you can decide whether, when, and how to involve these people (see the "Identifying the Drivers, Supporters, and Observers in Your Audience" section later in this chapter).

- ✔ **Include team members' functional managers.** Include the people to whom the project manager and team members directly report. Even though functional managers don't directly perform project tasks, they can help ensure that the project manager and team members devote the time they originally promised to the project.

- ✔ **Include a person's name on the audience list for every role she plays.** Suppose your boss will also provide expert technical advice to your project team. Include your boss's name twice — once as your direct supervisor and once as the technical expert. If your boss is promoted but continues to serve as a technical advisor to your project, the separate listings remind you that a new person now occupies your direct supervisor's slot.

- ✔ **Continue to add and remove names from your audience list throughout your project.** Your audience list evolves as you understand more about your project and as your project changes. Encourage people involved in your project to continually identify new candidates as they think of them.

- ✔ **When in doubt, write down a person's name.** Your goal is to avoid overlooking someone who may play an important part in your project. Identifying a potential audience doesn't mean you have to involve that person; it means that you must consider him. Eliminating the name of someone who won't be involved is a lot easier than trying to add a name of someone who should be.

## Making an audience list template

An *audience list template* is a predesigned audience list that contains typical audiences for projects similar to yours. The template reflects the cumulative experiences of a particular type of project. As you perform more projects, you can add audiences to the template that you overlooked in earlier projects and remove audiences that proved unnecessary. Using templates can save you time and improve your accuracy.

Suppose you prepare the budget for your department each quarter. After doing a number of these budgets, you know most of the people who give you the necessary information, who draft and print the document, and who have to approve the final budget. Each time you finish another budget, you revise your audience list template to include new information from that project. The next time you prepare your quarterly budget, you begin your audience list with that template. You then add and subtract names as appropriate for this particular budget preparation.

When using audience list templates, keep the following in mind:

- ✔ **Develop templates for frequently performed tasks and for entire projects.** Templates for kicking off the annual blood drive or submitting a newly developed drug to the Food and Drug Administration are valuable. But so are templates for individual tasks that are part of these projects, such as awarding a competitive contract or printing a document. Many times projects that appear totally new contain some tasks that you've done before. You can still reap the benefits of your prior experience by including the audience list templates for these tasks into your overall project audience list.

- ✔ **Focus on position descriptions rather than the names of prior audiences.** Identify an audience as *accounts payable manager* rather than *Bill Miller.* People come and go, but functions endure. For each specific project, you can fill in the appropriate names.

- ✔ **Develop and modify your audience list template from previous projects that actually worked, not from plans that looked good.** Often you develop a detailed audience list at the start of your project but don't revise the list during the project or add audiences that you overlooked in your initial planning. If you only update your template with information from an initial list, your template can't reflect the discoveries you made throughout the project.

- ✔ **Use templates as starting points, not ending points.** Make clear to your team that the template isn't the final list. Every project differs in some ways from similar ones. If you don't critically examine the template, you may miss people who weren't involved in previous projects but whom you need to consider for this one.

> ✔ **Continually update your templates to reflect the experiences from different projects.** The postproject evaluation (see Chapter 15) is an excellent time to review and critique your original audience list, so take a moment to be sure your template reflects your experience.

Templates can save time and improve accuracy. However, starting with a template that's too polished can suggest you've made up your mind about its contents, which may discourage people from sharing their thoughts freely about the list. Their lack of involvement may lead to their lack of commitment to the project's success.

# Identifying the Drivers, Supporters, and Observers in Your Audience

After identifying everyone in your project audience, determine which of the following groups they fall into. Then you can decide whether to involve them and, if so, how and when.

> ✔ **Drivers:** People who have some say in defining the results of your project. You're performing your project for these people.

> ✔ **Supporters:** The people who help you perform your project. Supporters include individuals who authorize the resources for your project and who actually work on it.

> ✔ **Observers:** People who are interested in the activities and results of your project. Observers have no say in your project and they're not actively involved in it. However, your project may affect them at some point in the future.

Categorizing audiences in this way helps you decide what information to seek from and share with each one and helps them clarify which project decisions to be involved in.

Consider that an information technology group has the job of modifying the layout and content of a monthly sales report for all sales representatives. The vice president of sales requested the project, and the chief information officer (CIO — the boss of the head of the information technology group) approved it. If you were the project manager for this project, you may consider categorizing your project's audiences as follows:

> ✔ **Drivers:** The vice president of sales is a driver because he has specific reasons for revising the report. The CIO is a potential driver because she may hope to develop certain new capabilities for her group through this project. Individual sales representatives are all drivers for this project because they'll use the redesigned report to support their work.

✓ **Supporters:** The systems analyst who designs the revised report, the training specialist who trains the users, and the vice president of finance who authorizes the funds for printing the changes in the manual are all supporters.

✓ **Observers:** The head of the customer service department is a potential observer because he hopes your project will improve the chances for an improved problem-tracking system this year.

Beware of supporters who try to act like drivers. In the previous example, the analyst that finalizes the content and format of the report may try to include certain items that she thinks are helpful. However, only the drivers should determine the specific data that go into the report. The analyst just determines whether it's possible to include the desired data and what it will cost.

Keep in mind that one person can be both a driver and a supporter. The vice president of sales is a driver for the project to develop a revised monthly sales report. But this same person is also a supporter if he has to transfer funds from the sales department budget to pay for developing the report.

This section helps you identify when you need to involve drivers, supporters, and observers, and the best ways to keep them involved.

## Deciding when to involve them

Projects pass through the following five stages as they progress from an initial idea to completion (see Chapter 1 for detailed explanations of these phases):

✓ Conceive

✓ Define

✓ Start

✓ Perform

✓ Close

Plan to involve drivers, supporters, and observers in each phase.

### Drivers

Involve drivers from the start to the finish of your project. Keeping them involved is critical because they define what your project should produce, and they evaluate your project's success when it's finished. Check out Table 3-2 to see how to keep drivers involved during the five phases.

# Include a project champion

A *project champion* is a person in a high position in the organization who strongly supports your project; advocates for your project in disputes, planning meetings, and review sessions; and takes whatever actions are necessary to help ensure the successful completion of your project.

As soon as you start planning, find out whether your project has a champion. If it doesn't, try to recruit one. An effective champion has the following characteristics:

✔ Sufficient power and authority to resolve conflicts over resources, schedules, and technical issues

✔ A keen interest in the results of your project

✔ A willingness to have his or her name cited as a strong supporter of your project.

---

**Table 3-2    Involving Drivers in the Different Phases of Your Project**

| Phase | Involvement Level | Rationale |
|-------|-------------------|-----------|
| Concept | Heavy | Identify and speak with as many drivers as possible. Their desires and your assessment of feasibility can influence whether you should pursue the project. If you uncover additional drivers later, explore with them the issues that led to the project; ask them to identify and assess any special expectations they may have. |
| Definition | Moderate to heavy | Consult with drivers to ensure your project plan addresses their needs and expectations. Have them formally approve the plan before you start the actual project work. |
| Start | Moderate | Announce and introduce the drivers to the project team. Having the drivers talk about their needs and interests reinforces the importance of the project and helps team members form a more accurate picture of project goals. Having the drivers meet team members increases the drivers' confidence that the members can successfully complete the project. |

*(continued)*

### Table 3-2 *(continued)*

| Phase | Involvement Level | Rationale |
|---|---|---|
| Perform | Moderate | Keep drivers apprised of project accomplishments and progress to sustain their ongoing interest and enthusiasm. Involving drivers during this phase also ensures that the results are meeting their needs. |
| Close | Heavy | Have drivers assess the project's results and determine whether their needs and expectations were met. Identify their recommendations for improving performance on similar projects in the future. |

### Supporters

Just as with drivers, involve supporters from start to finish. Because they perform and support the project work, they need to know about changing requirements so they can promptly identify and address problems. Involvement also sustains their ongoing motivation and commitment to the project. Check out Table 3-3 to see how to keep supporters involved during the five phases.

### Table 3-3    Involving Supporters in the Different Phases of Your Project

| Phase | Involvement Level | Rationale |
|---|---|---|
| Concept | Moderate | Wherever possible, have key supporters assess the feasibility of meeting driver expectations. If you identify key supporters later in the project, have them confirm the feasibility of previously set expectations. |
| Definition | Heavy | Supporters are the major contributors to the project plan. Because they facilitate or do all the work, have them determine necessary technical approaches, schedules, and resources. Also have them formally commit to all aspects of the plan. |
| Start | Heavy | Familiarize all supporters with the planned work. Clarify how the supporters will work together to achieve the results. Have supporters decide how they'll communicate, resolve conflicts, and make decisions throughout the project. |

| Phase | Involvement Level | Rationale |
|---|---|---|
| Performance | Heavy | Supporters perform the work of the project. Keep them informed of project progress, encourage them to identify performance problems they encounter or anticipate, and work with them to develop and implement solutions to these problems. |
| Closure | Heavy | Have supporters conclude their different tasks. Inform them of project accomplishments and recognize their roles in project achievements. Elicit their suggestions for more effective performances of future projects. |

### Observers

Choose the observers with whom you want to actively share project information. Involve them minimally throughout the project because they neither tell you what should be done nor help you do it. Table 3-4 shows how to keep observers involved.

| Table 3-4 | Involving Observers in the Different Phases of Your Project | |
|---|---|---|
| Phase | Involvement Level | Rationale |
| Concept | Minimal | Inform observers that your project exists and what it'll produce. |
| Definition | Minimal | Inform observers about the planned outcomes and timeframes. |
| Start | Minimal | Tell them that the project has started and confirm the dates for planned milestones. |
| Performance | Minimal | Inform observers of key achievements during the project. |
| Closure | Minimal | When the project is complete, inform observers about the project's products and results. |

# Using different methods to keep them involved

Keeping drivers, supporters, and observers informed as you progress in your project is critical to the project's success. Choosing the right method can stimulate a group's continued interest and encourage them to actively support your work. Consider the following approaches for keeping your project audiences involved throughout your project:

- ✔ **One-on-one meetings:** One-on-one meetings (formal or informal discussions with one or two other people about project issues) are particularly useful for interactively exploring and clarifying special issues of interest to a small number of people.

- ✔ **Group meetings:** These are planned sessions for some or all team members or audiences. Smaller meetings are useful to brainstorm project issues, reinforce team-member roles, and develop mutual trust and respect among team members. Larger meetings are useful to present information of general interest.

- ✔ **Informal written correspondence:** Informal written correspondence (notes, memos, letters, and e-mail) helps you document informal discussions and share important project information.

- ✔ **Written approvals:** Written approvals (such as a technical approach to project work or formal agreements about a product, schedule, or resource commitment) serve as a record of project decisions and achievements.

To maximize your audiences' contributions, consider the following guidelines throughout your project:

- ✔ **Involve an audience early in planning if they have a role later on.** Give your audience the option to participate in planning even if they don't perform until later in the project. Sometimes they can share information that'll make their tasks easier. At the least, they can reserve time to provide their services when you need them.

- ✔ **If you're concerned with the legality of involving a specific audience, check with your legal department or contracts office.** Suppose you're planning to award a competitive contract to buy certain equipment. You want to know whether prospective bidders typically have this equipment on hand and how long it'll take to receive it after you award the contract. However, you're concerned that speaking to potential contractors in the planning stage may tip them off about the procurement and lead to charges of favoritism by unsuccessful bidders who didn't know about the procurement in advance. Instead of ignoring this important audience, check with your contracts office or legal department to determine how you can get the information you want and still maintain the integrity of the bidding process.

- ✔ **Develop a plan with each key audience to meet their information needs and interests as well as yours.** Determine the information they want and the information you believe they need. Also decide when to provide that information and in what format. Finally, clarify what you want from them and how and when they can provide it.

✔ **Always be sure you understand each audience's *What's In It For Me* (WIIFM).** Clarify why it's in each audience's interest to see your project succeed. Throughout your project, keep reminding them of the benefits they'll realize when your project's complete and the progress your project's made towards achieving those benefits. See more about identifying project benefits for different audiences in Chapter 14.

# Getting People with Sufficient Authority

*Authority* is the right to make project decisions that others must follow. Having opinions about how an aspect *should be* addressed is different from having the authority to decide how it *will be* addressed. Mistaking a person's level of authority can lead to frustration as well as wasted time and money.

Confirm that the people you've identified as audiences can make the necessary decisions to perform their tasks. If they don't have that authority, find out who does and how to bring those people into the process. (Check out the nearby sidebar "Avoid a headache — involve the people who really have the authority" for an example.)

## Avoid a headache — involve the people who really have the authority

A client of mine attended a meeting to choose the color of his group's new offices. All of the people working on the project to renovate and upgrade his group's offices were present. After intense discussions, they agreed the walls should be light gray.

One week later, the team member from the facilities department informed the rest of the team that his boss had decided that color was too expensive and that they'd have to choose another one. The entire meeting a week earlier had been a complete waste of time. They had assumed that every member of the group had the necessary authority to support the group's decision. If they had they known that the facilities department rep didn't have this authority, they could have

✔ Asked the representative from the facilities department to find out the criteria for the color

✔ Developed and prioritized two or more alternatives and asked the rep to present them to his boss for final approval

✔ Invited the person who did have the authority

✔ Postponed the meeting until the right people could attend

In your own projects, take the following steps to define each audience member's authority:

1. **Clarify each person's tasks and decisions.**

   Define with each person his tasks and his role in those tasks. Will he only work on the task, or will he also approve the schedules, resource expenditures, and work approaches?

2. **Ask each person her authority regarding each decision and task.**

   Ask about individual tasks rather than all issues in a particular area. For example, a person can be more confident about her authority to approve supply purchases up to $5,000 than about her authority to approve all equipment purchases, no matter the type or amount.

   Clarify decisions that the person can make herself. For decisions needing someone else's approval, find out whose approval she needs. (Ask, never assume!)

3. **Ask people how they know what authority they have.**

   Does a written policy, procedure, or guideline confirm the authority? Did the person's boss tell him in conversation? Is the person just assuming? If the person has no specific confirming information, encourage him to check with the above sources to get it.

4. **Check the history.**

   Have you or other people worked with this person in the past? Has he been overruled on decisions that he said he was authorized to make? If so, ask him why he believes he won't be similarly overruled this time.

5. **Verify whether anything has recently changed.**

   Is there any reason to believe that this person's authority has changed? Is the person new to his current group? To his current position? Has the person recently started working for a new boss? If any of these situations is true, encourage the person to find specific documentation to confirm his authority for his benefit as well as yours.

Reconfirm the information in these steps when the audience's decision-making assignments change. Suppose, for example, that you initially expect all individual purchases on your project to be at or under $2,500. Bill, the team representative from the finance group, assures you that he has the authority to approve such purchases for your project without checking with his boss. Midway through the project, you find that you have to purchase a piece of equipment for $5,000. Be sure to verify with Bill that he can personally authorize this larger expenditure. If he can't, find out whose approval you need and plan how to get it.

# Chapter 4

# Developing Your Game Plan: Getting from Here to There

*In This Chapter*

▶ Breaking down your project

▶ Knowing how much detail is enough

▶ Developing and displaying a Work Breakdown Structure

▶ Dealing with unknown activities

*T*he keys to successful project planning and performance are completeness and continuity. You want to identify all important information in your project plan, and you want to address all aspects of your plan during project performance.

Your description of project work provides the basis for: scheduling and resource planning, defining roles and responsibilities, assigning work to team members, capturing key project performance data, and reporting on completed project work. This chapter gets you on the right track.

## Dividing and Conquering: Working on Your Project in Manageable Chunks

One of my major concerns when I start a new project is remembering to plan for all important pieces of work. Another concern is accurately estimating required time and resources. To address both issues, I develop a logical framework to define all work that is necessary to complete the project.

I have a friend who loves jigsaw puzzles. A while back, he told me about an acquaintance who had asked him to assemble a 5,000-piece puzzle of the United States. When his acquaintance suggested that he should determine whether any pieces were missing, my friend laughed. He had always determined whether a piece was missing by assembling the puzzle and then noting whether the picture had any holes. How else could he do it?

You've probably had the same experience with your project assignments. Suppose you're asked to design and present a training program. You and a colleague work intensely for a couple of months developing the content and materials, arranging for the facilities, and inviting the participants. A week before the session, you ask your colleague whether he's made arrangements to print the training manuals. He says he hadn't thought about it, and you say you hadn't either because you thought he was dealing with the final details. Unfortunately, both of you overlooked printing the manuals because you both thought the other person was handling it. Now you have a training session in a week but neither time nor money to print the needed materials. It's crisis time.

How can you avoid this situation? By using an organized approach in the planning stage to identify all necessary work. This section explains how to identify all required project work by breaking down activities into smaller pieces of work.

## Thinking in detail

The most important guideline when identifying and describing project work is: Think in detail! I find that people consistently underestimate the time and resources they need because they just don't recognize everything they have to do to complete their tasks.

Suppose you have to write a report of your team's most recent meeting. Your first task is to estimate the necessary time and resources to prepare this report. Because you've written many, you figure it'll take a few days. But how confident are you in this estimate? Are you sure you've considered all the activities the report will entail?

The key to describing your work is *decomposition,* breaking down a piece of work into its component parts. Preparing the report actually entails three separate activities: writing a draft, reviewing the draft, and preparing the final report. Preparing the final report, in turn, involves two separate activities: writing the final report and printing the final report.

Follow two guidelines to decompose an activity correctly:

✔ **No gaps:** Identify all work in the subelements. In the example of writing a report, *no gaps* means the three subelements encompass all the work that goes into writing the report. If you feel there's more work, define another subelement to include it.

✔ **No overlaps:** Don't include the same work in more than one of your subelements. For example, don't say that *writing* the draft involves having people review preliminary versions if all reviews are under *reviewing* the draft.

Detailing your work in this way increases your confidence that you haven't overlooked anything important and lets you develop more accurate estimates of the necessary time and resources.

## Thinking of hierarchy

Thinking in detail is critical but you also need to consider the big picture. If you fail to identify a major part of your project's work, you won't have the chance to detail it! You must be comprehensive and specific.

My friend's jigsaw puzzle dilemma (refer to the previous section) suggests an approach that can help you achieve your goal. He can count the pieces before assembling the puzzle to determine whether any piece is missing. However, knowing that he only has 4,999 pieces can't help him determine which piece is missing. He needs to divide the 5,000 pieces into smaller groups that he can examine and understand. Suppose he divides the puzzle of the United States into 50 separate puzzles, one for each of the 50 states, each comprising 100 pieces. Because he knows the United States has 50 states, he's confident that each piece of the puzzle can be in one and only one box.

Suppose he takes it a step further and divides each state into northeast, northwest, southeast, and southwest sections, each containing 25 pieces. He can then count the pieces in each box to see whether any are missing. Determining which one of 25 pieces is missing from the northeast sector of New Jersey is a lot easier than figuring out which piece is missing from the 5,000-piece puzzle of the entire United States.

Figure 4-1 shows a *Work Breakdown Structure,* which uses the approach of dividing an item into its component parts to describe the details of a project. A Work Breakdown Structure (WBS) is an organized, hierarchical representation of all work — broken out in sufficient detail — to support a project's planning, assignment of roles and responsibilities, and ongoing monitoring and control.

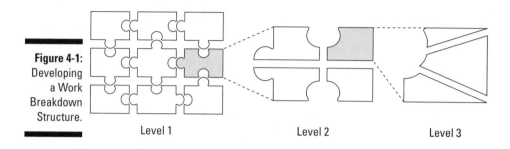

**Figure 4-1:**
Developing
a Work
Breakdown
Structure.

Level 1          Level 2          Level 3

The different WBS levels have had many different names. The very top element is typically a *project* and the lowest level of detail is typically a *work package*. However, the levels in between have been called *phases*, *subprojects*, *work assignments*, *tasks*, *subtasks*, *deliverables*, and *subdeliverables*. In this book, the top-level box is a *project*, the lowest level of detail is a *work package*, and all other levels are *Level 1*, *Level 2* and so forth.

Consider that you're planning to develop and present a new training program for your organization. Develop your WBS as follows.

1. **Determine the major pieces of work.**

   Ask yourself, "What major pieces of work does this project entail?"

   Identify the following pieces:

   - Determine the needs
   - Design the program
   - Develop the materials
   - Test the program
   - Present the program

2. **Divide each of these major pieces into its component parts in the same manner.**

   Choose any piece to begin. Suppose you choose *Determine the needs*.

   Ask, "What major pieces of work are necessary to complete this portion of the project?"

   Determine that you have to

   - Identify people who have an interest in the program.
   - Interview some of these people.
   - Review written materials that discuss needs for the program.
   - Prepare a report of the needs this program will address.

3. **Divide each of these work pieces into its component parts.**

   Suppose you choose to start with *Interview some of these people.*

   Ask, "What major pieces of work have to be done to complete this portion of the project?"

   Decide that you have to

   - Select the people you want to interview.
   - Prepare the questions to ask.
   - Schedule the interviews.
   - Conduct the interviews.
   - Write up the results of the interviews.

   But why stop here? You can break each of these five pieces of work into finer detail and then break those pieces into finer detail. How far should you go? The following sections can help.

### Asking three key questions

Determining how much detail you need isn't a trivial task. Experienced project managers often have difficulty deciding when to say *when*. A client told me of a situation she had experienced with overdetailing. Her boss had asked her to plan out her work for the next 12 months by breaking down her proposed activities into 20-minute intervals! She was a strong supporter of project management but she wondered, "Isn't this going a bit too far?"

 You want to describe your work in sufficient detail to support accurate planning and meaningful tracking. But the benefits of these details must justify the additional time you spend developing and maintaining your plans and reporting your progress. The following three questions can help you decide whether an activity has sufficient details.

   ✔ Can you accurately estimate the resources you'll need? (Resources include personnel, equipment, raw materials, money, facilities, information, and so on.)

   ✔ Can you accurately estimate how long the activity will take?

   ✔ If you have to assign the activity to someone else, are you confident that he'll understand exactly what to do?

If your answer to any one of these questions is *No,* break down the work into finer detail. Your answers to these questions depend on: how familiar you are with the work, how critical the activity is to the success of your project, what happens if something goes wrong, who you may assign to perform the activity, how well you know that person, and so on. In other words, the correct level of detail for your WBS depends upon your judgment.

If you're a little uneasy about answering these three questions, try this even simpler test: Break your activity into more detail when you feel either of the following applies:

✔ It'll take significantly longer than two calendar weeks to complete

✔ It'll require significantly more than 80 person-hours to complete.

Remember, these are just guidelines. Suppose you estimate calendar time of two weeks and two days to prepare a report — that's sufficient detail. But what if you figure two to three months to finalize requirements for your new product? Then you need to break your project into more detail because you may have so many activities in that period that you can't confidently plan your time, your resource estimates, or your ability to assign the task to someone else.

### Making assumptions to clarify planned work

Sometimes the work isn't defined in sufficient detail, but certain unknowns stop you from defining it further. How do you resolve this dilemma? Make assumptions regarding the unknowns! If your assumptions prove to be incorrect in time, you can change your plan to reflect the correct information.

For example, suppose you decide that *Conduct the interviews* from Step 3 earlier in this section needs more detail so you can estimate its required time and resources. However, you don't know how to detail it further because you don't know how many people you'll interview or how many separate sets of interviews you need to conduct. If you assume you'll interview five groups of seven people each, you can then develop specific plans for arranging and conducting each of these sessions. In most situations, consider a guess in the middle of the possible range. You may also analyze several different assumptions to determine how sensitive your results are to the different values.

Be sure to write your assumptions down so you remember to change your plan if you conduct more or less than five sessions. See the discussion in Chapter 2 for more information about detailing assumptions.

### Using action verbs at the lowest levels of detail

To clarify the nature of the work, use action verbs at the lowest levels of detail. Action verbs can improve: your time and resource estimates, your work assignments to team members, and your tracking and reporting because they provide a clear picture of an activity.

Consider the assignment to prepare a report. Suppose you choose to break this project into three work assignments: draft, reviews, and final. If that's all you provide, you haven't stated clearly whether *draft* includes any or all of the following activities:

✔ Collect information for the draft

✔ Determine length and format expectations and restrictions

✔ Handwrite the draft

✔ Review the draft

But, if you simply word the activity as *Design and handwrite the draft — voilà!* Your scope of work is instantly clearer. A few well-chosen words at this level go a long way.

### Using a Work Breakdown Structure for large and small projects

You develop a WBS for very large projects, very small projects, and everything in between. Building a skyscraper, designing a new airplane, researching and developing a new drug, and revamping your organization's information systems all need a WBS. So, too, do writing a report, scheduling and conducting a meeting, coordinating your organization's annual blood drive, and moving into your new office. The size of the WBS may vary immensely depending on the project, but the hierarchical scheme to develop each one is the same.

Occasionally your detailed WBS may seem to make your project more complex than it really is. I agree that 100 tasks (not to mention 10,000) written out can be a little unnerving! The truth is, though, the project's complexity was there all the time; the WBS just displays it. In fact, by clearly portraying all aspects of the work, the structure actually simplifies your project.

Check out the sidebar "Conducting a survey: Utilizing the Work Breakdown Structure" in this chapter for an illustration of how a WBS helps you develop a more accurate estimate of the time you need to complete your work.

## Dealing with special situations

With a little bit of thought, you can break most work into detailed components. However, this section looks a little more closely at several special situations that require some creativity.

### Representing a conditionally repeating activity

Suppose you plan an activity that requires an unknown number of repetitive cycles, such as obtaining approval of a report. In reality, you write a draft and submit it for review and approval. If the reviewers approve the draft, you proceed to the next activity (such as preparing the final version). But, if the reviewers don't approve the draft, you have to revise it to incorporate their comments and then resubmit it for a second review and approval. If they approve the second draft, you proceed to the final version. But if they still don't approve that draft, you have to repeat the process (or try to catch them in a better mood).

# Conducting a survey: Utilizing the Work Breakdown Structure

Suppose your boss asks you to estimate how long it'll take to survey people regarding characteristics of a new product that your company may develop. Based on initial thoughts, you figure you need to contact people at your headquarters, at two regional activity centers, and from a sampling of your current clients. You tell your boss, "Between one and six months."

Have you ever noticed that bosses aren't happy when you respond to their question of "How long?" with an answer of "Between one and six months"? You figure that finishing anytime before six months meets your promise, but your boss expects you can be done in a month, given some (okay, a lot of) hard work. The truth is, though, you don't have a clue how long the survey will take because you don't have a clue how much work you have to do.

Developing a WBS encourages you to define exactly what you'll do and, correspondingly, how long it'll take. In this example, you decide to conduct three different surveys: personal interviews with people at your headquarters, phone conference calls with people at the two regional activity centers, and a mail survey of a sample of clients. Realizing you need to describe each survey in more detail, you begin by considering the mail survey and realize it includes five activities:

✔ **Select a sample of clients to survey:** You figure it should take one week to select your sample of clients if the sales department has a current listing of all company clients. You check with them and they do.

✔ **Design and print a survey questionnaire:** You get lucky. A colleague tells you she thinks the company conducted a similar survey of a different target population a year ago and that extra questionnaires may still be around. You find that a local warehouse has 1,000 of these questionnaires and —yes! — they're perfect for your survey. How much time do you need to allow for designing and printing the questionnaires? Zero!

✔ **Send out the survey and receive the returns:** You determine you'll need a response rate of at least 70 percent for the results to be valid. You consult with people who've done these surveys before and find out that a minimum response rate of 70 percent needs a three-phased approach: First, mail out a set of questionnaires and collect responses for four weeks. Second, mail out another set of the same questionnaires to the nonrespondents and wait another four weeks. Finally, conduct phone follow-ups for two more weeks with the people who still haven't responded.

✔ **Enter and analyze the data:** You figure you need about two weeks to enter and analyze the data you expect to receive.

✔ **Prepare the final report:** You estimate two weeks to prepare the final report.

Now, instead of one to six months, your estimated time to complete your mail survey is 15 weeks. Because you've clarified the work and how you'll do it, you're more confident in your number and you've increased the chances that you'll achieve it!

Revising the draft is a *conditional activity;* it only occurs if a certain condition (in the report example, not receiving everyone's approval) comes to pass. Unfortunately, a WBS doesn't include conditional activities — you plan to perform every activity that you detail. So you can represent conditional activities in two ways.

✔ **You can define a single activity as** *Review/revise report* **and assign one duration to that activity.** You're saying, in effect, that you can perform as many reviews and revisions as possible within the established time period.

✔ **You can assume that you'll need a certain number of revisions and include each of these reviews and revisions as separate activities in your WBS.** This approach defines a separate milestone at the end of each review and revision, which also allows more meaningful tracking.

Assuming that your project needs three reviews and two revisions doesn't guarantee that your draft will be good to go after the third review. If your draft is approved after the first review, congratulations! You've bought some time in the schedule and can move on to the next activity immediately (that is, you don't perform two revisions just because the plan says so!).

However, if you still haven't received approval after the third review, you continue to revise it and submit it for further review until you do get that seal of approval. Of course, then you have to reexamine your plan to determine the impact of the additional reviews and revisions on the schedule and budget of future activities.

A plan isn't a guarantee of the future; it's your statement of what you'll work to achieve. If you're unable to accomplish any part of your plan, you must revise it accordingly (and promptly).

### Handling an activity with no obvious break points

Sometimes you can't see how to break down an activity into two-week intervals. And sometimes that detail just doesn't seem necessary. Even in these situations, divide the activity into smaller chunks to remind yourself to periodically verify that schedule and resource estimates are still valid.

No matter how carefully you plan, something unanticipated can always occur. The sooner you find out about such an occurrence, the more time you have to minimize any negative impact on your project.

# Keeping a closer eye on your project

A number of years back, I met a young engineer at one of my training sessions. Soon after he joined his organization, he received an assignment to design and build a piece of equipment for a client. When he asked his procurement office to order the raw materials he needed, he was told that the material would arrive in six months. He was to notify the procurement office if he hadn't received the raw materials by the promised date. Being young, inexperienced, and new to the organization, he wasn't comfortable trying to fight this established procedure. So he waited for six months.

When he hadn't received his raw materials after six months, he notified the procurement office. The procurement specialist discovered that there had been a fire in the vendor's facilities five months earlier that had caused all production to stop. Production had just resumed the previous week, and the vendor estimated his materials would be shipped in about five months!

The young engineer's Work Breakdown Structure had identified one activity, *Buy raw materials,* with a duration of six months. He reasoned that, after placing the order, nothing else was to happen until five and one-half months later, when he would start to work on his design and the final materials would arrive two weeks later. How was he to break this activity down further?

I suggested he could have divided the waiting time into one-month intervals and called the vendor at the end of each month to see whether anything could change the projected delivery date. Although checking wouldn't have prevented the fire, he would have known about it five months sooner and could have made other plans immediately.

### Planning a long-term project

A long-term project presents a different challenge. Often the activities you perform a year or more in the future depend on the results of the work you do between now and then. Even if you can accurately predict the activities you'll perform later, the farther into the future you plan, the more likely something will change and require you to modify your plans.

When developing a WBS for a long-term project, use a *rolling-wave* approach, which continually refines your plans throughout the life of your project as you understand the project and its environment better. The rolling-wave approach acknowledges that uncertainties may limit your plan's initial detail and accuracy, and it encourages you to reflect more accurate information in your plans as soon as you discover it. Take the following steps in a rolling-wave approach:

1. Break down the first three months' activities into components that take two weeks or less to complete.

2. Plan the remainder of the project in less detail, perhaps describing the work in packages you estimate to take between one and two months.

3. Revise your initial plan at the end of the first three months to detail your activities for the next three months in components that take two weeks or less to complete.

4. Modify any future activities as necessary, based on the results of your first three months' work.

5. Continue revising your plan in this way throughout the project.

# Creating and Displaying Your Work Breakdown Structure

You can use several different schemes to develop and display your project's WBS, and each one can be effective under different circumstances. This section looks at a few of those different schemes and provides some examples and advice on their application.

## Considering different hierarchal schemes for classifying activities

You can use many different schemes to subdivide a project and its activities. The following are four of the most common schemes and examples of each:

- **Product components:** Floor plan, training manuals, screen design, or promotional literature
- **Functions:** Design, launch, review, or test
- **Geographical areas:** Region 1 or the northwest
- **Organizational units:** Marketing, operations, or facilities

Product component and function are the most common schemes.

When you choose the scheme you want to use, stick with that scheme to prevent possible overlap in categories.

For example, consider that you want to develop finer detail for the activity *Prepare report*. You may choose to break out the detail according to function, such as *write the draft report, review the draft report,* and *write the final report.* Or, you may choose to break it out by product component, such as *Section 1, Section 2,* and *Section 3.*

However, don't try to break out details by using some elements from both schemes, such as *Section 1, Section 2, review the draft report,* and *write the final report.* This breakout creates confusion. For example, the activity *Prepare the final version of Section 2* could be included in either of two categories: *Section 2* or *Write the final report.*

Consider the following questions when choosing a detail scheme:

- ✔ What higher-level milestones will be most meaningful when reporting progress? For example, is it more helpful to report that *Section 1* is completed or that *the entire draft of the report* is done?

- ✔ How will responsibility be assigned? For example, is one person responsible for drafting, reviewing, and finalizing Section 1, or is one person responsible for all drafts of Sections 1, 2, and 3?

- ✔ How will the work actually be done? For example, is drafting, reviewing, and finalizing of Section 1 separate from the same activities for Section 2, or are all chapters drafted together, reviewed together, and finalized together?

## Developing your WBS

How you develop your WBS depends on how familiar you and your team are with your project, whether similar projects have been successful in the past, and how many new methods and approaches you'll use. Choose one of the following two approaches depending on your project's characteristics:

- ✔ **Top-down:** Start at the top level in the hierarchy and systematically break down activities into their component parts.

    This approach is very useful when people have a good idea of the work *beforehand.* It ensures that you thoroughly consider each category at each level, and it reduces the chances that you overlook activities in those categories.

✔ **Brainstorming:** Generate all possible activities for this project and then group them into categories.

Brainstorming is very helpful when people *don't have a clear sense at the outset* of a project's required activities. This approach encourages people to generate any and all possible activities that may have to be done, without worrying about how to organize them in the final WBS. After you decide that a proposed piece of work is a necessary part of the project, you can identify related activities that are also required.

In either case, consider using stickums to support your work. As you identify activities, write them on the notes and put them on the wall. Add, remove, and regroup the notes as you continue to think through your work. This approach encourages open sharing of ideas and helps all people appreciate — in detail — the nature of the work that needs to be done.

### Top-down approach

Use the top-down approach for projects that you or others are familiar with. Proceed as follows:

1. **Specify all work assignments for the entire project.**

2. **Determine all necessary tasks for each work assignment.**

3. **Specify the subtasks for each task as necessary.**

4. **Continue in this way until you've detailed your entire project.**

### Brainstorming approach

Use the following brainstorming approach for projects involving untested methods or for projects you and your team members haven't done before.

1. **Write all activities that you think are necessary for your project.**

   Don't worry about overlap or level of detail.

   Don't discuss activity wording or other details.

   Don't make any judgments about the appropriateness of the activity.

2. **Group the activities into a few major categories with common characteristics and eliminate any activities you don't have to perform.**

   These groupings are your *level 1* categories.

3. **Next divide the activities under each level 1 category into groups with common characteristics.**

   These groups are your *level 2* categories.

4. **Now use the top-down method to identify any additional activities that you overlooked in the categories that you created.**

5. **Continue in this manner until you have described all project work clearly and completely.**

## Taking different paths to the same end

Early in the development of your WBS, you can look at two or more different hierarchical schemes to describe your project. Considering your project from two or more perspectives helps you identify activities you may have over-looked.

Suppose a local community wants to open a halfway house for substance abusers. Figures 4-2 and 4-3 depict two different schemes to categorize the work for this community-based treatment facility. The first scheme classifies the work at the highest level by product component, and the second classi-fies the work by function.

Figure 4-2 defines the following *project components* as level 1 categories: staff, facility, residents (people who'll be living at the facility and receiving ser-vices), and community training.

**Figure 4-2:**
A product component scheme for a Work Breakdown Structure for preparing to open a community-based treatment facility.

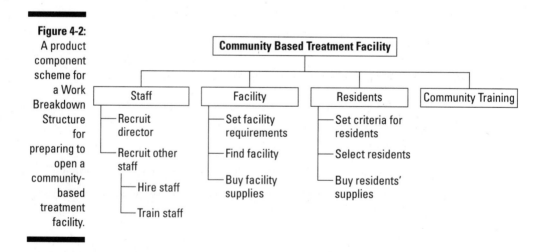

Figure 4-3 defines the *functions* as level 1 categories: planning, recruiting, buying, and training.

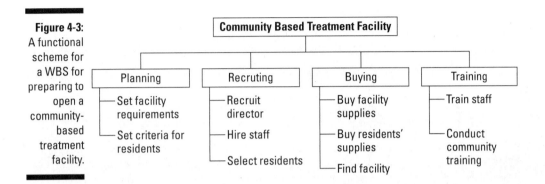

**Figure 4-3:**
A functional scheme for a WBS for preparing to open a community-based treatment facility.

The same lowest-level activities are in both WBSs.

When you think about your project in terms of major functions (rather than project components), you realize that you forgot the following activities:

✔ You have no planning activity for hiring of staff.

✔ You have no activity to buy staff supplies.

✔ You forgot an activity to plan your community training.

After you identify the activities you overlooked, you can represent them in either of the two WBSs.

Be sure you choose only one WBS before you leave your planning phase. Nothing confuses people faster than trying to use two or more different WBSs to describe the same project.

## Labeling your WBS entries

As the size of a project grows, its WBS becomes increasingly complex. It's often easy to lose sight of how a particular piece of work relates to other parts of the project. This problem can lead to poor coordination between related activities and lack of urgency on the part of people who must complete an activity.

Figure 4-4 illustrates a scheme for labeling your WBS entries so you can easily see their relationships with each other and their relative positions in the overall project.

✔ The first number refers to a level 1 category.

✔ The number after the first period refers to a level 2 category under that level 1 category.

✔ The number after the second period refers to a level 3 category under that level 2 category.

✔ The number after the third period refers to a work package under that level 3 category.

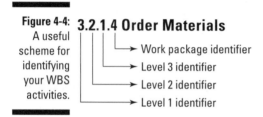

**Figure 4-4:**
A useful scheme for identifying your WBS activities.

# Displaying your WBS in different formats

You can use several different formats to display your WBS. This section looks at three of the most common.

### The organization-chart format

Figure 4-5 shows a WBS in an organization-chart format. This format effectively portrays an overview of your project and the hierarchical relationships of different categories at the highest levels. However, because this format generally requires a lot of space, it's less effective for displaying large numbers of activities.

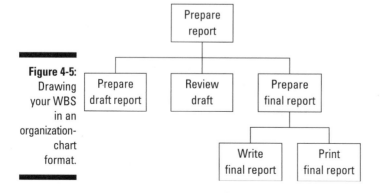

**Figure 4-5:**
Drawing your WBS in an organization-chart format.

### The indented-outline format

The indented-outline format in Figure 4-6 is another way to display your WBS. This format allows you to read and understand a complex WBS with many activities. However, you can easily get lost in the details of a large project with this format and forget how the different pieces all fit together.

**Figure 4-6:**
Drawing
your WBS in
an indented-
outline
format.

**Prepare Report**

1.0   Prepare draft report
2.0   Review draft report
3.0   Prepare final report
     3.1   Write final report
     3.2   Print final report

Both formats can display a WBS for a small project. For a large project, however, consider using a combination of the organization-chart and the indented-outline formats to explain your WBS. You can display the level 1 and level 2 categories in the organization-chart format and portray the detailed breakout for every level 2 category in the indented-outline format.

### The bubble-chart format

The bubble-chart format in Figure 4-7 is particularly effective for supporting the brainstorming process for both small and large projects. You interpret the bubble chart as follows:

✔ The bubble in the center represents your entire project.

✔ Lines from the center bubble lead to level 1 breakouts.

✔ Lines from each level 1 breakout lead to level 2 breakouts related to that level 1 breakout.

**Figure 4-7:**
Drawing
your WBS in
a bubble-
chart
format.

The freeform nature of the bubble chart makes it effective for easily recording thoughts generated in a brainstorming process. You can also easily rearrange activities as you proceed with your analysis.

The bubble chart isn't effective for displaying your WBS to audiences who aren't familiar with your project. Use the bubble chart to develop your WBS with your team but transpose it into an organization-chart or indented-outline format when you present it to people outside your team.

## *Improving the quality of your WBS*

You increase the chances for project success when your WBS is accurate and complete *and* when people who will be performing the work understand and agree with it. The following tips suggest some ways to improve a WBS's accuracy and acceptance.

- ✔ **Involve the people who'll be doing the work.** When possible, involve them during the initial development of the WBS. If they join the project after the initial planning, have them review and critique the WBS before they begin work.

- ✔ **Review and include information from WBSs from similar projects.** Review plans and consult people who've worked on projects similar to yours that were successful. Incorporate your findings into your WBS.

- ✔ **Keep your WBS current.** When you add, delete, or change activities during your project, be sure to reflect these changes in your WBS. (See "Gathering What You Need to Know about Your Activities" later in this chapter for more about sharing the updated structure with the team.)

- ✔ **Make assumptions regarding uncertain activities.** If you aren't certain whether you'll do a particular activity, make an assumption and prepare your WBS based on that assumption. Be sure to document that assumption. If your assumption proves to be wrong during the project, change your plan to reflect the true situation. (See the sections "Making assumptions to clarify planned work" and "Representing a conditionally repeating activity" earlier in this chapter for more about assumptions.)

- ✔ **Remember that your WBS only identifies the elements of activities; it doesn't depict their chronological order.** Nothing is wrong with including activities from left to right or top to bottom in the approximate order that you'll perform them. However, you may have difficulty showing detailed interrelationships among activities in complex projects in the WBS format. The purpose of the WBS is to ensure that you identify all activities. Check out Chapter 5 for more on developing the schedule for your project's activities.

# Using templates

A *WBS template* is an existing WBS that contains activities typical for a particular type of project. This template reflects people's cumulative experience from performing many projects of the same type. As people perform more projects, they add activities to the template that were overlooked and remove activities that weren't needed. Using templates can save you time and improve your accuracy.

Although templates can save time and improve accuracy, don't inhibit people's active involvement in the development of the WBS by using a template that's too polished. Lack of people's involvement can lead to missed activities and lack of commitment to project success.

This section looks at how you can develop a WBS template and improve its accuracy and completeness.

### Drawing upon previous experience

Suppose you prepare your department's quarterly budget. After doing a number of these budgets, you know most of the activities you have to perform. Each time you finish another budget, you revise your WBS template to include new information you gleaned from the recently completed project.

The next time you start to plan a quarterly budget-preparation project, begin with the WBS template that you've developed from your past projects. You then add and subtract activities as appropriate for this particular budget preparation.

By drawing on previous experience, you can prepare your WBS in less time and be more confident that you've included all the important activities.

### Improving your WBS templates

The more accurate and complete your WBS templates are, the more time they can save on future projects. This section offers several suggestions for continually improving the quality of your templates.

When using templates, keep the following in mind:

- ✔ **Develop templates for frequently performed tasks as well as for entire projects.** Templates for the annual organization blood drive or the submission of a newly developed drug to the Food and Drug Administration are valuable. So are templates for individual tasks that are part of these projects, such as awarding a competitive contract or having a document printed. You can always incorporate templates for individual tasks into a larger WBS for an entire project where you plan to perform these tasks.

✔ **Develop and modify your WBS template from previous projects that worked, not from initial plans that looked good.** Often you develop a detailed WBS at the start of your project, but you may forget to add activities that you overlooked in your initial planning. If you update your template from a WBS that you prepared at the *start* of your project, it won't reflect what you discovered *during* the actual performance of the project.

✔ **Use templates as starting points, not ending points.** Make it clear to your team members and others involved in the project that the template is only the start of your WBS, not the final version. Every project differs in some ways from similar ones in the past. If you don't critically examine the template, you miss activities that weren't in previous projects but that need to be in this one.

✔ **Continually update your templates to reflect your experiences from different projects.** The postproject evaluation is an excellent opportunity to review and critique your original WBS. (See Chapter 15 for information on how to plan and conduct this evaluation.) At the end of your project, take a moment to revise your WBS template to reflect what you discovered.

# Identifying Risks While Detailing Your Activities

In addition to helping you identify activities to perform, a WBS helps you identify unknowns that may cause problems. As you think through the work to complete your project, you often identify considerations that may affect how or whether you can perform certain project activities. Sometimes this information is certain and sometimes it's unknown. Identifying and dealing effectively with unknowns can dramatically increase your chances for success with your project.

Unknown information can fall into either of two categories:

✔ **A known unknown:** Information you don't have but someone else does.

✔ **An unknown unknown:** Information that you don't have because it doesn't yet exist.

You deal with known unknowns by finding out who has the information and determining the information. You deal with unknown unknowns by

- ✔ Buying insurance to minimize damage that occurs if something doesn't turn out the way you wanted.
- ✔ Developing contingency plans for when you do get the information.
- ✔ Trying to influence what eventually happens.

You've just become aware that twice in the past month a computer operator accidentally spilled some coffee when he was preparing to mount the tape on a tape drive, and it destroyed the tape. You also know that the survey you're going to conduct requires a tape mounted on a tape drive. So now you're concerned that Mr. Coffee will accidentally destroy your tape also.

Whether or not he'll spill coffee on your tape is an unknown unknown when you prepare your plan. You can't be certain whether he'll spill coffee on your tape because it's an unintended, unplanned act (at least we hope so!).

Because you can't find out whether or not it'll happen, you have to consider the following approaches to address this risk:

- ✔ **You can buy insurance.** For example, have one or more back-up tapes.

- ✔ **You can develop a contingency plan.** For example, have the statistician who guides the selection of the sample also develop a scheme for selecting names randomly by hand from the hard copy of the data tape.

- ✔ **You can take steps to reduce the likelihood that coffee is spilled on your data tape.** For example, on the morning that your data tape is to be run, check beforehand to see whether open cups of coffee are in the computer room.

Developing the WBS helps you identify a situation that may compromise your project's success. You then must decide how to deal with that situation. See Chapter 8 for more detailed information on how to identify and manage project risks and uncertainties.

# Gathering What You Need to Know about Your Activities

After detailing your project work, specify all important information about your lowest-level activities. You and your team will use this information to develop the remaining parts of your plan and refer to it during the project. To ensure easy access, keep this information in a WBS dictionary that's available to all members. The project manager (or her designee) should approve all changes to information in this dictionary.

The WBS dictionary contains the following information:

- **Work detail:** Narrative description of work processes and procedures to accomplish the activity
- **Inputs:** Work products from other activities that this activity will use
- **Outputs:** Products or results of this activity
- **Roles and responsibilities:** How team members will work with each other on this activity
- **Duration:** Estimated calendar time this activity will take
- **Required resources:** People, funds, equipment, facilities, raw materials, information, and so on that this activity needs

Sometimes the dictionary also includes the following information:

- **Immediate predecessors:** Activities that must be completed right before this activity can begin
- **Immediate successors:** Activities that can be started as soon as this activity is finished

# Part II
# Determining
# When and
# How Much

The 5th Wave                    By Rich Tennant

"My project plan has changed a little this year."

## In this part . . .

You have the greatest chance of achieving project success when you have a plan that meets your client's
needs and that you believe is possible to accomplish.

In this part, I show you how to develop a feasible and
responsive initial project schedule and how to respond
when you need to complete your project earlier than
planned. I discuss how to estimate the people, funds, and
other resources you'll need to perform the project work.
And last, but definitely not least, I discuss how you can
identify and deal with potential project risks.

# Chapter 5

# You Want This Project Done When?

*P*roject assignments always have deadlines. So even though you're not sure what your new project is to accomplish, you want to know when it has to be finished. Unfortunately, when you do find out the end date, your immediate reaction is often "But I don't have enough time!"

The truth is, when you receive your project assignment, you usually have no idea how long it'll take. First reactions tend to be based on fear and anxiety more than facts, especially if you're trying to juggle multiple responsibilities and the project sounds complex.

You need an organized approach to clarify how you plan to perform your project's activities, what schedules are possible, and how you'll meet deadlines that initially appear unrealistic. This chapter describes a technique that helps you proactively develop your schedule possibilities.

The discussion in this chapter on network diagramming to develop project schedules is the most technically detailed presentation in this book. Even though the technique takes about ten minutes to master, the explanations and illustrations can appear overwhelming. If this is your first contact with flowcharts, I suggest you initially scan this chapter and then read the different sections several times. The more you read the text, the more logical the explanations become. However, if you get frustrated with the technical details, put the book away and come back to it at another time. You'll be surprised how much clearer the details are the second or third time around!

# Illustrating Your Work Plan with a Network Diagram

Suppose you have a project consisting of ten activities and each takes one week. How long will it take you to complete your project? Truth is, you can't tell. You may finish the project in one week if you can perform all activities at the same time and have sufficient resources. You may take ten weeks if you have to do the activities one at a time in sequential order. Or you may take between one and ten weeks if you have to do some, but not all, activities in sequence.

In order to determine the amount of time for your project, you need two pieces of information:

 ✔ **Duration:** How long each individual activity takes

 ✔ **Sequence:** The order in which you perform the activities

To develop a schedule for a small project, you can probably consider the durations and interdependencies in your head. But projects with 15 to 20 activities or more — many of which you can perform at the same time — require a method to guide your analysis.

This section can help you develop feasible schedules by showing how to draw network diagrams and then how to choose the best one for your project.

## Defining a network diagram's elements

A *network diagram* is a flowchart that illustrates the order in which you perform project activities. Think of the network diagram as your project's test laboratory — it gives you a chance to try out different strategies before performing the work.

No matter how complex your project, its network diagram has the following three elements.

### Event

An *event* is a significant occurrence in the life of your project, sometimes called a *milestone* or a *deliverable*. Events take no time and consume no resources; they occur instantaneously. Think of them as signposts that signify a certain point in your trip to project completion. Events mark the start or finish of one activity or a group of activities. Examples of events are *draft report approved* and *design begun*.

The word *event* in this book is different from other contexts you may have seen. Suppose you read that the premier social *event* of a postelection year was the presidential inaugural ball. In project management terms, the inaugural ball is an *activity* rather than an *event* because it takes time and lots of resources!

### Activity

An *activity* is the work to go from one event to the next in your project. Activities take time and consume resources; they describe action. Examples of activities are *design report format* and *identify needs for new product.*

Make sure you define activities and events clearly. The more clearly you define them, the more accurately you can estimate time and resources, the more easily you can assign the task to someone else, and the more meaningful your tracking becomes.

### Span time

*Span time* is the actual calendar time to complete an activity, also called *duration.* The amount of work effort, people's availability, and whether people can work on an activity at the same time all affect the activity's span time. Capacity of nonpersonnel resources (for example, a computer's processing speed and the pages per minute that a copier can print) and availability of those resources also affect span time. Delay can also add to an activity's span time. If your boss spends one hour reading your memo after it sat in her inbox for four days and seven hours, the activity's span time is five days, even though she spent only one hour reading it.

Understanding the basis of a span-time estimate helps you to figure out ways to reduce it. For example, suppose you estimate that a software package must run for 24 hours on a computer to do a complete test. If you can use the computer only six hours in any one day, the span time for your software test is four days. Suppose you want to cut the span time for your software test in half. Doubling the number of people assigned to the activity won't do it, but getting approval to use the computer for 12 hours a day will.

The units of time describe two related, but different, activity characteristics. *Span time* is duration; *work effort* is the amount of time a person needs to work on the activity to complete it. (See Chapter 6 for more discussion of work effort.) Suppose four people had to work together full time for five days to complete an activity. The activity's span time is five days. The work effort is 20 person-days (four people multiplied by five days).

# Drawing your network diagram

Determining your project's end date requires you to choose the dates each activity starts and ends and the date each event is reached. These dates depend on the order in which you perform your activities and their span times. This section shows you how to draw a network diagram that represents the order in which you perform your project's activities so you can determine schedule possibilities.

### Activity-in-the-box approach

The *activity-in-the-box* technique (also called *activity-in-the-node, precedence diagramming,* or *dependency diagramming*) uses three symbols to describe the three elements of the diagram:

- ✔ Boxes represent events and activities. You can tell whether a box represents an event or an activity by its span time. If the span time is *0*, it's an event. *Note:* Event boxes are sometimes highlighted with lines that are bold, double, or otherwise more noticeable.

- ✔ The letter *t* represents span time.

- ✔ Arrows represent the direction work flows from one activity or event to the next.

Figure 5-1 presents a simple illustration. When you reach Event A (the box on the left), you can perform Activity 1 (the box in the middle). You estimate that Activity 1 will take two weeks to complete. Upon completing Activity 1, you reach Event B (the box on the right). The arrows indicate the direction of workflow.

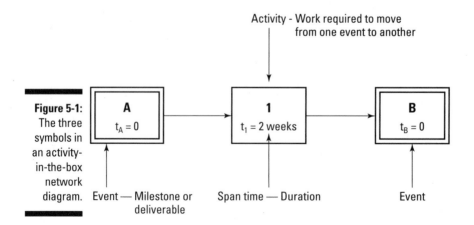

**Figure 5-1:** The three symbols in an activity-in-the-box network diagram.

Activity - Work required to move from one event to another

| A | 1 | B |
| $t_A = 0$ | $t_1 = 2$ weeks | $t_B = 0$ |

Event — Milestone or deliverable

Span time — Duration

Event

Figure 5-1 illustrates how you can use the activity-in-the-box approach to represent events and activities. In this approach, however, the use of events is optional; you can have one activity lead directly to another with no event between them.

### Activity-on-the-arrow approach

You can also draw your network diagram using the *activity-on-the-arrow* approach, (also called the *classical* or *traditional* approach). This method depicts the three elements of the diagram as follows:

- ✓ Circles represent events.
- ✓ Arrows represent activities.
- ✓ The letter *t* represents span time.

The two diagramming approaches are interchangeable; anything you can represent with one technique you can also represent with the other. If you choose, you can draw your entire project using only activities in the activity-in-the-box approach, but with the activity-in-the-arrow technique, all activities must start and end with an event.

Today, most integrated project-management software packages use the activity-in-the-box approach. Because many people find that format to be simpler and more intuitive, I use the activity-in-the-box technique in this book.

# Analyzing Your Network Diagram

Think of your project as a trip for you and several friends. Each of you has a car and will travel a different route to the final destination. During the trip, two or more of your routes will cross at certain places. You agree that all people who pass through a common point must arrive at that point before anyone can proceed on the next leg of the journey. The trip is over when all of you reach the final destination.

You certainly don't want to undertake a trip this complex without planning it out on a road map. Planning your trip allows you to

- ✓ Determine how long the entire trip will take.
- ✓ Identify potential difficulties along the way.
- ✓ Consider alternate routes to get to your final destination more quickly.

This section helps you plan your project by telling you how to read and interpret a road map (your network diagram) so you can determine the likely consequences of your approach.

# Reading your network diagram

Use the following two rules to draw and interpret your network diagram. After you understand these rules, analyzing the diagram is a snap:

- ✔ **Rule 1:** After you finish an activity or reach an event, you can proceed to the next activity or event, as indicated by the arrow(s).

- ✔ **Rule 2:** Before you can start an activity or reach an event, you must have first completed all activities and reached all events with arrows pointing to that activity or event.

Figure 5-2 illustrates a network diagram. According to Rule 1, from *Start,* you can work on Activity 1 or 3, which means you can do Activity 1 or Activity 3 or both Activities 1 and 3. In other words, they're independent of one another.

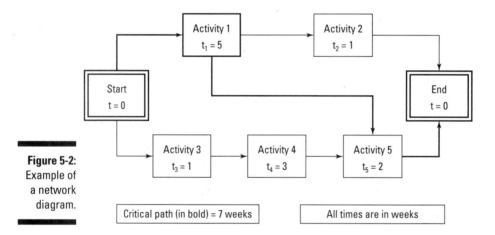

**Figure 5-2:**
Example of
a network
diagram.

Activity 1 — $t_1 = 5$
Activity 2 — $t_2 = 1$
Start — $t = 0$
End — $t = 0$
Activity 3 — $t_3 = 1$
Activity 4 — $t_4 = 3$
Activity 5 — $t_5 = 2$

Critical path (in bold) = 7 weeks

All times are in weeks

You may also choose to do neither of the activities. Rule 1 is an *allowing* relationship, not a *forcing* relationship. In other words, you can work on the activities that the *Start* arrows lead to, but it doesn't say that you *must* work on any of them. For example, suppose a part of your plan includes two activities to build a device: *receive parts* and *assemble parts.* As soon as you receive the parts, you can start to assemble them. However, suppose that you've received all of the parts you ordered. Nothing says that you *must* start to assemble them immediately; you can assemble them if you want to, but you can also wait.

Of course, if you work on neither activity, your project will be delayed. But that's your choice. According to Rule 2, you can start working on Activity 2 in Figure 5-2 as soon as you complete Activity 1 because the arrow from Activity 1 is the only one leading into Activity 2. Rule 2, therefore, is a forcing (or requiring) relationship. If arrows from three activities enter Activity 2, you must complete all three activities before you can start Activity 2. The diagram doesn't indicate that you can start working on Activity 2 by completing only one or two of the three activities.

## *Interpreting your network diagram*

The network diagram illustrates the order of your project's activities. Use the diagram to figure out when to start and end activities and when you'll finish the entire project if you perform the activities in this way. This section gives you the key information you need to determine your schedule.

You need the following information to find out the schedule that your approach will allow:

- ✔ **Critical path:** A sequence of activities that takes the longest time to complete

- ✔ **Noncritical path:** A sequence of activities that you can delay and still finish your project in the shortest possible time

- ✔ **Slack time:** The maximum amount of time that you can delay an activity and still finish your project in the shortest possible time

- ✔ **Earliest start date:** The earliest date you can start an activity

- ✔ **Earliest finish date:** The earliest date you can finish an activity

- ✔ **Latest start date:** The latest date you can start an activity and still finish your project in the shortest possible time

- ✔ **Latest finish date:** The latest date you can finish an activity and still finish your project in the shortest possible time

The lengths of your project's *critical path(s)* define your project's length. If you want to finish your project in less time, consider ways to shorten the critical path.

Monitor critical-path activities closely during performance because *any* delay in critical-path activities delays your project's completion.

Your project can have two or more critical paths at the same time. In fact, every path can be critical if they all take the same amount of time. However, when every path is critical, you have a high-risk situation; a delay in any activity immediately causes a delay in the completion of the project.

Critical paths can change as your project unfolds. Sometimes activities on a critical path finish so early that the path becomes shorter than one or more other paths. Also, activities on an initially noncritical path can be sufficiently delayed so that its completion time exceeds the time of the current critical path.

### The forward pass — determining critical paths, noncritical paths, and earliest start and finish dates

Your first step in analyzing your project's network diagram is to start at the beginning and see how quickly you can complete the activities along each path. This start-to-finish analysis is called the *forward pass*.

You can perform a forward pass through the diagram in Figure 5-2 as follows:

Using Rule 1 (check out "Reading your network diagram" earlier in this chapter for more info), you can consider working on Activity 1 or 3 as soon as the project starts. First consider Activities 1 and 2 in the upper path:

- ✔ The earliest you can start Activity 1 is the moment the project starts.

- ✔ The earliest you can finish Activity 1 is the end of week 5 (add Activity 1's estimated span time of five weeks to its earliest start time, which is the start of the project).

- ✔ According to Rule 2, the earliest you can start Activity 2 is the beginning of week 6 because the arrow from Activity 1 is the only one entering Activity 2.

- ✔ The earliest you can finish Activity 2 is the end of week 6.

So far, so good. Now consider the path of Activities 3, 4, and 5 at the bottom of the diagram:

- ✔ The earliest you can start Activity 3 is the moment the project starts.

- ✔ The earliest you can finish Activity 3 is the end of week 1.

- ✔ The earliest you can start Activity 4 is the beginning of week 2.

- ✔ The earliest you can finish Activity 4 is the end of week 4.

Ah, there's a catch. According to Rule 2, the two arrows entering Activity 5 indicate you must finish both Activity 1 and Activity 4 before you begin

Activity 5. Even though you can finish Activity 4 by the end of week 4, you can't finish Activity 1 until the end of week 5. Therefore, the earliest you can start Activity 5 is the beginning of week 6.

This situation illustrates the following guideline: If two or more activities lead to the same activity, the earliest you can start that activity is the latest finish date of the preceding activities.

In the example, the finish dates for Activity 4 and Activity 1 are the ends of weeks 4 and 5, respectively. Therefore, the earliest date you can start Activity 5 is the beginning of week 6.

Is your head spinning yet? Take heart, the end is in sight.

- ✔ The earliest you can start Activity 5 is the beginning of week 6.

- ✔ The earliest you can finish Activity 5 is the end of week 7.

- ✔ The earliest you can finish Activity 2 is the end of week 6. Therefore, the earliest you can finish the entire project (and reach the event called *End*) is the end of week 7.

So far you have the following information about your project:

- ✔ The length of the critical path (the shortest time in which you can complete the project) is seven weeks. Only one critical path takes seven weeks; it includes the event *Start,* Activity 1, Activity 5, and the event *End.*

- ✔ Activity 2, Activity 3, and Activity 4 aren't on critical paths.

- ✔ The earliest dates you can start and finish each activity in your project are summarized in Table 5-1.

| Table 5-1 | Earliest Start and Finish Dates for Figure 5-2 | |
|---|---|---|
| *Activity* | *Earliest Start Date* | *Earliest Finish Date* |
| 1 | Beginning of week 1 | End of week 5 |
| 2 | Beginning of week 6 | End of week 6 |
| 3 | Beginning of week 1 | End of week 1 |
| 4 | Beginning of week 2 | End of week 4 |
| 5 | Beginning of week 6 | End of week 7 |

### *The backward pass — determining slack times and earliest start and finish dates*

You're halfway home. In case resource conflicts or unexpected delays prevent you from beginning all the project activities at their earliest possible start times, you want to know how much you can delay the activities along each path and still finish the project at the earliest possible date. This finish-to-start analysis is called the *backward pass*.

You found out from the forward pass that the earliest date you can reach the event *End* is the end of week 7. However, Rule 2 says you can't reach that event until you have completed Activities 2 and 5. Therefore, to finish your project by the end of week 7, the latest you can finish Activities 2 and 5 is the end of week 7. Again, consider the lower path with Activities 3, 4, and 5.

- ✔ You must start Activity 5 by the beginning of week 6 to finish it by the end of week 7.

- ✔ According to Rule 2, you can't start Activity 5 until you finish Activities 1 and 4. Therefore, you must finish Activities 1 and 4 by the end of week 5.

- ✔ Hence, you must start Activity 4 by the beginning of week 3.

- ✔ You must finish Activity 3 before you can work on Activity 4. Therefore, you must finish Activity 3 by the end of week 2.

- ✔ You must start Activity 3 by the beginning of week 2.

Finally, consider the upper path.

- ✔ You must start Activity 2 by the beginning of week 7.

- ✔ You can't work on Activity 2 until you finish Activity 1. Therefore, you must finish Activity 1 by the end of week 6.

Now again, you see a catch. You must finish Activity 1 by the end of week 5 to start Activity 5 at the beginning of week 6. But, to start work on Activity 2 at the beginning of week 7, you must finish Activity 1 by the end of week 6. So, finishing Activity 1 by the end of week 5 satisfies both requirements. This situation illustrates the following guideline:

If two or more arrows leave the same activity, then the latest date to finish the activity or reach the event is also the earliest that you can start the next activity or reach the next event.

In Figure 5-2, the latest start dates for Activities 2 and 5 are the beginnings of week 7 and week 6, respectively. Therefore, the latest date to finish Activity 1 is the end of week 5. The rest is straightforward: You must start Activity 1 by the beginning of week 1 at the latest.

Table 5-2 summarizes the latest dates to start and finish each activity in our example.

| Table 5-2 | Latest Start and Finish Dates for Figure 5-2 | |
|---|---|---|
| *Activity* | *Latest Start Date* | *Latest Finish Date* |
| 1 | Beginning of week 1 | End of week 5 |
| 2 | Beginning of week 7 | End of week 7 |
| 3 | Beginning of week 2 | End of week 2 |
| 4 | Beginning of week 3 | End of week 5 |
| 5 | Beginning of week 6 | End of week 7 |

Sometimes you may feel that all these calculations are bogging you down. Consider writing the earliest and latest start dates and the earliest and latest finish dates at the top of each box. This step makes the whole process seem much simpler. See how this detail looks in Figure 5-3.

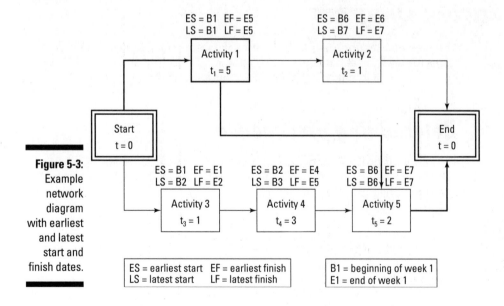

**Figure 5-3:** Example network diagram with earliest and latest start and finish dates.

Finally, determine the slack time of each activity in one of these two ways:

- ✔ Subtract the earliest possible start date from the latest allowable start date.
- ✔ Subtract the earliest possible finish date from the latest allowable finish date.

Activity 2, 3, and 4 have one-week slack times, while Activity 1 and 5 have no slack time. *Note:* If an activity's slack time is *0*, the activity is on a critical path.

An activity's slack time is the amount of time it can be delayed without causing a delay in your overall project completion time. However, slack time is actually associated with a sequence of activities rather than with an individual activity. Table 5-3 indicates that both Activities 2 and 3 (which are on the same path) have slack times of one week. If Activity 2 is delayed by a week, Activity 3 will have *0* slack time.

# Working with Your Project's Network Diagram

The previous sections in this chapter explain the general rules and procedures for drawing and analyzing any network diagram. This section tells you how to create and analyze the network diagram for your own project.

## Determining precedence

To draw your project's network diagram, decide the order of your project's activities. This section tells you different reasons why it may be necessary to perform activities in a particular order.

A *predecessor* to Activity 4 is an activity you must complete before you can work on Activity 4. An activity is an *immediate predecessor* to Activity 4 if you don't have any other activities between it and Activity 4.

When you determine the immediate predecessors for every activity, you have all the information you need to draw your project's network diagram. Several considerations affect the order in which you must perform your project's activities:

✔ **Required relationships:** Relationships that must be observed if project work is to be a success.

- **Legal requirements:** Federal, state, and local laws or regulations that require certain activities to be done before others.

  As an example, consider a pharmaceutical company that has developed a new drug in the laboratory and demonstrated its safety and effectiveness in clinical trials. The manufacturer wants to start producing and selling the drug immediately but can't. Federal law requires that the company obtain Food and Drug Administration (FDA) approval of the drug before selling it.

- **Procedural requirements:** Company policies and procedures that require certain activities to be done before others.

  Suppose you're developing a new piece of software for your organization. You've finished your design and want to start programming the software. However, your organization follows a systems development methodology that requires the management-oversight committee to formally approve your design before you can develop it.

✔ **Discretionary relationships:** Relationships you choose to establish between activities.

- **Logical relationships:** Performing certain activities before others because that procedure seems to make the most sense.

  Suppose you're writing a report. Because much of Chapter 3 depends on what you write in Chapter 2, you decide to write Chapter 2 first. You could write Chapter 3 first or work on both at the same time, but that plan increases the chance that you'll have to rewrite some of Chapter 3 after you finish Chapter 2.

- **Managerial choices:** Arbitrary decisions to work on certain activities before others.

  Perhaps one activity is harder, more apt to have problems, and so on. These reasons can influence the manager's decision to adjust the relationship of the project activities.

Decide on the immediate predecessors for your project's activities in one of two ways:

✔ **Front-to-back:** Start with the activities you can perform as soon as your project begins and work your way through to the end.

1. **Select the first activity or activities to perform as soon as your project starts.**

2. **Consider one of these activities and decide which activity or activities you can perform as soon as you finish your first ones.**

3. **Continue in this way until you've considered all activities in the project.**

✔ **Back-to-front:** Choose the activity or activities that will be done last on the project and continue backward toward the beginning.

1. **Identify the last activity or activities of your project.**

2. **Choose one of these activities and decide which activities to perform immediately before you start the last activity.**

3. **Continue in this manner until you've considered all activities in your project.**

In either case, record your project's immediate predecessors in a simple table as illustrated in Table 5-3.

| Table 5-3 | Immediate Predecessors | |
|-----------|------------------------|---|
| *Work Breakdown* | *Activity Description* | *Immediate Structure Code Predecessors* |
| 1 | (activity name) | None |
| 2 | (activity name) | 1 |
| 3 | (activity name) | None |
| 4 | (activity name) | 3 |
| 5 | (activity name) | 1, 4 |

Determine precedence based on the nature and requirements of the activities, not on the resources you think are available. Suppose Activities A and B can be performed at the same time but you plan to assign them to the same person. In this case, don't make Activity A the immediate predecessor for B, thinking that the person can work on only one activity at a time. Instead, let your diagram show that A and B can be done at the same time. Later, if you find out you have another resource who can help out with this work, you'll be able to evaluate the impact of performing Activities A and B at the same time. (See Chapter 6 for a discussion on how to determine when people are over-committed and how to resolve these situations.)

When you create your network diagram for simple projects, consider using stickum notes to represent your activities and events and attach them to chart paper or a wall. For more complex projects, consider using an integrated project-management software package. (See Chapter 17 for a discussion of how to use software to support your project planning and control, and check out *Microsoft Project For Dummies* by Martin Doucette [Wiley] for the lowdown on the most popular project-management software package.)

# Using a network diagram to analyze a simple example

Consider the following example of preparing for a picnic to illustrate the network diagram to determine schedules and meet expectations. (I'm not suggesting that you plan all your picnics this way, but it does illustrate the technique!)

It's Friday evening after a very tense week. You and your friend are considering what to do on the weekend to unwind and relax. The forecast for Saturday is sunny and mild weather, so you decide to visit a local lake for a picnic tomorrow. Because you want to get the most enjoyment possible from your picnic, you decide to plan this outing carefully by drawing and analyzing a network diagram.

Table 5-4 illustrates the seven activities you must perform to prepare your picnic and get to the lake.

| Table 5-4 | Activities for Your Picnic at the Lake | | |
|---|---|---|---|
| *Activity Identifier* | *Description* | *Who Will Do the Work* | *Duration (minutes)* |
| 1 | Load car | You and your friend | 5 |
| 2 | Get money from bank | You | 5 |
| 3 | Make egg sandwiches | Your friend | 10 |
| 4 | Drive to lake | You and your friend | 30 |
| 5 | Decide which lake | You and your friend | 2 |
| 6 | Buy gasoline | You | 10 |
| 7 | Boil eggs (for egg sandwiches) | Your friend | 10 |

In addition, you agree to observe the following constraints:

- ✔ You and your friend will start all activities at your house at 8 a.m. Saturday — you can't do anything before that time.
- ✔ You must complete all activities.
- ✔ You can't change who does the activities.
- ✔ The two lakes you're considering are in opposite directions from your house, so you have to choose before you begin your drive.

First, you decide the order of these various activities. In other words, you determine the immediate predecessors for each activity. Two dependencies are required: Your friend must boil the eggs before he can make the egg sandwiches (Duh!), and you must agree on which lake to visit before you start your drive.

The order of the rest of the activities is up to you. You may consider the following approach:

- ✔ Decide which lake before you do anything else.
- ✔ After you agree on the lake, you drive to the bank to get money.
- ✔ After you get money from the bank, you get gasoline.
- ✔ After you agree on the lake, your friend starts to boil the eggs.
- ✔ After the eggs are boiled, your friend makes the sandwiches.
- ✔ After you get back with the gas and your friend finishes the egg sandwiches, you both load the car.
- ✔ After you both load the car, you drive to the lake.

Table 5-5 illustrates these predecessor relationships.

| Table 5-5 | Predecessor Relationships for Your Picnic | |
|---|---|---|
| *Activity Identifier* | *Description* | *Immediate Predecessors* |
| 1 | Load car | 3, 6 |
| 2 | Get money from bank | 5 |
| 3 | Make egg sandwiches | 7 |
| 4 | Drive to lake | 1 |
| 5 | Decide which lake | None |
| 6 | Buy gasoline | 2 |
| 7 | Boil eggs (for egg sandwiches) | 5 |

Draw the network diagram for your project from the information in this table as follows:

1. **Start your project with a single event, *Start*.**

2. **Find all activities that have no immediate predecessors — they can all start as soon as you begin your project.**

   In this case, Activity 5 is the only activity that has no immediate predecessors.

3. **Start your diagram by representing these relationships, as illustrated in Figure 5-4.**

   Represent Activity 5 in a box and draw an arrow from *Start* to this box.

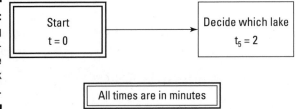

4. **Find all activities that have your first activity as an immediate predecessor.**

   In this case, your table shows two activities (2 and 7) have Activity 5 as an immediate predecessor. Represent them in boxes and draw arrows from Activity 5 to these boxes.

5. **Continue on in the same way with the remaining activities.**

   Recognize from Table 5-5 that only Activity 6 has Activity 2 as an immediate predecessor. Draw a box representing Activity 6 and draw an arrow from Activity 2 to Activity 6.

   The table shows further that only Activity 3 has Activity 7 as an immediate predecessor. Draw a box representing Activity 3 and draw an arrow from Activity 7 to Activity 3. Figure 5-5 depicts your diagram-in-progress.

   Now you realize that Activity 1 has both Activities 3 and 6 as immediate predecessors.

6. **Draw a box representing Activity 1 and draw arrows from Activity 3 to Activity 1 and from Activity 6 to Activity 1.**

   The rest is pretty straightforward. Only Activity 4 has Activity 1 as its immediate predecessor.

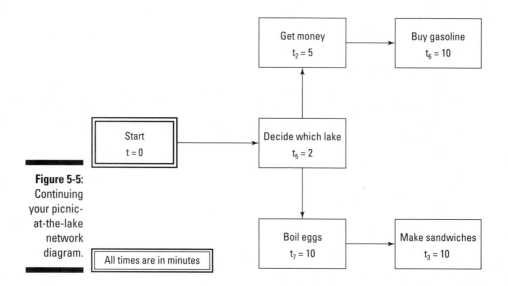

**Figure 5-5:**
Continuing
your picnic-
at-the-lake
network
diagram.

7. **Draw a box representing Activity 4 and draw an arrow from Activity 1 to Activity 4.**

8. **Draw a box representing the event called *End* and draw an arrow from Activity 4 to that box.**

Figure 5-6 depicts your project's complete network diagram.

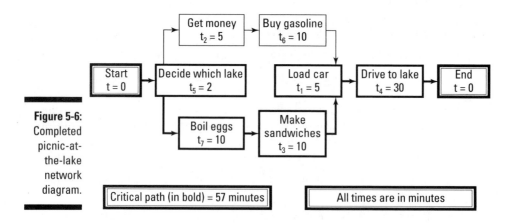

**Figure 5-6:**
Completed
picnic-at-
the-lake
network
diagram.

Now for the important questions. First, how long will you take to get to the lake for your picnic? The upper path (Activity 2 and 6) takes 15 minutes to complete. The lower path (Activity 7 and 3) takes 20 minutes to complete. Because the critical path is the longest path through your project, the path with Activity 5, 7, 3, 1, and 4 is the critical path. Your trip will take 57 minutes if you follow your network diagram.

Next, can you delay any activities and still get to the lake in 57 minutes? If so, which ones?

✔ The upper path (Activity 2 and 6) is a noncritical path.

✔ The network diagram reveals that Activity 5, 7, 3, 1, and 4 are on the critical path. Therefore, you can't delay any of them if you want to get to the lake in 57 minutes.

✔ However, Activity 2 and 6 can be performed at the same time as Activity 7 and 3. Activity 7 and 3 take 20 minutes to perform, while Activity 2 and 6 take 15 minutes. Therefore, Activity 2 and 6 have a total slack time of 5 minutes.

# Developing Your Project's Schedule

Developing your schedule requires a combination of activities, resources, and activity-performance sequences that gives you the greatest chance of meeting your client's expectations with the least amount of risk. This section helps you start making a schedule. It also focuses on some potential pitfalls and meeting time crunches.

## Taking the first steps

After you've specified your project's activities (see the discussion on creating Work Breakdown Structures in Chapter 4), take the following steps to develop an initial project schedule.

1. **Identify immediate predecessors for all activities.**

   Immediate predecessors define the structure of your network diagram.

2. **Estimate span times for all activities.**

   See the section on estimating activity duration later in this chapter.

3. **Identify all intermediate and final dates that must be met.**

   These define the criteria that your schedule must meet.

4. **Identify all activities or events outside your project that affect your project's activities.**

   Once you know these, you can set up the appropriate dependencies between them and your project's activities and events.

5. **Draw your network diagram.**

   Use the network diagram to determine what schedules your project can achieve.

6. **Analyze your project's network diagram to identity all critical paths and their lengths and to identify the slack times of noncritical paths.** (See the section *Interpreting your network diagram* earlier in this chapter for additional information on critical and noncritical paths.)

   This information helps you choose which project activities to monitor how often. It also suggests strategies for getting back on track if you encounter unexpected schedule delays.

If the completion date is acceptable to your client, you're done with your scheduling. However, if your client wants you to finish faster than your initial schedule allows, your analyses are just beginning.

## *Avoiding the pitfall of backing in to your schedule*

Beware of developing a schedule by *backing in,* that is, starting at the end of a project and working your way back toward the start to identify activities and estimate durations that allow you to meet your client's desired end date. Using this approach substantially decreases the chances that you'll meet the schedule for the following reasons:

- ✔ You may miss activities because your focus is on meeting a time constraint, not ensuring that you've identified all required work.

- ✔ You base your span-time estimates on what you can *allow* activities to take rather than what they'll *require*.

- ✔ The order for your proposed activities may not be the most effective one.

I was reviewing a colleague's project plan a while back and noticed that she had allowed one week for her final report's review and approval. When I asked her whether she thought this estimate was realistic, she replied that it certainly wasn't but she had to put it in for the project plan to work out. In other words, she was using time estimates that totaled to the number she *wanted to* reach rather than one she *could* reach.

# *Meeting an established time constraint*

Suppose your initial schedule has you finishing your project in three months, but your client wants the results in two months. Consider the following options for reducing the length of your critical paths:

- ✓ **Recheck the original span-time estimates.**

  - Be sure you have clearly described the activity's work.

  - If you used past performance as a guide for developing the span times, recheck to be sure all characteristics of your current situation are the same as those of the past performance.

  - Ask other experts to review and validate your estimates.

  - Ask the people who'll actually be doing the work on these activities to review and validate your estimates.

- ✓ **Consider using more-experienced personnel.** Sometimes more-experienced personnel can get work done in less time. Of course, using more-experienced people may cost you more money. Further, you're not the only one in your organization who needs those more-experienced personnel; they may not always be available!

- ✓ **Consider different strategies for performing the activities.** As an example, if you estimate a task you're planning to do internally to take three weeks, see if you can find an external contractor who can perform it in two weeks.

- ✓ **Consider *fast tracking* — removing tasks from the critical path and doing them in parallel with other tasks on the path.** Fast tracking reduces the time to complete the remaining path and may change the path to a noncritical one.

The technical term for performing activities in parallel to reduce the time is called *fast tracking*. Although you can finish faster by fast tracking, you increase the risk of having to redo portions of your work because finishing some tasks before others may have an impact on them.

As you find ways to reduce the lengths of critical paths, monitor paths that aren't initially critical to ensure that they haven't become critical. If one or more paths have become critical, use these same approaches to reduce their length.

# Illustrating ways to shorten a schedule

If your initial schedule doesn't meet your requirements, consider changing your network diagram to reduce the length of your project's critical paths. Consider the example of preparing for a picnic to see how you can approach this task.

Figure 5-6 illustrates your initial 57-minute plan. If arriving at the lake in 57 minutes is okay, your analysis is done. But suppose you and your friend agree that you must reach the lake no later than 45 minutes after you start on Saturday morning. What changes can you make to save you 12 minutes?

You may be tempted to change the estimated time for the drive from 30 minutes to 18 minutes, figuring that you'll just drive faster. Unfortunately, doing so doesn't work if the drive really takes 30 minutes. Remember, your plan represents an approach that you believe has a chance to work (though not necessarily one that's guaranteed). If you have to drive at speeds in excess of 100 miles per hour over dirt roads to get to the lake in 18 minutes, reducing the time has no chance of working. (However, it does have an excellent chance of getting you a speeding ticket.)

To develop a more realistic plan to reduce your project's schedule, take the following steps:

1. **Start to reduce your project's time by finding the critical path and reducing its time until a second path becomes critical.**

2. **To reduce your project's time further, shorten both critical paths by the same amount until a third path becomes critical.**

3. **To reduce the time still further, shorten all three critical paths by the same amount of time until a fourth path becomes critical, and so on.**

## Performing activities at the same time

One way to shorten a path's length is by taking one or more activities off the path and doing them in parallel with the remaining activities. However, often you have to be creative to successfully perform activities in parallel.

Consider the 57-minute solution to the picnic example in Figure 6-1. Assume an automatic teller machine (ATM) is next to the gas station that you use. If you use a full-service gas island, you can get money from the ATM while the attendant fills your gas tank. This strategy allows you to perform Activities 2 and 6 at the same time — in a total of 10 minutes rather than the 15 minutes you indicated in the initial diagram.

At first glance, it appears you can cut the total time down to 52 minutes by making this change. But look again. These two activities aren't on the critical path, so reducing their time has no impact on the overall project schedule. (In case you think you can save five minutes by helping your friend make the sandwiches, remember: You agreed that you can't swap jobs.)

Try again. This time, remember you must reduce the length of the critical path if you want to save time. Here's another idea: On your trip to the lake, you and your friend are in the car, but only one of you is driving. The other person is just sitting there. If you agree to drive, your friend can load the fixings for the sandwiches into the car and make the sandwiches while you drive. This adjustment appears to take ten minutes off the critical path. But can it?

The diagram in Figure 5-6 reveals that the upper path (Activity 2 and 6) takes 15 minutes, and the lower path (Activity 7 and 3) takes 20 minutes. Because the lower path is the critical path, removing five minutes from it can reduce the time to complete the overall project by five minutes. However, reducing the lower path by five minutes makes it the same length (five minutes) as the upper path. Therefore, both paths take five minutes and both are now critical.

Taking an additional 5 minutes off the lower path (because the sandwiches take 10 minutes to make) doesn't save more time for the overall project because the upper path still takes 15 minutes. However, you do have five minutes of added slack to the lower path.

Figure 5-7 reflects this change in your network diagram. Consider using your first idea to get money at the ATM while an attendant fills your car with gas. This move now can save you five minutes because the upper path is now critical.

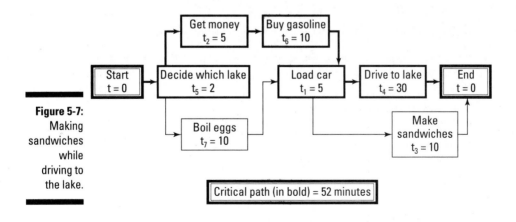

**Figure 5-7:**
Making sandwiches while driving to the lake.

Finally, you can decide which lake to visit and load the car at the same time, which saves you an additional two minutes. The final 45-minute solution is illustrated in Figure 5-8.

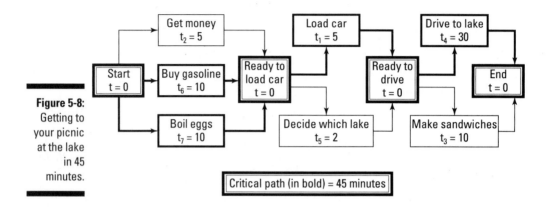

**Figure 5-8:**
Getting to your picnic at the lake in 45 minutes.

Consider a situation where you have to complete two or more activities before you can work on two or more new ones. Show this relationship in your diagram by defining an event that represents the two or more completed activities and then draw arrows from the completed activities to this event. Then draw arrows from that event to the new activities (see Figure 5-8).

In the example, you first complete the activities *Get money, Buy gasoline,* and *Boil eggs,* and then you can perform the activities *Load car* and *Decide which lake.* You represent this relationship by drawing arrows from each of the first three activities to a newly defined event, *Ready to load car,* and by drawing arrows from that event to the activities *Load car* and *Decide which lake.*

If you think this analysis is getting complicated, you're right. You pay a price to perform a group of activities faster. This price includes

- ✔ **Increased planning time:** You have to precisely detail all the activities and their interrelationships because you can't afford to make mistakes.

- ✔ **Increased risks:** The list of assumptions grows, increasing the chances that one or more will turn out to be wrong.

In the picnic-at-the-lake example, you make the following assumptions to arrive at a possible 45-minute solution:

- ✔ You can get right into the full-service island at a little after 8 a.m.

- ✔ Attendants are available to fill up your tank as soon as you pull into the full-service island.

✔ The ATM is available and working when you pull into the full-service island.

✔ You and your friend can load the car and make a decision together without getting into an argument that takes an hour to resolve.

✔ Your friend can make sandwiches in the moving car without totally destroying the car's interior in the process.

However, when you identify assumptions, you can increase the chances that they'll be true or develop contingency plans in case they don't happen.

Consider your assumption that you can get right into a full-service island about 8 a.m. on Saturday. You can call the gas station owner and ask whether your assumption is reasonable. If the gas station owner tells you he has no any idea of how long you'll have to wait, you may ask him whether it would make a difference if you paid him $200 in cash. When he immediately promises to cordon off the full-service island from 7:55 a.m. until 8:20 a.m. and assign two attendants to wait there, one with a nozzle and the other with a charge receipt ready to be filled out, so you'll be out in ten minutes, you realize you can reduce most uncertainties for a price! Your job is to determine how much you can reduce the uncertainty and what its price will be.

### Devising an entirely new strategy

So you have a plan for getting to the lake in 45 minutes. You can't guarantee the plan will work, but at least you have a chance. However, suppose your friend now tells you he really needs to get to the lake in 10 minutes, not 45! Your immediate reaction is probably "Impossible!" You figure creative planning is one thing, but how can you get to the lake in 10 minutes when the drive alone is 30 minutes?

By deciding that there is no way to arrive at the lake in 10 minutes when the drive alone takes 30 minutes, you have just redefined your criterion for project success. The true indicator of success in this project is arriving at the lake for your picnic, not performing a predetermined set of activities. The seven activities you originally formulated were fine, as long as they allowed you to get to the lake within your established constraints. But if the activities won't allow you to achieve success as you now define it (arriving at the lake in ten minutes), consider changing the activities.

Suppose you decide to seek out modes other than driving to the lake. After some checking, you discover that you can rent a helicopter for $500 per day that'll fly you and your friend to the lake in ten minutes. However, you figure that you both were thinking about spending a total of $10 on your picnic (for admission to the park at the lake). Clearly, spending $500 to get to a $10 picnic is absurd. So you don't even tell your friend about the possibility of renting the helicopter; you just reaffirm that getting to the lake in ten minutes is impossible. Unfortunately, you didn't know the reason your friend wanted to get to the lake in ten minutes. You find out that he can make a $10,000 profit on a business deal if he can get to the lake in ten minutes. Is spending $500 worth making $10,000? Sure. But you didn't know about the $10,000.

When developing schedule options, it's not your job to preempt someone else from making a decision. Instead, you want to present all options and their associated costs to the decision maker so he can make the best decision. In this instance, you should have told your friend about the helicopter option so he could have taken the relevant facts into account when he made the final decision.

### Subdividing activities

You can often reduce the time to complete a sequence of activities by subdividing one or more of the activities and performing parts of them at the same time. Figure 5-9 illustrates how your friend can save seven minutes when boiling the eggs and preparing the egg sandwiches by using this approach:

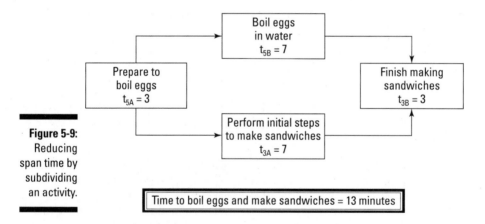

**Figure 5-9:** Reducing span time by subdividing an activity.

✔ **Divide the activity of boiling into two parts.**

- Prepare to boil eggs: Remove the pot from the cupboard, take the eggs out of the refrigerator, put the water and eggs in the pot, put the pot on the stove, and turn on the heat — estimated span time of three minutes.

- Boil eggs in water: Allow the eggs to boil in a pot until they're hard — estimated span time of seven minutes.

✔ **Divide the activity of making the egg sandwiches into two parts.**

- Perform initial steps to make sandwiches: Take the bread, mayonnaise, lettuce, and tomatoes out of the refrigerator; take the wax paper out of the drawer; put the bread on the wax paper; put the mayonnaise, lettuce, and tomatoes on the bread — estimated span time of seven minutes.

- Finish making sandwiches: Take the eggs out of the pot; shell, slice, and put them on the bread; slice and finish wrapping the sandwiches — estimated span time of three minutes.

✔ **First "Prepare to boil eggs"; next "Boil eggs in water" and "Perform initial steps to make sandwiches" at the same time; finally "Finish making sandwiches".**

As Figure 5-9 illustrates, the total time to boil the eggs and prepare the sandwiches is (3 minutes + 7 minutes + 3 minutes) = 13 minutes. *Note:* The total time for the original activity to boil the eggs is still ten minutes (three minutes to prepare and seven minutes in the water), and the total time for the original activity to make the sandwiches is also still ten minutes (seven minutes for the initial steps and three minutes to finish up). By specifying exactly how to perform these activities, you can complete them in 13 minutes rather than 20.

# *Estimating Activity Duration*

A span-time estimate is your best sense of how long you need to actually perform an activity. The estimate is not how long you want the activity to take or how long someone tells you it must take; the estimate is how long you think it really will take.

Unrealistically short span-time estimates can actually cause an activity to take longer than necessary.

✔ Because unrealistic estimates appear to comfortably meet your schedule targets, you don't seek realistic alternative strategies that increase the chances of accomplishing activities in their declared span times.

✔ If people believe span-time estimates are totally unrealistic, they'll stop trying to achieve them. When delays occur during an activity, people will accept them as inevitable instead of trying to find ways to overcome them.

Check out the nearby sidebar "Estimating isn't negotiating or bartering" for an example of estimating activity duration.

This section looks more closely at what you need to accurately estimate activity duration, including underlying factors, important resources, historical information, and your personal estimating skills.

## Determining the underlying factors

The underlying makeup of an activity determines how long it will take. Therefore, accurately estimating that activity's span time requires you to describe its different aspects and determine the effect of each one.

When estimating an activity's span time, consider past experience, expert opinion, and other available sources of information to clarify the following components:

- ✔ **Work performed by people:** Physical and mental activities that people perform. Examples include writing a report, assembling a piece of equipment, and thinking of ideas for an ad campaign.
- ✔ **Work performed by nonhuman resources:** Testing software on a computer and printing a report on a high-speed copy machine are examples.
- ✔ **Physical processes:** Physical or chemical reactions. Concrete curing, paint drying, and chemical reactions in a laboratory are examples.
- ✔ **Time delays:** Passage of time where no resource is performing. Time delays are typically due to the availability of resources. The need to reserve a conference room two weeks prior to holding a meeting is an example.

## Considering resource characteristics

Knowing the types of resources an activity requires can improve your estimate of the activity's span time. For example, not all reproduction machines generate copies at the same rate. Specifying the characteristics of the particular machine you'll use can improve the activity's span-time estimate.

You may need the following types of resources to support project work:

- ✔ Personnel
- ✔ Equipment
- ✔ Facilities
- ✔ Raw materials
- ✔ Information
- ✔ Funds

## Estimating isn't negotiating or bartering

Suppose your boss asks you to complete a project in six months. You explore all alternative strategies and determine you can't complete the project in less than 12 months. After some back-and-forth negotiating, you and your boss agree that you'll complete the project in nine months.

If you were both being honest initially, you just guaranteed the project's failure. You have agreed to complete the project three months before you can possibly finish it. Your boss has agreed to accept the final product three months after she needs it.

If you weren't honest initially, you each discovered something about the other. You found out that you need to add 50 percent to any end date your boss gives you (nine months is 50 percent more than six months). And your boss figured out that she can subtract 25 percent from your earliest date (nine months is 25 percent less than 12 months).

At the worst, you've reached an agreement that defines a performance target that's unacceptable to both of you. At the best, you've figured out not to trust the information you share with each other!

For each resource you need, determine its

- ✔ **Capacity:** Productivity per unit time period
- ✔ **Availability:** On the calendar; when a resource will be available

For example, a reproduction machine that produces 1,000 copies per minute can complete a job in half the time a machine that produces 500 copies per minute requires. Likewise, a large printing job can take half as long if you have access to a reproduction machine for four hours a day rather than two hours a day. (See Chapter 7 for more information on estimating project requirements for nonhuman resources.)

## *Finding sources of supporting information*

The first step toward improving your estimate's accuracy is recognizing the need to consider particular information when estimating span time. However, the accuracy also depends on the accuracy of the information you base that estimate on.

The information you need often has no single authoritative source. Therefore, compare information from the following sources as you prepare your estimates:

✔ Historical records of how long similar activities have taken in the past

✔ People who've performed similar activities in the past

✔ People who'll be working on the activities

✔ Experts familiar with the type of activity, even if they haven't performed work exactly like it before

## *Improving activity span-time estimates*

In addition to ensuring accurate and complete data, do the following to improve the quality of your span-time estimates (see Chapter 4 for further discussion of how to define and describe your project's activities):

✔ **Define your activities clearly.** Minimize the use of technical jargon and describe work processes fully.

✔ **Subdivide your activities until your lowest-level activity estimates are two weeks or less.**

✔ **Define activity start and end points clearly.**

✔ **Involve the people who'll perform an activity when estimating its duration.**

✔ **Minimize the use of fudge factors.** A *fudge factor* is an amount of time you add to your best estimate of span time *just to be safe*. Automatically estimating your final span-time estimates to be 50 percent greater than your initial ones is an example. Fudge factors compromise your planning for several reasons:

• Work tends to expand to fill the allotted time. If you're able to finish an activity in two weeks but use a 50 percent fudge factor to indicate a span time of three weeks, the likelihood that you'll finish in less than three weeks is almost zero.

• People use fudge factors to avoid studying activities in sufficient depth; as a result they can't develop viable performance strategies.

• Team members and other project audiences lose faith in the accuracy and feasibility of your plan because they know you're playing with numbers rather than thinking activities through in detail.

No matter how hard you try, estimating span time accurately can be next to impossible for some activities. Examples are activities you haven't done before, activities you'll perform in the future, and activities with a history of unpredictability. In these cases:

✔ Make the best estimate you can by following the approaches and guidelines in this section.

✔ Monitor activities closely as your project unfolds to identify details that may affect your initial estimate.

✔ Reflect any changes in your project schedule as soon as you become aware of them.

# Displaying Your Project's Schedule

Your network diagram doesn't contain your schedule — it presents information to consider as you develop your schedule. After you've selected your actual dates, choose one of the following formats to present your schedule:

✔ **Key-events list:** A table that lists events and the dates you plan to reach them

✔ **Activities list:** A table that lists activities and the dates you plan to start and end them

✔ **Combined key-events/activities list:** A table that includes events and activity dates

✔ **Gantt chart:** A timeline that illustrates when each activity starts, how long it continues, and when it ends

✔ **Combined milestone chart and Gantt chart:** A timeline that illustrates when activities start, how long they continue, when they end, and when selected events are achieved

Your 45-minute schedule for your picnic at the lake is presented in a key-events/activities list and a combined milestone and Gantt chart in Figures 5-10 and 5-11 (where triangles represent milestones), respectively.

Each format can be effective in particular situations. Consider the following when choosing the format to display your schedule:

✔ Key-events lists and activities reports are more effective for indicating specific dates.

✔ The Gantt chart provides a clearer picture of the relative lengths of activities and when they overlap.

✔ The Gantt chart provides a better high-level overview of a project.

| | Key Event/Activity | Person Responsible | Start Date (minutes after project start) | End Date (minutes after project start) | Comments |
|---|---|---|---|---|---|
| | 1. Get money | You | 0 | 5 | |
| | 2. Buy gasoline | You | 0 | 10 | Critical path |
| | 3. Boil eggs | Your friend | 0 | 10 | Critical path |
| | **A. Ready to load car** | **You and your friend** | - | **10** | **Critical path** |
| | 4. Load car | You and your friend | 10 | 15 | Critical path |
| | 5. Decide which lake | **You and your friend** | 10 | 12 | |
| | **B. Ready to drive** | You and your friend | - | **15** | **Critical path** |
| | 6. Make egg sandwiches | Your friend | 15 | 25 | |
| | 7. Drive to lake | You and your friend | 15 | 45 | Critical path |
| | **C. End – arrived at lake** | **You and your friend** | - | **45** | **Critical path** |

**Figure 5-10:**
Representing your picnic-at-the-lake schedule in a key-events/activities list.

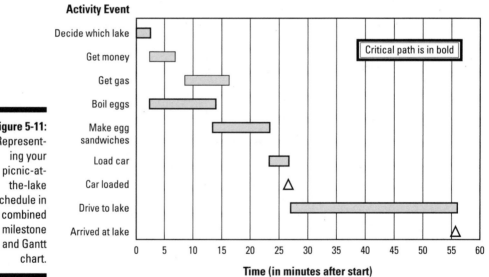

**Figure 5-11:**
Representing your picnic-at-the-lake schedule in a combined milestone and Gantt chart.

# Chapter 6

# Establishing Whom You Need, How Much, and When

. . . . . . . . . . . . . . . . . . . . . . . . . . . . . . . . . . . . . . . . . . . . . . . . . . .

### In This Chapter

▶ Focusing first on people's abilities

▶ Accurately planning your project's personnel needs

▶ Striking a balance among all those commitments

. . . . . . . . . . . . . . . . . . . . . . . . . . . . . . . . . . . . . . . . . . . . . . . . . . .

*I* remember reading the following declaration from a stressed-out project manager: "We've done so much with so little for so long [that] they now expect us to do everything with nothing!"

The truth is, of course, you can't accomplish anything with nothing; everything has a price. You live in a world of limited resources and not enough time. You always have more work to do than time and resources allow. You need to decide which tasks to pursue and then do everything possible to succeed at those activities. By identifying and planning the resources you need to perform your project, you can

✔ Explain team members' contributions to the project.

✔ Ensure that the resources are available when they're needed.

✔ Develop more accurate and realistic schedules.

✔ Monitor resource expenditures to identify and address possible overruns.

Some organizations have procedures that detail and track every resource on every project. Other organizations don't formally plan or track project resources at all. However, planning your resource needs is invaluable to your project's success, whether or not your organization requires it.

This chapter helps you figure out whom you need on your project, when, and for how long. The chapter also discusses how you can identify and manage conflicting demands for people's time.

# Determining People's Skills and Knowledge

Your project's success rests on your ability to enlist the help of the right people to perform necessary work. Take the following steps to clarify the work and to get qualified people to perform it.

- ✔ Identify the skills and knowledge needed to perform your project's activities.

- ✔ Specify the people who'll work on each activity.

- ✔ Determine how much effort they have to invest to complete their assignments.

- ✔ For those tasks on which they are less than fully committed, determine when they need to invest their time.

If you can influence the selection of team members, the personnel planning in the following sections can help you get the most qualified people. When you're arbitrarily assigned people or when your team already exists, the planning in the next sections can help you make the best use of their individual skills and knowledge.

## Working with a Skills Roster

The first requirement for selecting appropriate people for your project is knowing the skills and knowledge of potential candidates. A Skills Roster, illustrated in Figure 6-1, is a convenient format to display the skills and knowledge of people who may work on your project.

**Figure 6-1:** Displaying people's skills, knowledge, and interests in a Skills Roster.

|  | Bill | Mary | Sue | Ed |
|---|---|---|---|---|
| **Technical writing** |  |  | ▲● | △ |
| **Legal research** | △ | △ |  | ● |
| **Graphic design** | ▲● |  | ○ | ▲● |
| **Questionnaire design** | ○ |  |  | △ |

● – Primary skill or knowledge    ○ – Secondary skill or knowledge    △ – Interest

The left-hand column identifies skill and knowledge areas and the top row lists people's names. At the intersection of the rows and columns, you identify the level of each person's particular skills, knowledge, and interests.

You can use the following symbols to represent people's skill, knowledge, and interest levels:

- ✔ **Primary capability:** Person is able to assume a lead role in an assignment requiring this skill or knowledge.

- ✔ **Secondary capability:** Person has some training or experience in the skill or knowledge area but should work under another's guidance.

- ✔ **Interest:** Person would like to work on assignments involving this skill or knowledge.

The Skills Roster in Figure 6-1 shows that Sue is qualified to lead technical writing assignments and that she wants to work on this type of assignment. Ed is qualified to lead legal research tasks, but he'd prefer not to work on them. He prefers working on questionnaire design activities, but he has no skills or knowledge in this area.

By the way, you may figure that you'll never assign Ed to work on a questionnaire design activity because he has no relevant skills or knowledge. However, if you're trying to find more people who can develop questionnaires, Ed is a prime candidate. Because he wants to work on these types of assignments, he most likely is willing to put in extra effort to acquire the necessary capabilities.

## Depicting skill and knowledge levels in more detail

You can use a variety of numerical or alphanumeric codes to describe a person's skill, knowledge, or interest level. As an example, you can represent relative levels with the following numerical scale:

   5: Outstanding

   4: Above Average

   3: Average

   2: Limited

   1: Minimal

You may also indicate people's experience on activities that require skills and knowledge.

In addition to helping you request the appropriate people, a Skills Roster can reveal gaps and weaknesses in staff skills and knowledge. This information can guide the following:

- **Training:** The organization can develop or make available training to address the deficiencies.

- **Career development:** Individuals can develop skills and knowledge that are in short supply in order to increase their opportunities for greater responsibilities in the organization.

- **Recruiting:** When looking to hire staff for specific assignments, recruiters can look for candidates who have skills and knowledge in areas that the organization is deficient in.

## Creating the Skills Roster

Because Skills Rosters can be useful in different areas, your organization's group managers and supervisors, training departments, and employee-recruiting departments may already have rosters for some or all of the staff. If you decide to create a roster or help someone else in your organization create one, proceed as follows:

1. **Develop a complete list of the skill and knowledge areas that may be required for anticipated project assignments.**

   Determine these areas by consulting with subject-matter experts, your human resources department, and staff people who have done similar work in the past.

2. **Develop a list of all people who'll be included in the Skills Roster.**

   Include all people who may be assigned to your project.

3. **Have the people on your list rate their *proficiency* in each skill and knowledge area and then their *interest* in working on assignments in each area.**

4. **Have each person's direct supervisor rate the person's skill, knowledge, and interest.**

5. **Compare the ratings made by the person and his supervisor and reconcile any differences.**

   Consult the person being rated and his supervisor to determine the reasons for differences in ratings; choose the rating that you feel most accurately describes the person's proficiency.

6. **Prepare a final version of the Skills Roster.**

In a project environment, you often work with people you don't know well or haven't spent much time with. Making a special effort to find out about their skills, knowledge, and interests helps you to make more appropriate use of their special talents. In turn, this effort improves the team members' morale and productivity.

## Reconciling ratings: When a person and her supervisor's views differ

Comparing a person's ratings of her own skills, knowledge, and interests with those made by her supervisor can help identify situations that may lead to future performance problems. The following are typical situations, potential problems, and possible solutions:

✔ **A person rates her skills and knowledge in an area higher than her supervisor rates them.**

- Potential situation: She may feel that her supervisor is unfair, choosing not to give her challenging assignments with greater responsibility.

- Possible solution: Her supervisor can give her a more challenging assignment and monitor her performance closely. If all goes well, her supervisor's opinion of her capabilities can improve. If she has problems with the assignment, she can work out a plan with her supervisor to develop any skills or knowledge that she may be lacking.

✔ **A person rates her skills and knowledge in an area lower than her supervisor rates them.**

- Potential situation: She checks with her supervisor about the smallest issues and decisions because she feels she's not qualified to deal with them herself.

- Possible solution: Her supervisor can explain to her why he feels she's qualified to handle her assignment; her supervisor can point out when she's handling issues correctly and why.

✔ **A person has interests in areas that her boss doesn't know about.**

- Potential situation: She misses out on opportunities to work on assignments.

- Possible solution: The person can frequently talk with her supervisor about her interests and why she thinks she may perform well on assignments in these areas.

✔ **A person's boss thinks she has interests in areas where she doesn't.**

- Potential situation: The person's boss repeatedly gives her assignments in which she has little or no interest; she becomes bored and disinterested in work, and her productivity suffers.

- Possible solution: The person can discuss her interests with her boss; she can ask her boss whether she can work in those areas in addition to her normal assignments.

# Estimating Needed Commitment

Just because a person has the right skills and knowledge doesn't assure success. That person must be given an adequate amount of time to perform all the necessary work.

This section tells you how to prepare a Human Resources Matrix to display the people you need and the effort they'll have to put in to complete their tasks. In addition, it explains how you can take into account productivity, efficiency, and availability to make your estimates more accurate.

## Using a Human Resources Matrix

Planning your personnel needs begins with identifying whom you need and how much effort they have to invest. You can display this information in a Human Resources Matrix, as illustrated in Figure 6-2. The Human Resources Matrix displays the people assigned to each project activity and the work effort each person will contribute to each assignment.

**Figure 6-2:** Displaying personnel needs in a Human Resources Matrix.

| Activity | | Personnel (Person-hours) | | |
|---|---|---|---|---|
| Work Breakdown Structure Code | Description | J. Jones | F. Smith | Analyst |
| 2.1.1 | Design questionnaire | 32 | 0 | 24 |
| 2.1.2 | Pilot questionnaire | 0 | 40 | 60 |
| 2.2.1 | Prepare instructions | 40 | 24 | 10 |

*Work effort* or *person effort* is the actual time a person spends doing an activity. Express work effort in units of person-hours, person-days, person-weeks, and so forth. (You may still hear people express work effort as *man*-hours or *man*-days. Same concept — just outdated and politically incorrect!)

Work effort is related to, but different from, *span time* (duration). Work effort is a measure of resource use; span time is a measure of time passage (see Chapter 5 for more discussion of span time). Consider the work effort to complete the *design questionnaire* in the Human Resources Matrix in Figure 6-2. According to the matrix, J. Jones works on this activity for 32 person-hours and an unnamed analyst works on it for 24 person-hours.

This information alone, however, doesn't tell you the span time of the activity. If both people can work on the activity at the same time, if they're both assigned 100 percent to the project, and if no other aspects of the task take additional time, then the activity may be finished in four days. However, if either person is available for less than 100 percent time, if one or both people must work overtime, or if one person has to finish her work before the other can start, the span time won't be four days.

## Describing needed personnel

Gather the different personnel for the top row of the Human Resources Matrix as follows. In your Work Breakdown Structure (see Chapter 4 for further discussion), a lowest-level activity is one that's not subdivided any further. From your Linear Responsibility Chart (see Chapter 10 for further discussion), identify all personnel who will play a role on each lowest-level activity in your project. You can specify these people by listing the following:

- **Name:** The person who'll do the work

- **Position description:** The position or title of the person who'll do the work

- **Skills and knowledge:** The specific skills and knowledge that the person must have

Early in your planning, try to specify needed skills and knowledge, such as *must be able to develop work process flow charts* or *must be able to use Microsoft PowerPoint*. If you can identify the exact skills and knowledge that a person must have for a particular task, you increase the chances that the proper person will be assigned.

On occasion, you may use a position description or title (such as *operations specialist*) to identify a needed resource. In doing so, you assume anyone with that title has the necessary skills and knowledge. Unfortunately, titles are often vague and position descriptions are frequently out of date. Therefore, using titles or position descriptions are risky ways to get the right person for the job.

Very often, you identify people you want on your project by name. The reason is simple: If you've worked with someone before and she's done a good job, you want to work with her again. Unfortunately, although it's great for that person's ego, this method often reduces the chances that you'll get the best person for your project. People who develop reputations for excellence often get more requests than they can handle. When you don't specify the particular skills and knowledge needed for the activity, the manager — who has to find a substitute for that overextended person — doesn't know what skills and knowledge the substitute needs to have.

## Estimating required work effort

For all lowest-level activities, estimate the work effort that each person has to invest and enter the numbers in the appropriate boxes in the Human Resources Matrix. Develop your work-effort estimates as follows:

✔ **Describe in detail all work to perform the activity.** Include work directly and indirectly related to the activity.

Examples of work directly related to an activity include writing a report, meeting with clients, performing a laboratory test, and designing a new logo. Examples of indirect work include training to perform activity-related work and preparing periodic activity-progress reports.

✔ **Consider history.** Past history doesn't guarantee future performance. It does, however, provide a guideline for what's possible.

Determine whether an activity has been done before. If it has, review written records to determine the work effort. If written records weren't kept, ask people who've done the activity before to estimate the work effort they invested.

When using prior history to support your estimates, be sure

- The people had qualifications and experience similar to those of the people who'll work on your project.

- The facilities, equipment, and technology were similar to those that'll be used for your project.

- The time frame was similar to the one you anticipate for your project activity.

✔ **Have the person who'll do the work participate in estimating the required work effort.** Having people contribute to their work-effort estimates provides several benefits: Their understanding of the activity improves; the estimates are tailored for a person with their particular skills, knowledge, and prior experience; and their commitment to do the work for that level of work effort increases.

If you know who'll be working on the activity, have those people participate during the initial planning. If people don't join the project team until the start or during the project, have them review and comment on the plans you've developed.

✔ **Consult with experts familiar with this type of activity, even when they haven't performed work exactly like it before.** Experience and knowledge from all sources improve the accuracy of your estimate.

## Factoring in productivity, efficiency, and availability

Being assigned to a project full time doesn't mean a person can perform project work at peak productivity 40 hours per week, 52 weeks per year. Additional personal and organizational activities reduce the amount of work he produces. Therefore, consider each of the following factors when you determine the number of hours that people need to complete their project assignments:

✔ **Productivity:** The results a person produces per unit of time that he spends on an activity. The following affect his productivity:

  • **Knowledge and skills:** The raw talent and capability he has to perform a particular task.

  • **Prior experience:** His familiarity with the work and the typical problems of a particular task.

  • **Sense of urgency:** A person's drive to generate the desired results within established time frames. Urgency influences a person's focus and concentration on an activity.

  • **Ability to switch among several tasks:** A person's level of comfort moving to a second task when she hits a roadblock in her first one so she doesn't sit around stewing about her frustrations and wasting time.

  • **The quality and setup of the physical environment:** Proximity and arrangement of a person's furniture and the support equipment he uses; also the availability and condition of the equipment and resources.

✔ **Efficiency:** The proportion of time that a person spends on project work as opposed to organizational tasks that aren't related to specific projects. The following factors affect a person's efficiency:

- **Non-project-specific professional activities:** Time spent attending general organization meetings, handling incidental requests, and reading technical journals and periodicals about her field of specialty.

- **Personal activities:** Time spent getting a drink of water, going to the restroom, organizing her work area, conducting personal business on the job, and talking about non-work-related topics with co-workers.

The more time a person spends each day on non-project-specific and personal activities, the less time he has to work on his project assignments. (Check out the "How workers really spend their time" sidebar in this chapter for more info.)

✔ **Availability:** The portion of time a person is at the job as opposed to on leave. Organization policy regarding employee vacation days, sick days, holidays, personal days, mental health days, administrative leave, and so on define a person's availability.

When deciding how many work-hours to allow a person to do a particular task, adjust the number required at peak performance to allow for actual levels of productivity, efficiency, and availability.

# How workers really spend their time

A number of years ago, I read a study that determined the typical employee spends an average of four hours of an eight-hour work day on pre-planned project activities and work assignments. The interviewers in this study spoke with people with a wide range of job responsibilities from more than 100 organizations. In other words, the typical employee in this study averaged a work efficiency of 50 percent!

Since then I have found several organizations that conducted similar studies of their own operations. These organizations all found workers'

efficiency to be about 75 percent. You may think the workers in these companies were more efficient than the ones in the previous study. But, in fact, these studies were biased. The people surveyed wanted their organizations to think they were spending most of their time working on project assignments, and the organizations wanted to believe this was the case. Still, the organization studies found that people spent about 25 percent of each day doing something other than preplanned, project-related activities!

## Reflecting efficiency when you use historical data

How you reflect efficiency in your personnel planning depends on whether and how you track your work effort. If you base your estimate on historical data from time sheets and if either of the following situations is true, you don't have to factor in a separate measure for efficiency:

✔ **Time sheets have one or more categories to show time spent on non-project-specific work *and* people accurately report the actual time they spend on their different activities.**

If this is the case, the historical information represents the actual number of hours people worked on the activity in the past. You can comfortably use these numbers to estimate the actual level of effort this activity will require in the future, as long as people continue to record in separate categories the hours they spend on non-project-specific activities.

✔ **Your time sheet has no category for recording your time on non-project-specific work. However, you report accurately (by activity) the time you spend on work-related activities, and you apportion in a consistent manner your non-project-specific work among the available project activities.**

This historical information reflects the number of hours that people *recorded* they spent on the activity in the past, which includes time they actually spent on the activity and a portion of the total time they spent on non-project-specific work.

Again, if people's time-recording practices haven't changed, you can use these numbers to estimate the hours that people record for this activity in the future.

When collected properly, time-sheet data provide the most reliable source of past experience. However, the following time-sheet practices can cause the data to be inaccurate:

✔ People aren't allowed to record overtime, so some hours actually spent on an activity may never be known.

✔ People fill out their time sheets for a period several days before the period is over, so they must guess their hourly allocations for those several days.

✔ You copy the work-effort estimates from the project plan onto your time sheet each period instead of recording the actual number of hours you spend.

If any of these situations exist in your organization, don't use historical data from time sheets to support your work-effort estimates for your current project.

## *Factoring efficiency into personal estimates*

If you base estimates on the opinions of people with experience in similar activities or people who'll do the activities instead of on historical records, you have to factor in a measure of efficiency.

First, ask the person to estimate the required work effort assuming 100 percent efficiency. (In other words, don't worry about normal interruptions during the day, having to work on multiple tasks at a time, and so on.) Then modify the estimate to reflect efficiency as follows:

- ✔ If the person will use a time sheet that has one or more categories for non-project-specific work, then use her original estimate.

- ✔ If she'll use a time sheet that doesn't have categories to record non-project-specific work, add an additional amount to her original estimate to account for her efficiency.

---

# Be wise to the difference between efficiency and availability

A while back, a person in one of my training sessions was convinced that he took efficiency into account when he estimated levels of resources for his projects. His organization had performed an internal study and determined that a typical employee spent about 25 percent of his time on a combination of sick days, holidays, vacation time, personal days, and administrative leave. Therefore, he defined *full-time availability* to be 120 person hours each month for an employee, or 75 percent of the available 160 person hours. (He derived his estimate of 160 person hours by multiplying 8 hours per day by five days a week by four weeks per month — admittedly, this is an approximation.)

I explained that employees don't work at 100 percent efficiency even though they're available 120 person-hours each month. I told him that people actually have about 90 productive hours each month if they work at 75 percent efficiency. (I determined 90 person-hours by multiplying the 160 hours by the 75 percent availability factor and that number by the 75 percent efficiency factor.)

His reaction to my suggestion was interesting: He completely rejected my analysis! He said he refused to tell people that they only had to do six hours of work for every eight hours they charged to his project.

Unfortunately, he didn't realize that it wasn't about *allowing* people to bill eight hours while only working six. They were already doing this. He needed to decide whether to *recognize* the fact and reflect it in his plans or *ignore* it and pretend it wasn't happening. But ignoring the fact wouldn't change the reality.

As an example, suppose a person estimates that he needs 30 person-hours to perform a task (if he can be 100 percent efficient) and his time sheets have no categories for recording non-project-specific work. If you estimate that he'll work at about 75 percent efficiency, allow him to charge 40 person-hours to your project to complete the task. (75 percent of 40 person-hours is 30 person-hours — the amount you really need.)

Failure to consider efficiency in work-effort estimates and reviews can lead to incorrect conclusions about people's performance. Suppose your boss assigns you a project on Monday morning. He tells you the project will take about 40 person-hours, but he really needs it by Friday close of business. Suppose further that you work intensely all week and finish the task by Friday close of business. In the process, you record 55 hours for the project on your time sheet.

If your boss doesn't realize that his initial estimate of 40 person-hours was based on your working at 100 percent efficiency, he'll think you took 15 hours longer than you should have. On the other hand, if your boss recognizes that 55 person-hours *on the job* translates into about 40 person-hours of work *on specific project tasks,* your boss will appreciate that you invested extra effort to meet his aggressive deadline.

Although your performance is the same, overlooking the impact of efficiency makes you appear less capable, while correctly considering it makes you appear intensely dedicated.

The longer your involvement in an assignment, the more important efficiency and availability become. Suppose you decide you have to spend one hour on an assignment. You can reasonably figure your availability is 100 percent and your efficiency is 100 percent, so you charge your project one hour for the assignment. If you need to spend six hours on an assignment, you can figure your availability is 100 percent, but you must consider 75 per cent efficiency (or a similar planning figure). Therefore, charge one workday (eight work hours) to ensure that you can spend the six hours on your assignment.

However, if you plan to devote one month or more to your assignment, you'll most likely take some leave days during that time. Even though your project budget doesn't have to pay for your annual or sick leave, one person-month means you have about 97 hours for productive work on your assignment, assuming 75 percent efficiency and 75 percent availability (2,080 hours total in a year ÷ 12 months in a year × .75 × .75).

The numbers in Table 6-1 depict productive person-hours available at different levels of efficiency and availability.

## Beware of the hierarchical work-effort estimate

Reflecting reality in your plan increases the chances that you'll actually accomplish it. However, in your effort to consider all important influences, sometimes you overcompensate and actually make the plan less realistic.

Suppose you plan to assign a task to Harry's group. However, Harry passes the assignment to Mary, who passes it to Beth, who passes it to Joe, who actually does the required work. You ask Harry to estimate the work effort to complete the task. Harry in turn asks Mary, who asks Beth, who asks Joe. Joe estimates it'll take two person-weeks of actual work to complete the task. However, Joe, Beth, Mary, and Harry all know the

organization has determined that people work at 75 percent efficiency, so each of them reflects this factor in his or her estimate to be realistic. So Joe tells Beth it'll take 2.7 person-weeks; Beth tells Mary it'll take 3.6 person-weeks; Mary tells Harry it'll take 4.8 person-weeks; and Harry tells you it'll take 6.4 person-weeks!

The problem, of course, was communication (or the lack of it!). Each person separately factored in efficiency without telling the other members of the group. Including this factor one time is appropriate; including it four times is wasteful and misleading.

| Table 6-1 | Person-Hours Available for Project Work | | |
|---|---|---|---|
| | *Productive Person-Hours Available* | | |
| | *100 Percent Efficiency, 100 Percent Availability* | *75 Percent Efficiency, 100 Percent Availability* | *75 Percent Efficiency, 75 Percent Availability* |
| 1 person-day | 8 | 6 | 4.5 |
| 1 person-week | 40 | 30 | 22.5 |
| 1 person-month | 173 | 130 | 98 |
| 1 person-year | 2080 | 1560 | 1170 |

Develop your own planning figures if your organization uses different levels of efficiency or availability.

In addition to reflecting the influence of efficiency and availability, improve the accuracy of your work-effort estimates by doing the following:

✔ **Define your activities clearly.** Minimize the use of technical jargon and describe associated work processes (see Chapter 4 for further discussion).

✔ **Subdivide your activities.** Do so until you estimate that your lowest-level activities will take two person-weeks or less.

✔ **Update work-effort estimates when project personnel or task assignments change.**

# Ensuring You Can Meet Your Resource Commitments

If you work on only one activity at a time, determining whether or not you're overcommitted can be straightforward. But suppose you plan to work on several activities that partially overlap during a particular time period. Then you must decide when to work on each activity to see whether your multitasking has left you overcommitted.

This section shows how to schedule your work effort for a task, how to identify resource overloads, and how to resolve those overloads.

## Planning your initial allocations

The first step in making sure you can handle all project commitments is to decide when you'll work on each activity. If your initial plan has you working on more than one activity at the same time, your next task is to determine the total level of effort you'll have to devote to meet your multiple commitments.

Begin planning out your workload by developing

✔ A Human Resources Matrix (see "Using a Human Resources Matrix" earlier in this chapter for more info).

✔ A Person-Loading Graph or Person Loading Chart for each individual in the Human Resource Matrix.

A *Person-Loading Graph is* a bar graph that depicts the level of work effort you'll spend each day, week, or month of an activity. A *Person-Loading Chart* presents the same information in a table. The graphical format highlights peaks, valleys, and overloads more effectively while the tabular format presents exact work-effort amounts more clearly. Prepare Person-Loading Charts or Graphs for each project team member.

Suppose you plan to work on Tasks 1, 2, and 3 of a project. Table 6-2 depicts the person-hours you plan to spend on each task (consider that efficiency has already been reflected in these estimates — see the previous section "Estimating Needed Commitment" for more on efficiency).

| Table 6-2 | Proposed Work Effort on Three Activities |
|---|---|
| *Activity* | *Level of Effort (person-hours)* |
| Task 1 | 60 |
| Task 2 | 40 |
| Task 3 | 30 |

The Gantt Chart (see Chapter 5) in Figure 6-3 illustrates a plan to perform Task 1 in Weeks 1, 2, and 3, Task 2 in Weeks 2 and 3, and Task 3 in Weeks 3, 4, and 5. The chart shows Task 1 and Task 3 take three weeks and Task 2 takes two weeks. Table 6-2 indicates 60 person-hours on Task 1 (50 percent of your available time over the task's three-week period), 40 person-hours on Task 2 (50 percent of your available time over the task's two-week period), and 30 person-hours on Task 3 (25 percent of your available time over the task's three-week period). Therefore, if you don't have to work on the tasks at the same time, you should have no problem completing your work on each one.

But your initial plan has you working on both Tasks 1 and 2 in week 2 and on all three tasks in week 3. You have to decide how much effort you'll put in each week on each of the three tasks to see whether you can work on all three activities as they're currently scheduled.

As a starting point, assume you'll spend your time evenly over the life of each task. That means you'll work 20 hours a week on Task 1 during Weeks 1, 2, and 3, 20 hours a week on Task 2 during Weeks 2 and 3, and 10 hours a week on Task 3 during Weeks 3, 4, and 5.

Determine the total effort you'll have to devote to the overall project each week by adding up the hours you'll spend on each task each week as follows:

- ✔ In Week 1, you'll work 20 person-hours on Task 1 for a total commitment to the project of 20 person-hours.

- ✔ In Week 2, you'll work 20 person-hours on Task 1 and 20 person-hours on Task 2, for a total commitment to the project of 40 person-hours.

- ✔ In Week 3, you'll work 20 person-hours on Task 1, 20 on Task 2 and 10 on Task 3, for a total commitment to the project of 50 person-hours.

- ✔ In Weeks 4 and 5, you'll work 10 person-hours on Task 3, for a total commitment to the project of 10 person-hours.

These commitments are displayed in the *Person Loading Chart* of Figure 6-3. A quick review reveals that this plan has you working 10 hours of overtime in Week 3. If you're comfortable putting in this overtime, this plan works. If you aren't, you have to come up with an alternative strategy to reduce your Week 3 commitments.

# Resolving potential resource overloads

If you don't change your allocations for Week 3 and you're unwilling to work 10 hours of overtime, you'll accomplish less on one or both of the activities than you planned because you'll only put in 80 percent of the total effort required. This lower per cent delays at least one of the two activities.

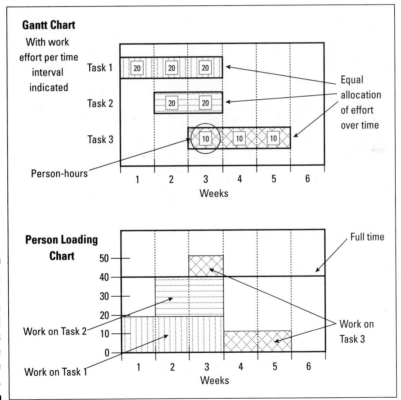

**Figure 6-3:** Planning to work on several activities over the same time period.

Consider the following strategies to eliminate your overcommitment:

✔ **Allocate your time unevenly over the duration of one or more activities.** Instead of spending the same number of hours on a task each week, plan to spend more hours some weeks than others.

Suppose you choose to spend your hours unevenly over the duration of Task 1 by increasing your commitment by 10 hours in the first week and reducing it by 10 hours in the third week, as depicted in Table 6-3. Figure 6-4 illustrates how this uneven distribution removes your overcommitment in week 3.

| Table 6-3 | Proposed Work Effort Each Week on Task 1 |
|---|---|
| *Time Period* | *Level of Effort (person-hours)* |
| Week 1 | 30 |
| Week 2 | 20 |
| Week 3 | 10 |

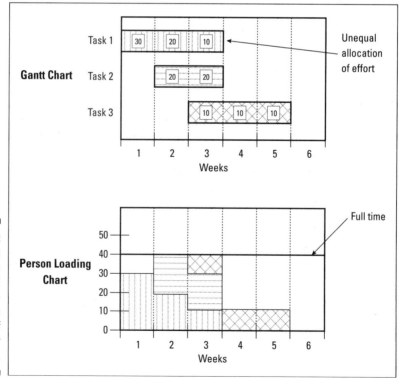

**Figure 6-4:** Eliminating a resource overload by changing the allocation of hours over the task life.

✔ **Take advantage of any slack time that may exist in your assigned activities.** Consider starting one or more activities earlier or later.

Figure 6-5 illustrates how you can remove the overcommitment in Week 3 by taking advantage of slack time that may be associated with Task 3. If Task 3 has at least one week of slack time, you can reduce your total work on the project in Week 3 to 40 person-hours by delaying both the start and the end of Task 3 by one week. (See Chapter 5 for a detailed definition and discussion of slack time.)

✔ **Assign some of the work you were planning to do in Week 3 to someone else on your project, or to a newly assigned team member of an external vendor, or to a contractor.** Reassigning 10 person-hours of your work in Week 3 removes your overcommitment.

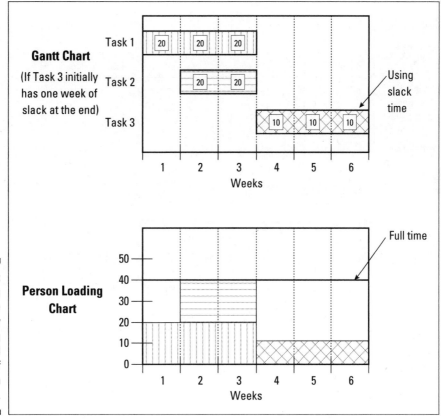

**Figure 6-5:** Eliminating a resource overload by changing the start and end dates of a task with slack time.

Show the total hours that each person will spend on your project in a Summary Person Loading Chart as illustrated in Figure 6-6. This chart helps you to

- ✔ Identify who may be available to share the load of overcommitted people.

- ✔ Determine the personnel budget for your project by multiplying the number of hours people work on the project by their weighted labor rates. (See Chapter 7 for more information.)

**Figure 6-6:** Illustration of a Summary Person Loading Chart.

|  | Person-hours | | | | | |
|---|---|---|---|---|---|---|
|  | Week 1 | Week 2 | Week 3 | Week 4 | Week 5 | Total |
| You | 20 | 40 | 50 | 10 | 10 | 130 |
| Bill | 10 | 20 | 10 | 30 | 10 | 80 |
| Mary | 15 | 10 | 20 | 10 | 30 | 85 |
| Total | 45 | 70 | 80 | 50 | 50 | 295 |

## Coordinating assignments across multiple projects

Working on overlapping tasks can place conflicting demands on a person, whether the tasks are on one project or several. Although successfully addressing these conflicts can be more difficult when more than one project manager is involved, the techniques for analyzing them are the same. This section illustrates how you can use the techniques and displays from the previous sections to resolve resource conflicts that arise from working on multiple projects at the same time.

You can manage resource assignments across projects if you prepare Person Loading Graphs or Charts for each project.

Figure 6-7 illustrates a Person Loading Chart for each person in your group. This chart is derived from the summary Person Loading Charts for each person's projects.

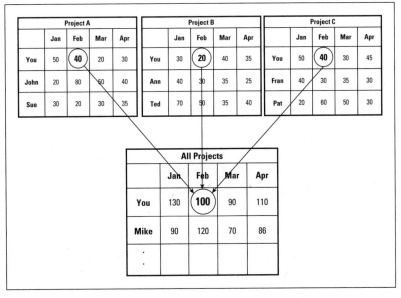

**Figure 6-7:**
Using
Person
Loading
Charts to
plan your
time on
several
projects.

Suppose you'll be working on three projects in January, February, and March. Consider your current plans for February. You're already committed to work on Projects A, B, and C for 40, 20, and 40 person-hours, respectively. If someone wants you to devote 80 person-hours to Project D in February, you have several options:

✔ If you assume that you have a total of 160 person-hours available in the month, then you can devote 60 person-hours to Project D with no problem.

✔ However, you don't currently have the other 20 hours available. You may consider the following:

• Find someone to assume 20 person-hours of your commitments to Projects A, B, or C in February.

• Shift your work on one or more of these projects to January or March.

• Work overtime.

# Chapter 7

# Planning for Other Resources and Developing the Budget

. . . . . . . . . . . . . . . . . . . . . . . . . . . . . . . . . . . . . . . . . . . . .

*In This Chapter*

▶ Accounting for the project's nonpersonnel costs

▶ Preparing a detailed budget

. . . . . . . . . . . . . . . . . . . . . . . . . . . . . . . . . . . . . . . . . . . . .

*A* key part of effective project management is ensuring that resources are available throughout the project when and where they're needed and according to specifications. When people are available for a scheduled task but the necessary computers and laboratory equipment aren't, your project can have costly delays and unanticipated expenditures. Also, your team members may experience frustration that leads to their reduced commitment.

The final requirement for a successful project is sufficient funds to secure the necessary people and resources. All major project decisions (including whether to undertake it, whether to continue it, and — after it's done — to determine how successful it was) must consider the project's costs.

This chapter looks at how you can determine, specify, and display your non-personnel resource needs and then how to develop your project budget.

# Planning for Nonpersonnel Resources

In addition to personnel, your project may require a variety of other resources (such as furniture, fixtures, equipment, raw materials, and information) that are important to your project's success. Plan for these nonpersonnel resources the same way you plan to meet your personnel requirements. (Check out Chapter 6 for more on meeting your personnel needs.) Develop the following:

 ✔ A resources matrix for all nonpersonnel resources

 ✔ Individual usage charts for each nonpersonnel resource

 ✔ A summary usage chart for all nonpersonnel resources

Figure 7-1 illustrates a resources matrix for nonpersonnel resources. The matrix displays the following information for every lowest-level activity in your project Work Breakdown Structure (WBS; see Chapter 4 for a discussion of a WBS):

 ✔ The nonpersonnel resources to perform the activity (in this illustration, computers, copiers, and use of a test laboratory)

 ✔ The required amount of each resource

| Activity | | Amount of Resource Required (Hours) | | |
|---|---|---|---|---|
| **Work Breakdown Structure Code** | **Description** | **Computer** | **Copier** | **Test Lab** |
| 1.2.1 | Design layout | 32 | 0 | 0 |
| 2.1.4 | Prepare report | 0 | 40 | 0 |
| 3.3.1 | Design device | 40 | 0 | 32 |

**Figure 7-1:** An illustration of a resources matrix for non-personnel resources.

Figure 7-1 suggests you'll need 40 hours of computer time and 32 hours of the test laboratory to design a device.

Estimate the amount of each resource you need by examining the nature of the task and the capacity of the resource. For example, determine the amount of copier time you need to reproduce a report as follows:

 ✔ Estimate the number of report copies.

 ✔ Estimate the number of pages per copy.

 ✔ Specify the copier capacity in pages per unit of time.

 ✔ Multiply the first two numbers and divide the result by the third number to determine the amount of copier time to reproduce your reports.

Figure 7-2 illustrates a computer usage chart for your task. The chart indicates that Task 1 requires ten hours of computer time in Weeks 1, 2, and 3, respectively.

|  | Computer Time Required (Hours) | | | | | |
|---|---|---|---|---|---|---|
|  | Week 1 | Week 2 | Week 3 | Week 4 | Week 5 | Total |
| Task 1 | 10 | 10 | 10 |  |  | 30 |
| Task 2 |  | 20 | 20 |  |  | 40 |
| Task 3 |  |  | 10 | 20 | 30 | 60 |
| Total | 10 | 30 | 40 | 20 | 30 | 130 |

**Figure 7-2:** Illustration of a computer usage chart.

Figure 7-3 summarizes the weekly usage of all resources for the project.

|  | Amount of Resource Required (Hours) | | | | | |
|---|---|---|---|---|---|---|
|  | Week 1 | Week 2 | Week 3 | Week 4 | Week 5 | Total |
| Computer | 10 | 30 | 40 | 20 | 30 | 130 |
| Copier | 10 | 20 | 10 | 30 | 10 | 80 |
| Test lab | 15 | 10 | 20 | 10 | 30 | 85 |

**Figure 7-3:** Illustration of a summary usage chart for non-personnel resources.

# Making Sense of the Dollar: Project Costs and Budgets

All project resources cost money. In a world of limited funds, you're constantly deciding how to get the most return for your investment. Therefore, estimating a project's costs is important for several reasons:

✔ It enables you to weigh anticipated benefits against anticipated costs to see whether the project makes sense.

✔ It allows you to see whether the necessary funds are available to support the project.

✔ It serves as a guideline to help ensure that you have sufficient funds to complete the project.

Although you may not develop and monitor detailed budgets for all your projects, knowing how to work with project costs can make you a better project manager and increase your chances of project success.

This section looks at different types of project costs that you may encounter. It then offers helpful tips for developing your own project budget.

## Looking at different types of project costs

A *project budget* is a detailed, time-phased estimate of all resource costs for your project. You typically develop a budget in stages — from an initial rough estimate to a detailed estimate to a completed, approved project budget. On occasion, you may even revise your approved budget while your project is in progress (check out "Refining your budget as you move through your project" later in this section for more info).

*Direct costs* are expenditures for resources solely used for your project. Direct costs include salaries for team members on your project; specific materials, supplies, and equipment for your project; travel to perform work on your project; and subcontracts that provide support exclusively to your project.

*Indirect costs* are expenditures that may support more than one project but aren't individually allocated to them. Indirect costs fall into two categories:

✔ **Overhead costs:** Expenditures that are difficult to subdivide and allocate directly. Examples include employee benefits, office space rent, general supplies, and the costs of furniture, fixtures, and equipment.

You need an office to work on your project activities and office space costs money. However, your organization has an annual lease for office space, the space has many individual offices and work areas, and people work on numerous projects throughout the year. Because you have no clear record of your office's rent, your office space is treated as an indirect project cost.

✔ **General and administrative costs:** Expenditures that keep your organization operational (if your organization doesn't exist, you can't perform your project). Examples include salaries of your contracts department, finance department, and top management as well as fees for accounting and legal services.

Suppose you're planning to design, develop, and produce a company brochure. Direct costs for this project may include the following:

- ✔ **Labor:** Salaries for you and other team members for the hours you work on the brochure
- ✔ **Materials:** The special paper stock for the brochure
- ✔ **Travel:** The costs for driving to investigate firms that may design your brochure cover
- ✔ **Subcontract:** The services of an outside company to design the cover art

Indirect costs for this project may include the following:

- ✔ **Employee benefits:** Benefits in addition to your salary while you're working on the brochure
- ✔ **Rent:** The cost of the office space you use when you're developing the copy for the brochure
- ✔ **Equipment:** The computer you use to compose the copy for the brochure
- ✔ **Management and administrative salaries:** A portion of the salaries of upper managers and staff who perform the administrative duties necessary to keep your organization functioning

## Developing your project budget

Organization decision makers would love to have a detailed and accurate budget when someone proposes a project so they can assess its relative benefits to the organization and decide whether they have sufficient funds to support it. Unfortunately, you can't prepare such an estimate until you develop a clear understanding of the work and resources the project will require.

But in reality, decisions of whether to go forward and how to undertake projects must be made before people can prepare highly accurate budgets. However, you can develop and refine your project budget in the following stages to provide the best information in time for these key project decisions:

- ✔ **Rough order-of-magnitude estimate:** An initial estimate of costs based on a general sense of the project work. This estimate is made without detailed data. Depending on the nature of the project, the final budget may wind up 100 per cent (or more!) higher than this initial estimate.

  Prepare a rough order-of-magnitude estimate by considering: the costs of similar projects (or similar activities that will be part of your project) in the past; applicable cost and productivity ratios (such as the number of assemblies that can be produced per hour), and other methods of approximation.

This estimate sometimes expresses what someone wants to *spend* rather than what the project will really *cost*. You typically don't detail this estimate by lowest-level project activity because you prepare it in a short amount of time and before you've identified the project activities.

Whether or not people acknowledge it, initial budget estimates in annual plans and long-range plans are typically rough order-of-magnitude estimates. As such, these estimates may change significantly as the planners define the project in greater detail.

✔ **Detailed budget estimate:** An itemization of the estimated costs for each project activity. You prepare this estimate by developing a detailed WBS (see Chapter 4) and estimating the costs of all lowest-level activities. (See Chapter 6 for information on estimating work effort and the section "Planning for Nonpersonnel Resources" earlier in this chapter for ways to estimate the needs for nonpersonnel resources.)

✔ **Completed, approved project budget:** A detailed project budget that essential people approve and agree to support.

### Refining your budget as you move through your project

A project moves through five phases as it evolves from an idea to a reality: *conceive, define, start, perform,* and *close.* (See Chapter 1 for more discussion of these phases.)

Prepare and refine your budget as your project moves through its different phases.

1. **Prepare a rough order-of-magnitude estimate in the *conceive* phase.**

   Use this estimate to decide whether the organization should consider this project further by entering the *define* phase to develop a detailed plan.

   Rather than an actual estimate of costs, this number often represents an amount that your project can't exceed in order to have an acceptable return for the investment. Your confidence in this estimate is low because you don't base it on detailed analyses of the project activities.

2. **Develop your detailed budget estimate in the *define* phase after you specify your project activities and get approval for your detailed budget.**

   Check with your organization to find out who must approve project budgets. At a minimum, the budget is typically approved by the project manager, the head of finance, and possibly the project manager's supervisor.

3. **Review your approved budget in the *start* phase — when you identify the people who will be working on your project and when you start to develop formal agreements for the use of equipment, facilities, vendors, and other resources.**

   Check Chapter 12 for suggestions on what to look for when reviewing the budget at the start of your project.

4. **Get approval for any required budget changes before you move to the *perform* phase.**

   Submit a request for any changes to the original budget to the same people who approved the original budget in Step 2.

5. **Monitor project activities and related occurrences throughout the *perform* and *close* phases to determine when budget revisions are necessary.**

   Check Chapter 12 for how to monitor project expenditures during your project's performance and how to determine whether budget changes are needed. Submit requests for necessary budget revisions as soon as possible to the same people identified in Step 2.

You may not personally work on all steps in your project budget. If you join your project after the initial planning, be sure to review the budget plans and resolve any questions and issues you may identify.

### *Estimating project costs*

Use a combination of the following approaches to develop a detailed budget:

- ✔ **Bottom-up:** Develop detailed cost estimates for each lowest-level activity in the WBS (refer to Chapter 4 for more information on this structure) and total these estimates to obtain the total project-budget estimate.

- ✔ **Top-down:** Examine the estimated cost of each major work assignment in the WBS to confirm its reasonableness.

Develop your bottom-up budget estimate as follows:

1. **Consider each lowest-level activity.**

2. **Determine direct labor costs for each activity by multiplying the number of hours each person will work on the activity by the person's hourly salary.**

   You can estimate direct labor costs by one of the following methods:

   - Using the salary of each person on the project
   - Using the average salary for people with a particular job title or in a certain department, and so on

Suppose you need a graphic artist to design overheads for your presentation. The head of the graphics department estimates the person will spend 100 hours on your project. If you know Harry (with a salary rate of $30 per hour) will work on the activity, you can estimate your direct labor costs to be $3,000. However, if the director doesn't know who'll work on your project, then use the average salary of a graphic artist in your organization to estimate the direct labor costs.

3. **Estimate the direct costs for materials, equipment, travel, contractual services, and other resources for each activity.**

   See the section "Planning for Nonpersonnel Resources" earlier in this chapter for information on how to determine nonpersonnel resources you need for your project. Consult with your procurement department, administrative staff, and finance department to determine the costs of these resources.

4. **Determine the indirect costs associated with each activity.**

   You typically estimate indirect costs as a fraction of the planned direct-labor costs for the activity. In general, your organization's finance department determines this fraction annually by the following method:

   • Estimating organization direct labor costs for the coming year.

   • Estimating organization indirect costs for the coming year.

   • Dividing the estimated indirect costs by the estimated direct labor costs.

   Choose your method of estimating indirect costs by weighing the potential accuracy of the estimate against the effort to develop it. See the nearby "Two approaches for estimating indirect costs" sidebar.

Table 7-1 illustrates a typical budget estimate. Suppose you're planning a project to design and produce a company brochure. You already have the following information:

✔ You estimate that you'll spend 200 person-hours on the project at $30 per hour and Mary will spend 100 person-hours at $25 per hour.

✔ You estimate your stationery for the brochures to be $1,000.

✔ You estimate $300 in travel costs to visit vendors and suppliers.

✔ You expect to pay a vendor $5,000 for the brochure's artwork.

✔ Your organization has a combined indirect cost rate of 60 percent.

| Table 7-1 | Project Budget for a Company Brochure | |
|---|---|---|
| *Cost Category* | *Cost* | *Total* |
| Direct Labor | You: 200 hours ($30 per hour) | $6,000 |
| | Mary: 100 hours ($25 per hour) | $2,500 |
| | Total Direct Labor | $8,500 |
| Indirect Costs (60 percent) | | $5,100 |
| Other Direct Costs | Materials | $1,000 |
| | Travel | $300 |
| | Subcontract | $5,000 |
| | Total Other Direct Costs | $6,300 |
| Total Project Costs | | $19,900 |

The top-down budget estimate encourages you to consider the relative emphases of different aspects. As an example, suppose you plan to develop a new piece of equipment. You develop a bottom-up cost estimate that suggests the project will cost $100,000 as follows:

- ✔ Design ($60,000)
- ✔ Development ($15,000)
- ✔ Testing ($5,000)
- ✔ Production ($20,000)

However, experience with similar projects suggests that approximately 40 percent of the total budget is devoted to design, not 60 percent. So your numbers indicate a design phase for a $150,000 project rather than a $100,000 project.

You have two choices: You can try to devise an alternative strategy for the design, or you can request an additional $50,000 for your project. But whichever you choose, you can't just arbitrarily change the numbers. You need a strategy for arriving at your new numbers!

# Two approaches for estimating indirect costs

Accurately determining the true cost of a project requires all activity and resource costs to be allocated appropriately. However, the cost of tracking and recording all expenditures can be considerable. Therefore, organizations developed methods for approximating the amounts of certain expenses assigned to different projects.

Following are two approaches for estimating indirect costs associated with an activity: The first approach defines two different indirect rates; it's more accurate but requires more detailed record keeping, so it's also more costly.

**Option 1: Use one rate for overhead costs and another rate for general and administrative costs.**

✔ Your finance department determines the overhead rate by calculating the ratio of all projected overhead costs to all projected direct salaries.

✔ Your finance department determines the general and administrative rate by calculating the ratio of all projected general and administrative costs to the sum of all projected direct salaries, overhead costs, and other direct costs.

✔ You determine overhead costs of an activity by multiplying its direct salaries by the overhead rate.

✔ You determine general and administrative costs of an activity by multiplying the sum of its direct salaries, overhead costs, and other direct costs by the general and administrative rate.

**Option 2: Use one indirect-cost rate for all overhead and general and administrative costs.**

✔ Your finance department determines the combined indirect-cost rate by calculating the ratio of all projected overhead costs to all projected direct salaries.

✔ You determine an activity's indirect costs by multiplying its direct salaries by the indirect cost rate.

Some organizations develop *weighted labor rates*, which combine hourly salary and associated indirect costs. As an example, suppose your salary is $30 per hour and your organization's indirect cost rate is 0.5. Your weighted labor rate is $45 per hour ($30 + 0.5 × $30).

# Chapter 8

# Dealing with Risk and Uncertainty

*Y*our first step toward a successful project is to develop a plan to produce the desired results on time and within budget. If your project lasts a relatively short time and you're thorough and realistic in your planning, then most likely your project will be a success.

However, the larger, more complex, and longer your project is, the more likely some aspects won't work out as you envisioned. Remember, "The best laid plans . . . ." You have the greatest chance for success if you confront the possibility of changes head-on *and* if you plan how to minimize the consequences of those changes from the outset.

This chapter discusses how to consider potential risks when you're deciding whether you'll undertake your project, when you're developing your project plan, and while you're performing your project's work. This chapter shows you how to identify and assess the impact of project risks, and it explores strategies for minimizing their consequences. Finally, this chapter gives pointers for preparing your own risk-management plan.

# Defining Risk and Risk Management

*Risk* is the possibility that you may not achieve your product, schedule, or resource targets because something unexpected occurs or something planned doesn't occur. All projects have some degree of risk because predicting the future with certainty is impossible. However, project risk is greater

- ✔ The longer your project lasts.
- ✔ The longer the time between preparing your project plan and starting the work.
- ✔ The less experience you, your team members, or your organization may have with similar projects.
- ✔ The newer your project's technology.

*Risk management* is the process of identifying possible risks, assessing their potential effect, and then developing and implementing plans for minimizing those negative effects. Risk management can't eliminate risks, but it offers the best chance for successfully accomplishing your project despite the uncertainties of a changing environment.

So how do you address your project's risks? Take the following steps to determine, evaluate, and manage the risks that may affect your project:

1. **Identify risks.**

   Determine which aspects of your plan or project environment may change.

2. **Assess their potential effect on your project.**

   Assess what will happen if those aspects don't work out the way you envision.

3. **Develop plans for mitigating the effect of the risks.**

   Decide how you can protect your project from the consequences of risks.

4. **Monitor the status of your project's risks throughout performance.**

   Determine whether existing risks are still present, whether the likelihood of these risks is increasing or decreasing, and whether new risks are arising.

5. **Inform key audiences.**

   Explain the status and potential effect of all project risks — from the initial concept to the project's completion.

## Don't put all of your eggs in one basket

I met a man who was starting a large project that was a top priority for his organization. His project's success heavily depended on one person who would work on the project full time for six months and perform all the technical development. I asked whether he had considered the consequences of this person leaving the project before it was finished. He said he didn't have to worry about that because he just wouldn't allow the man to leave.

It occurred to me that his approach for dealing with risk was similar to the one of a woman who cancelled her health insurance for a year — because she wasn't planning on getting sick! He may have gotten top management to agree that the person would have no other assignments for the duration of his project. However, he still couldn't guarantee that the person wouldn't get sick or decide to leave the organization!

# *Focusing on Risk Factors and Risks*

The first step toward controlling risks is identifying them. However, not all risks pose the same degree of concern to all projects, and using a scatter-gun approach to identify risks that may affect your project leaves a significant chance that you'll overlook some important ones.

This section shows you how to identify potential risks on your project by recognizing the special situations that are most likely to occur.

## *Recognizing risk factors*

A *risk factor* is a situation that may give rise to one or more project risks. A risk factor itself doesn't cause you to miss a product, schedule, or resource target. However, it increases the likelihood that you'll miss one.

The fact that you and your organization haven't undertaken projects similar to the present one is a risk factor. Because you have no prior experience, you may overlook activities you need to perform or you may underestimate the time and resources to perform them. Having no prior experience doesn't guarantee you'll have these problems. However, it increases the chance that you'll have a problem.

Start to manage risks at the outset of your project and continue throughout its performance. At each point during your project, identify risks by recognizing your project's risk factors. Your plan and your current project phase can both suggest risk factors.

All projects progress through the following five phases:

- **Conceive:** An idea is born.
- **Define:** A plan develops.
- **Start:** A team forms.
- **Perform:** The team does the work.
- **Close:** The project ends.

(See Chapter 1 for a detailed discussion of these phases.)

Table 8-1 illustrates risk factors related to managing your project through these phases.

| Table 8-1 | Possible Risk Factors during Your Project's Evolution |
|---|---|
| *Life-Cycle Phase* | *Possible Risk Factors* |
| All | Insufficient time on one or more phases |
| | Key information not in writing |
| | Move to a subsequent phase without completing one or more of the earlier phases |
| Conceive | Some background information and plans not in writing |
| | No formal cost-benefit analysis |
| | No formal feasibility study |
| | Unknown originator of project idea |
| Define | Plan prepared by people unfamiliar with similar projects |
| | Plan not in writing |
| | Missing parts to the plan |
| | All or some aspects of plan not approved by all key audiences |
| Start | Plan not prepared by people on the project team |
| | Plan not reviewed or questioned by team members who didn't participate in its development |
| | No effort to establish team identity and focus |
| | No team procedures to resolve conflicts, reach decisions, or maintain communication |

| Life-Cycle Phase | Possible Risk Factors |
|---|---|
| Perform | Change of primary client's needs |
| | Incomplete or incorrect information regarding schedule performance and resource expenditures |
| | Inconsistent project-progress reporting |
| | Reassignment of one or more key project-supporters |
| | Replacement of team members |
| | Change of marketplace characteristics or demands |
| | Changes handled informally, with no consistent analysis of their effect on the overall project |
| Close | Project results not formally approved by one or more project drivers |
| | Workers assigned to new projects before completion of this project |

Table 8-2 depicts risk factors that different parts of your project plan may suggest.

| Table 8-2 | Possible Risk Factors |
|---|---|
| **Planning Information** | **Possible Risk Factors** |
| Project audiences | New client |
| | Prior problems with your client |
| | Only mild interest in your project by upper management or other key drivers (see Chapter 3 for a definition and discussion of project drivers and supporters) |
| | No project champion |
| | Unidentified project audiences |
| Project background | Project derived from a spontaneous decision, not a well-thought-out assessment |
| | No conclusive proof that your project can eliminate the problem it addresses |
| | Your project's beginning preceded by other, completed activities |

*(continued)*

**Table 8-2 (continued)**

| Planning Information | Possible Risk Factors |
|---|---|
| Project scope | Unusually large project |
| | Variety of skills and knowledge required |
| | Different organizational units involved |
| Project strategy | No declared strategy |
| | New, untested technology or approach |
| Project objectives | Missing objective(s) |
| | Unclear or missing performance measures |
| | Difficult-to-quantify performance measures |
| | Missing performance targets or specifications |
| Constraints | No identified constraints |
| | Vague constraints |
| | In general, risk factors in all constraints |
| Assumptions | Vague assumptions |
| | Risk factors in all assumptions |
| Work packages | Insufficiently detailed work packages |
| | Work package descriptions not developed by some or all team members |
| Roles and responsibilities | Roles and responsibilities not developed by all supporters |
| | Overdependence on one or more people |
| | No primary responsibility for one or more activities |
| | Two or more people with primary responsibility for same activity |
| | No one person with overall responsibility for project |
| Schedule (activity-duration estimates) | Time estimates backed into from an established end-date |
| | No historical database of performance times |
| | New procedures or technologies for part of project |
| | Activities performed by team members unfamiliar to you |

| Planning Information | Possible Risk Factors |
|---|---|
| Schedule (activity interdependencies) | Interdependencies not specifically considered during schedule development |
| | Partially related activities scheduled simultaneously to save time |
| | No formal analytical approach to assess effect of interdependencies on schedule |
| Personnel | No estimates for actual work effort to perform activities |
| | No formal consideration of availability and efficiency |
| | No planned work schedules for people working simultaneously on two or more tasks |
| | New or inexperienced team members |
| Other resources | No plans to identify the type, amount, or timing of necessary nonpersonnel resources |
| Funds | No project budget |

## *Identifying risks*

As the next step in your risk assessment, identify the specific risks that may result from each of your risk factors. With this information, you can determine the particular effects the risk may have on your project and decide how you want to manage the risk.

Separately describe how each risk factor may cause you to miss your product, schedule, or resource targets.

Suppose you plan to use a new technology in your project. Using a new technology is a risk factor. Possible product, schedule, and resource risks that may arise from this risk factor are as follows:

- ✔ **Product risk:** The technology may not produce the desired results.

- ✔ **Schedule risk:** Tasks using the new technology may take longer than you anticipate.

- ✔ **Resource risk:** Existing facilities and equipment may not be adequate to support the use of the new technology.

When identifying potential risks, do the following:

- **Review past records of problems in similar situations.** If a risk factor actually resulted in an unexpected occurrence in the past, you definitely want to be prepared for it this time.

- **Brainstorm with experts and other people who have related experiences.** The more sources of expert opinion you consult, the less chance you'll overlook something important.

- **Be specific.** The more specifically you describe a risk, the better you can assess its potential effect. As an example:

   Specific: "Delivery may take three weeks rather than two."

   Nonspecific: "Activities may be delayed."

Try to eliminate potential risk factors as soon as possible. For example, suppose a key audience hasn't approved your project's objectives. Instead of just noting the risk that you may not correctly address audience needs, try to get the audience's approval!

# Assessing Risks: The Likelihood and Consequences

The expected consequences from a risk depend upon the *effect* of the risk if it becomes a reality and the *probability* that it will become a reality. Consider the expected consequences of different risks to choose which risks you want to actively manage and which risks you'll leave alone. This section discusses how to determine the probability that a particular risk will occur on your project.

## Gauging the likelihood of a risk

The weather forecaster saying that it may snow isn't sufficient reason to go out and buy a $1,000 snow thrower. First, you want to know the chances that it'll snow, and second, you want to know how much snow is likely to fall. If the weather forecaster is sure the total accumulation will be at least 20 inches but the chances of it snowing at all are only one in 1,000, you may decide not to spend $1,000 for such an unlikely situation.

The first step in deciding whether to deal proactively with a risk is assessing the likelihood that it will occur. Use one of the following schemes to describe the chances that a risk will occur:

- ✔ **Probability of occurrence:** You can express the likelihood that a risk will occur as a *probability*. Probability is a number between 0 and 1, with 0.0 signifying a situation will never happen, and 1.0 signifying it will always occur. (You may also express probability as a percentage, with 100 percent meaning the situation will always occur.)

- ✔ **Category ranking:** Classify risks into categories that represent their likelihood. You may use *high, medium,* and *low,* or *always, often, sometimes, rarely,* and *never.*

- ✔ **Ordinal ranking:** Order the risks so the first is the most likely to occur, the second is the next most likely, and so on.

- ✔ **Relative likelihood of occurrence:** If you have two possible risks, you can project a relationship. For example, you can declare the first as *twice as likely* to occur.

### Relying on objective info

You can estimate the likelihood of a risk by comparing the number of times the risk actually occurred on similar projects.

Suppose you designed 20 computer-generated reports over the past year for new clients. Eight times, when you submitted your design for final approval, new clients wanted at least one change. If you're planning to design a computer-generated report for another new client, you may conclude the chances are 40 percent that you'll have to make a change in the design you submit.

When using objective information to determine the likelihood of different risks,

- ✔ Consider previous experience with similar projects.

- ✔ Consider as many similar situations as possible.

- ✔ Keep in mind that the more similar situations you consider, the more confidence you can have in your conclusions.

### Counting on personal opinions

In the absence of objective data, solicit the opinions of experts and people who have worked on similar projects in the past.

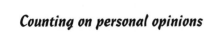

You can estimate the likelihood of a particular risk by soliciting the opinions of ten people who have worked on projects similar to yours. You can, for example, ask them to rate the likelihood of a specific risk as *high, medium,* or *low.* Suppose six people choose *high,* two choose *medium,* and two choose *low.* You may then develop your estimate of the likelihood by assigning values of 3, 2, and 1, to *high, medium,* and *low,* respectively, and determining the weighted average of the responses as follows:

$$(6 \times 3) + (2 \times 2) + (2 \times 1) = (18 + 4 + 2) \div 10 = 2.4$$

This formula suggests the risk has medium to high likelihood of occurring.

To increase the accuracy of these estimates, try the following:

- ✔ **Define the category name as clearly as possible.** You may suggest that *low* means the likelihood of the risk is between 0 and 33 percent, *medium* means 33 to 66 percent, and *high* means 66 to 100 percent.

- ✔ **Consider the opinions of as many people as possible.** The more data points you have, the higher your confidence in the estimate.

- ✔ **Be sure the projects your respondents have worked on are truly similar to yours.** Otherwise you have no reason to assume you can use their experience to predict what'll happen on your project.

- ✔ **Don't allow people to discuss their estimates with each other before they share them with you.** You're looking for their individual opinions, not a group consensus.

- ✔ **After they've submitted their initial estimates to you, consider having the people discuss their reasons for their estimates with each other and then asking them whether they want to revise their estimates.** Some people may choose to modify their original estimates if they realize they failed to take into account certain important considerations.

Precision is different from accuracy. *Precision* refers to the detail of a number. *Accuracy* refers to how correct the number is. You may estimate the likelihood of a particular risk to be 67.23 percent. However, even though you express the risk to two decimal places, your guess has little chance of being accurate if you have no prior experience with similar projects.

Unfortunately, people often assume that more-precise numbers are also more accurate. You can help avoid misinterpretations when you share your assessments of likelihood by using round numbers, categories, or relative rankings.

The more factors that suggest a particular risk may occur, the higher the likelihood that it will occur. For example, ordering from a vendor that you haven't worked with before raises the possibility that delivery times will be longer than he promised. However, the likelihood of those delays is greater if the item is also a special order, if you want delivery during a busy period for the vendor, and if the vendor has to order several parts to make the item.

## Estimating the extent of the consequences

Not long ago, I was waiting to see my doctor when the nurse came out and told me the doctor had to attend to an emergency and would be slightly delayed. Imagine my shock when, after waiting for three hours for the doctor, I learned that he had gone to a hospital that was an hour away several hours earlier and was currently in the middle of an emergency operation! If I had known the doctor was going to be gone for several hours, I would have rescheduled my appointment. Instead, because I didn't know how long the delay would be, I wasted three hours. And, unless I wanted to wait the rest of the afternoon, I'd have to make a new appointment anyway.

After you identify the likelihood that a particular risk will affect your project, be sure to determine the magnitude of the consequences that may result. That magnitude directly influences how you choose to deal with the risk. Determine the specific effect that each risk may have on your project's product, schedule, and resource performance. When evaluating these effects, do the following:

- ✔ **Consider the effect of a risk on the total project rather than on just a portion of it.** Taking one week longer than you planned to complete an activity may cause you to miss intermediate milestones (and cause the personnel waiting for the results of that activity to sit idle). However, the effect on the project is even greater if the delayed activity is on your project's critical path (see Chapter 5), which means the one-week delay also causes a one-week delay for your entire project.

- ✔ **Consider the combined effect of related risks.** The likelihood that you'll slip your schedule is greater if three activities on the same critical path have a significant risk of slippage rather than just one.

Be sure to describe risks and their associated consequences as specifically as possible. For example, suppose a key piece of equipment you ordered for your project may arrive later than expected. You can describe that risk as *the delivery may be late,* or as *the delivery may be delayed by two weeks.* Just stating that the delivery may be late doesn't give you enough information to determine the effect of that delay on the overall project. It also makes estimating the possibility of that risk more difficult. Are you talking about a delay of one day? One month? Stating that delivery may be delayed by two weeks allows you to determine the effect on the overall schedule and resources more precisely. Starting early also allows you to decide how much you're willing to spend to avoid that delay.

A variety of formal techniques can support your risk estimation and assessment:

✔ **Decision trees:** Diagrams that illustrate different situations that may occur as your project unfolds, the likelihood of each situation occurring, and the consequences to your project if it does.

Figure 8-1 illustrates a simple decision tree to help determine which of two vendors to buy a piece of equipment from. Both vendors have proposed a price of $50,000 if the equipment is delivered on the agreed-upon date. Both vendors have also proposed they receive an incentive for delivering early and absorb a penalty for delivering late, but the amounts of the incentives and penalties differ.

Multiplying the base price plus the performance incentive for early delivery by the probability of early delivery yields the expected value of the price you pay if delivery is early. You can calculate the total expected prices for Vendors A and B by totaling the expected prices if each is early, on time, and late, respectively.

This analysis suggests that you can expect to pay Vendor A $45,000 and have a 70 percent chance he'll deliver on time or early. You can expect to pay Vendor B $56,000 and have a 70 percent chance he'll deliver on time or early. It looks like Vendor A is the better choice!

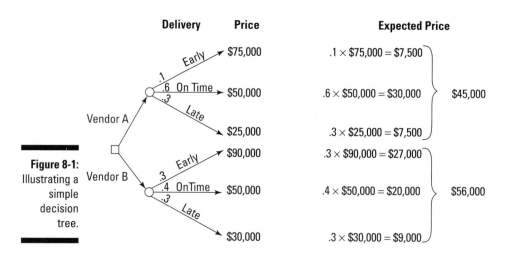

**Figure 8-1:** Illustrating a simple decision tree.

- ✔ **Risk assessment questionnaires:** Formal data-collection instruments that elicit expert opinion about the likelihood of different situations occurring and their associated effects.

- ✔ **Automated impact assessments:** Computerized spreadsheets that consider — in combination — the likelihood that different situations will occur and the consequences if they do.

# Managing Risk

Recognizing risks that pose a threat to your project is the first step toward controlling them. You also, however, have to develop specific plans for reducing their potential effect on your project.

This section helps you select the risks you'll manage proactively, develop a plan for addressing them, and share your plan with your project's audiences.

## Choosing the risks you want to manage

All identified risks affect your project in some way *if they occur* (after all, that's the definition of a risk). However, you may determine that anticipating and averting the problems of a particular risk actually takes more time and effort than just dealing with the problems, should they arise.

So, your first step in developing a risk-management strategy is to choose those risks that you need to address proactively. When making this choice, do the following:

- ✔ **Consider the likelihood of a risk *and* its potential effect on your project.** If the effect of a risk would be great and if the chances it will occur are high, you probably want to develop plans to manage it. If the effect is low and the likelihood is low, you may decide not to worry about it.

When the effect would be high but the likelihood is low or vice versa, consider the situation more carefully. A more formal approach for considering the combined effect of likelihood of occurrence and potential consequence is to define the *expected value of the risk,* as follows:

Expected value of the risk = (quantitative measure of the effect if it occurs) × (probability it will occur)

Suppose you need to buy certain materials for a device you're planning to build. When you place your order, you think you have an 80 percent chance of receiving the materials by the date promised. However, this means you have a 20 percent chance that something will go wrong and that you'll have to pay a premium to get the materials from another vendor by the date that you need them. You estimate that the materials normally cost $1,000 and that you'll have to pay an additional $500 to get them from another vendor at the last minute. Determine the expected value of this risk as follows:

> Expected value of risk = Additional cost incurred if you use another vendor at the last minute × probability that you'll have to use this vendor

> Expected value of risk = $500 × .2 = $100

You may conclude that, all things being equal, spending more than $100 to reduce the chances of this risk isn't a wise financial decision.

✔ **Decide whether a potential consequence is so unacceptable that you're not willing to take the chance even if it's very unlikely to occur.**

Suppose your company wants to build a new plant in an area that has been hit hard by hurricanes. The estimated cost of the new plant is $50 million, and the likelihood that a hurricane will totally destroy the building is 0.1 percent. The expected value of this risk is $50,000 ($50,000,000 × 0.001), which the company can easily absorb. However, if a hurricane actually destroys the building, the associated $50 million loss would put the company out of business. So, even though the expected value of the loss is relatively small, the company may feel that even a 0.1 percent chance of being ruined is unacceptable.

If you choose to build the plant, be sure you develop a strategy to manage the risk of the plant being totally destroyed (see the next section). You may want to reconsider whether you want to undertake the project at all.

## Developing a risk-management strategy

You can take several different approaches to minimize the negative effects risks can have on your project. However, if these approaches are to work, you must choose your strategies and plan their implementation at the earliest time possible in your project.

Choose one of the following approaches for dealing with the risks you decide to manage:

✔ **Minimize the chances they'll occur.** Take actions to reduce the chances that an undesirable situation will come to pass. For example, consider that you have a person on your project who's new to your organization.

Consequently, you feel the person may take longer to do her assigned task than you planned. Consider following steps to reduce the chances that the person will require more time:

- Explain the task and the desired results very clearly to the person before she begins to work on it.

- Develop frequent milestones and monitor the person's performance often so you can deal with any problems as soon as they occur.

- Have her attend training to refresh the skills and knowledge she needs to perform the assignment.

✔ **Develop contingencies.** Develop one or more alternative action plans in the event an undesirable situation does come to pass. Suppose you plan to have your organization's publication department reproduce 100 copies of the manual for your training program. If you're concerned that the department may have higher-priority projects at the same time, locate an external vendor that can reproduce the manuals if the need arises. Finding the vendor beforehand can reduce any time delay resulting from the switch to another resource.

✔ **Buy insurance.** Pay a price to reduce the effect when an undesirable situation occurs. For example, suppose you need a piece of equipment on a specific date. You may decide to order the same part from two different vendors to increase the likelihood that at least one of the vendors will deliver on time.

✔ **Transfer the risk.** Pay someone else to assume some or all of the effect of the risk. Suppose you choose to proceed with your plans to build a new $50,000,000 facility (see the example in the earlier section "Choosing the risks you want to manage"). You can buy disaster insurance on the facility so the company doesn't have to assume the full burden of a total loss if a hurricane destroys the facility.

Although the following approaches may sometimes seem appealing, they don't work:

✔ **The ostrich approach:** Ignore risks or pretend they don't exist.

✔ **The prayer approach:** Look to a higher being to solve all your problems or to make them disappear.

✔ **The denial approach:** Recognize that certain situations may cause problems for your project, but refuse to accept that these situations may occur.

Though it may require a bit of work upfront, proactively planning to manage your project's risks always pay dividends down the line.

## Communicating about risks

People often share information about project risks ineffectually or not at all. As a result, their projects suffer unnecessary problems and setbacks that proper communication may have avoided.

You may be reluctant to deal with risk because the concept is hard to grasp. If your project's a one-time deal, what difference does a risk that occurs 40 times out of 100 make? You may also feel that focusing on risks suggests you're looking for excuses for failure rather than ways to succeed.

Communicate about project risks early and often. In particular, share information with drivers and supporters at the following points in your project (see Chapter 1):

✔ **Conceive:** To support the process of deciding whether or not to undertake the project

✔ **Define:** To guide the development of all aspects of your project plan

✔ **Start:** To allow team members to discuss potential risks and to encourage them to recognize and address problems as soon as those problems occur

✔ **Perform:** To update the likelihood that identified risks will occur, to reinforce how people can minimize the negative effect of project risks, and to guide the assessment of change requests

You can improve your communications with your project's drivers and supporters by

✔ Explaining in detail the nature of a risk, how it may affect your project, and how you estimated the likelihood of its occurrence.

✔ Telling people the current chances that certain risks will occur, how you're minimizing the chances of problems, and how they can reduce the chances of negative consequences.

✔ Encouraging people to think and talk about risks, always with an eye toward minimizing the negative effects of those risks.

✔ Documenting in writing all the information about the risk.

You can discuss this information at regularly scheduled team meetings; in regularly scheduled progress reports and upper management reviews; and in special meetings to address issues that arise. (See Chapter 13 for more on sharing project information.)

# Preparing a Risk-Management Plan

A *risk-management plan* lays out strategies to minimize the negative effects that uncertain occurrences can have on your project. Develop your risk-management plan in the define phase of your project, refine it in the start phase, and continually update it during the perform phase (see Chapter 1 for more on these phases). Include the following in your risk-management plan:

- Risk factors
- Associated risks
- Your assessment of the likelihood of occurrence and the consequences for each risk
- How you plan to manage selected risks
- How you plan to keep people informed about those risks throughout your project

Table 8-3 illustrates a portion of a risk-management plan.

| Table 8-3 | A Portion of a Risk-Management Plan |
|---|---|
| *Plan Element* | *Description* |
| Risk factor | You haven't worked with this client before. |
| Risks | **Product:** Chance for miscommunication leads to incorrect or incomplete understanding of client's needs. |
| | **Schedule:** Incomplete understanding of client's business operation leads to an underestimate of your time to survey their current operations. |
| | **Resources:** Inaccurate understanding of client's technical knowledge leads to assigning tasks to client that he can't perform; you need additional staff to perform these tasks. |
| Analysis | Chances of misunderstanding the client's needs = high. |
| | Chances of underestimating the time to survey operations = low. |
| | Chances of misunderstanding the client's technical knowledge = low. |

*(continued)*

**Table 8-3** *(continued)*

| Plan Element | Description |
|---|---|
| Strategy | Only deal with the risk of misunderstanding the client's needs. Reduce the chances of this risk by |
| | 1. Reviewing past correspondence or written problem reports to identify the client's needs. |
| | 2. Having at least two team members present in every meeting with the client. |
| | 3. Speaking with different staff in the client's organization. |
| | 4. Putting all communications in writing. |
| | 5. Sharing progress assessments with the client every two weeks throughout the project. |

# Part III
# Putting Your Team Together

The 5th Wave                    By Rich Tennant

"Before we start this project, I'd like to clarify what metaphors we'll be speaking in. Last time we used sports metaphors. How about using cooking metaphors? 'Half baked', 'burnt', 'simmering', that sort of thing?"

## In this part . . .

The key to successful projects is people — using their capabilities to the fullest, encouraging their mutually supportive work efforts, and sustaining their ongoing commitment to your project's success.

In this part, I identify the people who affect the work environment in a project-oriented organization. I also suggest ways to define team member roles, and I offer approaches that encourage team members to maintain a supportive environment. Finally, I describe how to start your project off on the right foot.

# Chapter 9

# Aligning the Key Players for Your Project

. . . . . . . . . . . . . . . . . . . . . . . . . . . . . . . . . . . . . . . . . . . . . . . . .

## In This Chapter

▶ Stepping from traditional to project organizations

▶ Establishing order in the matrix organization

▶ Building a successful matrix

. . . . . . . . . . . . . . . . . . . . . . . . . . . . . . . . . . . . . . . . . . . . . . . . .

*I*n the traditional work environment, your supervisor assigned your work, completed your performance appraisals, approved your salary increases, and authorized your promotions. However, increasing numbers of organizations are moving toward a structure where a variety of people direct the work assignments. The greatest advantage of this new structure? It supports faster and more effective responses to the diverse projects in an organization.

Success in this new project-oriented organization requires you to

✔ Recognize the people who define and influence your work environment.

✔ Understand their unique roles.

✔ Know how to work effectively with them to create a successful project.

This chapter helps you define your organization's environment and understand everyone's roles. I also provide ways to ensure your project's success by focusing on the matrix structure.

## Defining the Organizational Environment

Over the years, projects have evolved from organizational afterthoughts to major vehicles for conducting business and developing future capabilities. Naturally, the approaches for organizing and managing projects have evolved as well.

This section focuses on one organizational approach for handling projects, the matrix, which is extensively used in organizations today. At the end of the section, I discuss two additional organizational structures that are used occasionally.

## Matrix structure

With increasing frequency, projects today involve and affect many functional areas within an organization. As a result, personnel in these different units must work in concert to successfully address people's individual and collective needs. The matrix structure facilitates the participation of people from different areas of the organization in projects that need their expertise.

As Figure 9-1 illustrates, in a *matrix structure* people from different areas of the organization are assigned to lead or work on projects. Project managers guide the performance of project activities while people's direct supervisors perform administrative tasks (such as formally appraising people's performances and approving promotions, salary increases, or requests for leave). Because an individual can be on a project for less than 100 percent of his time, he may work on more than one project at a time.

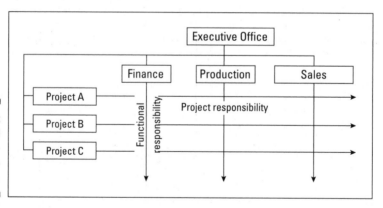

**Figure 9-1:**
General matrix-organization structure.

A matrix environment is classified as *weak, strong,* or *balanced,* depending on the amount of authority the project managers have over their teams.

- ✔ **Weak matrix:** Project managers have little if any direct authority over team members and actually function as project coordinators rather than managers.

- ✔ **Strong matrix:** Companies with a strong matrix structure choose project managers for new projects from a pool of people whose only job is to manage projects. These people are never asked to serve as a team member. Often these people form a single organizational unit that reports to a manager of project managers. In addition to directing and guiding project work, these project managers have certain administrative authority over the team members, such as the right to participate in their performance appraisals.

✔ **Balanced matrix:** This environment is a blend of the weak and strong environments. People are assigned to lead a project or serve as a team member based on the project's needs and not their job descriptions. Although the project manager may have some administrative authority over team members (such as approving leave requests), for the most part he guides, coordinates, and facilitates the project.

### Advantages of a matrix structure

A matrix environment offers many benefits, including the following:

✔ **Teams can assemble rapidly.** Because you have a larger resource pool from which to choose your project team, you don't have to wait for a few people to finish current assignments before they can start on your project. Additionally, this approach reduces the time-consuming process of hiring someone from the outside.

✔ **Scarce expertise can be available for several different projects.** Projects often require a small amount of effort from a person with highly specialized knowledge or skills. If your project can't support this person full time, several projects may be able to support her part time.

✔ **Getting buy-in from team members' functional units is easier.** Unit personnel who work on a project or are affected by its outcome are more likely to support the project if they're confident that the team hears their concerns and issues.

### Disadvantages of a matrix structure

However, a matrix environment also introduces challenges that the project manager must successfully address:

✔ **Team members working on multiple projects respond to two or more managers.** Each team member has at least two people giving her direction — a project manager (who coordinates project work and team support) and a functional manager (who coordinates the member's project assignments, completes her performance appraisal, and approves requests for leave). When these two managers are at similar levels in the organization, resolving conflicting demands for the member's time can be difficult.

✔ **Team members may not be familiar with each other's styles and knowledge.** Because team members may not have worked extensively together, they may require some time to become comfortable with each other's work styles and behaviors.

> ✔ **Team members may focus more on their individual assignments and less on the project and its goals.** For example, a procurement specialist may be responsible for buying equipment and supplies for all of her projects. In such a case, the specialist may be less concerned about a project's target date for the purchases and more concerned about correctly following her department's procurement procedures.

## Other structures

Although organizations use the matrix structure (see the previous section) extensively today, two other structures are available for handling projects. Both structures offer benefits, but they're less flexible than the matrix and less able to readily accommodate the variety of people and skills typically required on projects today.

### Centralized structure

The *centralized* structure (see Figure 9-2) is also called the *traditional* or *fixed-group* structure because the specialty units are established parts of the organization. In this structure, specialty units (such as human resources, training, and information systems) perform all projects in their specialty areas.

**Figure 9-2:**
A centralized structure for administering projects.

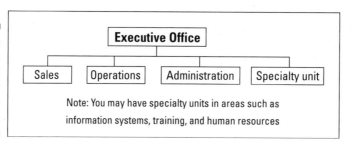

Executive Office

Sales  |  Operations  |  Administration  |  Specialty unit

Note: You may have specialty units in areas such as information systems, training, and human resources

In the centralized structure, each unit reports to a manager at the corporate level, and all specialty service requests are submitted to the appropriate specialty unit. For example, if the manufacturing group needs a new production-control system, they ask the information systems unit to develop it. The major difference between centralized and matrix structures is that the matrix allows people to work on multiple projects managed by different people from different parts of the organization; the centralized structure gives the head of the specialty unit ultimate administrative and project control over all projects.

*Advantages of the centralized structure*

Working on projects within this structure offers certain benefits:

- **Consistent criteria guide project selection.** A specialty unit's manager receives all project requests. The manager then chooses which projects to perform based on their expected benefits to the overall organization, staff availability, and his group's priorities (such as impact on other projects and his group's focus).

- **People can mesh into an effectively performing team more quickly.** The people in the unit start out knowing each other's skills, knowledge, and operating styles as a result of working together on previous projects. They also come to know which people live up to their commitments.

- **Priorities can be set and conflicts can be resolved more easily.** The specialty unit's manager makes or approves all personnel assignments for his unit's projects. Therefore, he also decides how to resolve conflicting demands for a unit member's time.

- **Clear lines of authority more strongly encourage people to honor their commitments.** The specialty unit manager reviews and approves her staff's performance appraisals. Therefore, she can easily ensure that a unit member's performance appraisal reflects his project performance.

*Disadvantages of the centralized structure*

However, working in a centralized structure also presents challenges.

- **Project review and approval is often slow.** Units throughout the organization compete against each other for the services of a specialty unit that has a fixed number of staff.

- **Specialty-unit members may not be familiar with the special processes and characteristics of areas that request the unit's services.** As an example, a person from an information-services unit who must develop a repair-parts inventory-control system may have extensive experience developing inventory-control systems but little or no experience with the procedures and operating practices of the repair-parts operation in the organization.

- **Individual members of the specialty unit often have more work than they can handle or not enough work to keep them busy.** People in specialty units only work on projects performed by their units. Unfortunately, project requests don't always come in a smooth stream, and the skills and knowledge required for the requests may not match those of the people available. As a result, even though members may average 100 percent of their available time working on assignments, they vary between working overtime to finish an assignment and sitting around with nothing to do.

### Functional structure

Unlike the centralized structure (see the previous section) that has specialty units that provide a particular type of support to the entire organization, the *functional structure* has multiple units that provide the same specialized support to the organization's different functional groups, as illustrated in Figure 9-3. For example, separate information-services units may support sales, operations, and administration, respectively. Each specialty unit only performs projects for its functional group.

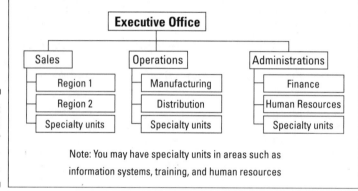

**Figure 9-3:**
A functional structure for administering projects.

### Advantages of the functional structure

The functional structure is a fixed-group structure because the specialty units are permanent parts of their functional groups. As such, the functional structure offers many of the same advantages of the centralized structure. In addition, the functional structure has these pluses:

- ✔ **People in the specialty unit have a better understanding of the functional area that they support.** Because each specialty unit only addresses the needs of one functional group, unit members are technically proficient in the unit's area of expertise and experienced in the functional group's operations.

- ✔ **Functional groups have less competition for their specialty units' support.** A specialty unit addresses only the needs of its functional group. This limited demand reduces the competition and tension that arise when groups compete for scarce resources.

### Disadvantages of the functional structure

However, the functional structure also has the following drawbacks:

✔ **Specialty unit members may have difficulty getting buy-in and support for their project from other functional groups that must support or will be affected by the project.** Each functional group can initiate a project without consulting other functional groups. As a result, people in these other areas may be reluctant to support such a project because it doesn't address their needs most effectively. They may also be reluctant to support it because the project may be competing with projects from their own functional group for scarce resources.

✔ **Making major investments to support a specific specialty unit's technical work is more difficult.** Suppose your organization's sales and marketing group and operations group both have a publications unit. Furthermore, suppose both units want to buy a new document printer and sorter that costs $100,000. Both groups have $75,000 in their budgets for such a machine, and each group has enough work to keep the machine busy about 60 percent of the time. But neither group has sufficient workload to justify the purchase or sufficient funds to make the purchase. However, the two units together have sufficient needs and sufficient funds to buy one machine.

✔ **Chances increase for overlap or duplication among projects in the same specialty area for different functional groups.** Specialty units providing the same type of support to different functional groups in the organization are under no obligation to tell each other about their individual work activities. As a result, different groups may perform similar or overlapping projects. In fact, one group may undertake a project similar to one being performed by another unit just to retain technical and administrative control of the work. Unfortunately, this power play often results in duplicate or wasted effort.

# Recognizing the Key Players in a Matrix Environment

The matrix structure encourages people from different parts of the organization to bring their expertise to projects. However, working in a matrix requires the project manager to deal with the styles, interests, and demands of more people who have some degree of control over their project's resources, goals, and objectives.

In a matrix environment, the following people play critical roles in every project's success:

- ✔ **Project manager:** The person ultimately responsible for the successful completion of the project.

- ✔ **Project team members:** People responsible for successfully performing individual project activities.

- ✔ **Functional managers:** The team members' direct-line supervisors.

- ✔ **Upper management:** People in charge of the organization's major business units.

This section discusses how each of these people can help your project to succeed.

## Project manager

If you're the project manager, you're responsible for all aspects of the project. (See Chapter 10 for definitions of authority, responsibility, and accountability.) Being responsible doesn't mean you have to do the whole project yourself, but you do have to see that every activity gets done satisfactorily. In this role, you're specifically responsible for the following:

- ✔ Determining objectives, schedule, and resource budgets

- ✔ Ensuring you have a clear, feasible project plan to reach your performance targets

- ✔ Identifying and managing project risks

- ✔ Creating and sustaining a well-organized, focused, and committed team

- ✔ Selecting or creating your team's operating practices and procedures

- ✔ Accomplishing objectives within time and budget targets

- ✔ Monitoring performance against plans and dealing with any problems that arise

- ✔ Resolving priority, work approach, or interpersonal conflicts

- ✔ Controlling project changes

- ✔ Reporting on project activities

- ✔ Keeping your clients informed and committed

- ✔ Contributing to your team members' performance appraisals

On occasion, you may hear people use the terms project *director* and project *leader,* both of which sound similar to project *manager*. Check with your organization, but usually *manager* and *director* describe the same position. Project *leader,* however, is a different story. People often think of *management* as focusing on issues and *leadership* as focusing on people; *management* also deals with established procedures and *leadership* deals with change. Therefore, calling someone a project *leader* emphasizes her responsibility to focus and energize the people supporting the project, as opposed to the more technical tasks of planning and controlling.

But again, check with your organization to be sure the term *leader* is meant to convey this message. (Often project leader is just another term for project manager — go figure!)

## Project team members

Project team members must satisfy the requests of both their functional managers and their project manager. Team-member responsibilities related to project assignments include the following:

- ✓ Performing tasks in accordance with the highest standards of technical excellence in your field
- ✓ Performing assignments on time and within budget
- ✓ Maintaining the special skills and knowledge to do the work

In addition, you're responsible for working with and supporting your team members' project efforts. Such help may entail the following:

- ✓ Considering the effect your actions may have on your team members' tasks
- ✓ Identifying situations and problems that may affect team members' tasks
- ✓ Keeping your team members informed of your progress, accomplishments, and any problems you encounter

## Functional managers

Functional managers are responsible for orchestrating their staff's assignments among different projects. In addition they provide the necessary resources for their staff to perform their work in accordance with the highest standards of technical excellence. Specifically, functional managers are responsible for the following:

- Developing or approving plans that specify the type, timing, and amount of resources to perform tasks in their area of specialty
- Ensuring team members are available to perform their assigned tasks for the promised amount of time
- Providing technical expertise and guidance to help team members solve problems related to their project assignments
- Actually providing the equipment and facilities for a person to do his work
- Helping people maintain their technical skills and knowledge
- Ensuring members of the functional group use consistent methodological approaches on all their projects
- Completing team members' performance appraisals
- Recognizing performance with salary increases, promotions, and job assignments
- Approving team members' requests for annual leave, administrative leave, training, and other activities that take time away from the job

## Upper management

Upper management creates the organizational environment; oversees the development and use of operating policies, procedures, and practices; and encourages and funds the development of required information systems. More specifically, upper management is responsible for the following:

- Creating the organizational mission and goals that provide the framework for selecting projects
- Setting policies and procedures for addressing priorities and conflicts
- Creating and maintaining labor and financial information systems
- Providing facilities and equipment to support project work
- Defining the limits of managers' decision-making authority

# Working Successfully in a Matrix Environment

Achieving success in a matrix environment requires that you align and coordinate the people who support your project, deflecting any forces that pull those people in different directions. This section can help you get the highest-quality work from your team members along with timely and effective support from the functional and senior managers.

The following tips can help you be successful in a matrix environment:

- **Create and continually reinforce a team identity.** Committing to work with others to achieve a common goal encourages people to overcome problems they may encounter along the way.

  - **Clarify team vision and working relationships.** As soon as you have a team, work with the members to develop a project mission that members can understand and support. Give people an opportunity to become familiar with each other's work styles.

  - **Define team procedures.** Encourage your team to develop its own work procedures instead of allowing people to use the approaches of their respective functional groups.

  - **Clarify each person's authority.** Team members may have to represent their functional areas when making project decisions. Clarify each team member's level of independent authority to make such decisions and determine who outside the team can make any decisions that are beyond the purview of the team member.

  - **Be aware of and attend to your team's functioning.** Help people establish comfortable and productive interpersonal relationships. Continue to support these relationships throughout your project.

  - **Be sure one person is assigned the role of project manager — with overall coordinative responsibilities.** The project manager continually reminds team members of the overarching project goals and focuses their attention on how they influence and affect each other's work.

- **Get team-member commitment.** Team members typically have little or no authority over each other in a matrix environment. Therefore, they perform their project assignments because they choose to, not because they must. Work with people initially and throughout your project to encourage them to commit to your project's goals (see Chapter 14 for more on how to encourage team member buy-in).

✔ **Elicit support from other people in the environment.**

- **Get a champion.** Because you most likely don't have authority over all the people who affect the chances for your project's success, get an ally who does have that authority as soon as possible. This *project champion* can resolve team members' schedule and interpersonal conflicts and raise your project's visibility in the organization. (See Chapter 3 for more on the project champion and how to get one for your project.)

- **Ask for and acknowledge your team members' functional managers' support.** By thanking functional managers for supporting their staff and allowing the staff to honor their project commitments, you are encouraging those managers to provide similar support for you and others in the future.

✔ **Develop procedures in advance that address the more common problems likely to arise during your project.**

- **Plan in sufficient detail.** Work with team members to define clearly and concisely the project work and each person's specific roles and responsibilities for all activities. This planning helps people more accurately estimate their amount of effort and the timing of that effort for each assignment.

- **Identify and address conflicts promptly.** Conflicts frequently arise in a matrix environment, given people's diverse responsibilities, different styles, and lack of experience working together. Encourage people to identify and discuss conflicts as soon as they occur. Develop systems and procedures to deal with conflicts promptly — before they get out of hand.

- **Encourage open communication among team members, especially regarding problems and frustrations.** The earlier you hear about problems, the more time you have to deal with them. Discussing and resolving team issues encourages working relationships that are more enjoyable and productive.

- **Encourage upper management to establish an oversight committee to monitor project performance and address resource and other conflicts.** Project and functional managers must focus on the goals for their respective areas of responsibility. Often, both groups rely on the same pool of people to reach these goals. But these diverse needs can place conflicting demands on people's time and effort. An upper-management oversight committee can ensure that the needs of the entire organization are considered when addressing these conflicts.

# Chapter 10

# Defining Team Members' Roles and Responsibilities

*Y*our project team typically includes people with different skill sets and operating styles who work in different parts of the organization. You may not have worked extensively with these people before. In addition, your project usually has a tight time schedule, and team members most likely are working on several other projects at the same time.

Success in this environment requires that you all agree how to work with each other to maximize contributions and minimize wasted time and mistakes. The team needs an approach that gives everyone confidence that members will live up to their commitments. The team leader and every team member must understand and be comfortable with the planned roles.

This chapter explains different degrees of team-member task involvement, how to make key assignments, how to encourage people to keep their promises, how to present an overall picture of team members' roles and responsibilities, and how to handle a micromanager.

## Understanding the Key Concepts

A typical project activity entails performing specific pieces of work, making decisions, and coordinating the activities of others. To accomplish the activity with a minimum of time and resources, each piece of work must be done in the correct order and each person must work at peak efficiency, being sure not to repeat or duplicate unnecessarily work that others have done. The more complex the task and the greater the number of people working on it, the more difficult it is to ensure people don't step on each other's toes along the way.

As a first step in coordinating people's efforts, this section defines three different roles that team members can play when working on a project activity and their similarities and differences.

## Distinguishing authority, responsibility, and accountability

The following concepts can help you define and clarify how team members should relate to each other and to their assigned tasks:

- ✔ **Authority:** The ability to make binding decisions about your project's products, schedule, resources, and activities. Examples include your ability to sign purchase orders not to exceed $3,000 and your ability to change a scheduled date by no more than two weeks.

- ✔ **Responsibility:** The commitment to achieve specific results. An example is your promise to have a draft report ready by March 1.

- ✔ **Accountability:** Bringing consequences to bear in response to people's performance. An example: Your boss notes in your annual performance appraisal that you solved a difficult manufacturing problem.

   Unfortunately, many people think accountability means paying the price when you foul up. This fear often causes people to avoid situations where they'll be accountable for their performance. Paying a price when you foul up is certainly half of the concept, but the other half is being rewarded for doing a good job. This positive reinforcement is far more effective than negative reinforcement to encourage high-quality results.

Although these three terms are related, each term is a distinct and necessary element for defining and reinforcing team roles.

## Comparing authority and responsibility

Authority and responsibility are similar, yet different. Both authority and responsibility are upfront agreements. Before you start your project, you agree who can make which decisions and who will ensure particular results.

However, authority focuses on process, while responsibility focuses on outcomes. Authority defines the decisions you can make but does not mention the results you have to achieve. Responsibility addresses the results you must accomplish with no mention of the decisions you can make to reach those results. Remember, too, that you can transfer the authority to make decisions to another person, but you can't transfer the responsibility for the results of those decisions. (For more about delegating authority and sharing responsibility, check out the next section.)

Suppose you have the authority to issue purchase orders up to $5,000 for your project. Assume no policy or instructions specifically prevent you from giving some or all of this authority to someone else, so you give Matt authority to sign purchase orders for your project not to exceed $4,000. However, if Matt mistakenly issues a $3,000 purchase order for ten reams of specialty paper instead of a $1,500 purchase order for the five reams that he really needs, you're still responsible for his error.

You can always take back authority that you gave to someone else, but you can't blame the person for exercising that authority while he has it.

# Making Project Assignments: Everything You Need to Know (And More)

Effectively eliciting the help and support of others in the work you do is essential to get the most out of all team members. This section focuses specifically on what you need to know about defining project roles, including deciding what can and can't be delegated, assigning roles with confidence, sharing responsibility, and keeping everyone accountable.

## Deciding what to delegate

*Delegating* is giving away something you have. (I know other definitions of delegating exist, but to keep it simple: *to delegate* is to give away.)

You can delegate authority, but you can only share responsibility. You can completely transfer your decision-making power to someone else so he can make the decisions with no or involvement or approval from you. However, when another person agrees to assume a responsibility of yours, you're still obligated to ensure that he achieves the desired results.

You delegate for three reasons:

✔ To free yourself up to do other tasks

✔ To have the most qualified person make decisions

✔ To develop another person's ability to handle additional assignments prudently and successfully

Although the potential benefits of delegating can be significant, not every task can or should be delegated. Consider the following guidelines when deciding which tasks are appropriate candidates:

✔ **Assign yourself to the tasks that you do best.** Suppose you're the best lawyer in town and there is more demand for your services at a fee of $500 per hour than you can meet. Suppose also that you can type twice as fast as the next fastest typist in town, who charges $200 per hour. Should you type all of your own legal briefs? The answer is no. Your choice is whether to spend an hour providing legal services or typing. If you spent your hour typing, you would save the $400 you would have to pay the typist (who would require two hours at a cost of $200 per hour to do the same work). However, if you spent the same one hour providing legal services, you'd earn $500, which would allow you to pay the typist $400 for the work and still have $100 left over. (This is referred to as the *Law of Comparative Advantage.*)

✔ **If possible, assign yourself to tasks that aren't on a project's critical path.** (See Chapter 5 for a discussion of critical path.) If any activity on a project critical path is delayed, it will push back the estimated date for project completion. Therefore, if you have to stop working on a critical path task to deal with problems on a task that's not critical, you'll immediately delay the entire project.

✔ **Don't assign other people to work on a task that you can't clearly describe yourself.** The time you save by not working on the task will be more than offset by the time you'll spend answering questions and continually redirecting the person.

Delegation doesn't have to be an all-or-nothing proposition, where you either make all decisions yourself or you withdraw from the situation entirely. Consider the following six degrees of delegation, each of which builds on and extends the ones that come before it:

✔ **Get in the know.** Get the facts and bring them to me for further action.

✔ **Show me the way to go.** Develop alternative actions to take based on the facts you've found.

✔ **Go when I say so.** Be prepared to take one or more of the actions you have proposed, but don't do anything until I say so.

✔ **Go unless I say *no*.** Tell me what you propose to do and when; take your recommended actions unless I tell you otherwise.

✔ **How'd it go?** Analyze the situation, develop a course of action, take action, and let me know the results.

✔ **Just go!** Here's a situation; deal with it.

Each level entails some degree of independent authority. As manager, when I ask you to find the facts about a situation, you choose what information sources to consult, which information to share with me, and which to discard. The primary difference between the levels is the degree of checking with the manager before taking action.

## Supporting your delegations of authority

You must actively reinforce and support your delegations of authority or you can suddenly find yourself doing the task that you thought you had assigned to someone else.

Suppose you've been a manager of a project for the past two months and Mary has been your assistant. Mary has been dealing with people's technical issues. When someone runs into a technical problem, he discusses it with Mary. She analyzes the problem and decides how to address it. She then discusses it with you and explains her proposed solution. If you agree with her solution, you ask her to implement it. If you don't agree with Mary's suggestion, you work with her to develop a more acceptable approach.

Yesterday, you told Mary that you want to change the way she deals with technical issues. You explain that, from now on, she doesn't have to pass her proposed solutions by you before implementing them. After discussing this with her, you told the other team members about the new procedure.

This morning, Joe came to Mary to discuss a problem he was having with a contractor. After listening to the problem, Mary gave Joe very specific instructions for how to deal with it. As soon as Joe left Mary's office, however, he called you on the phone. He recounted the problem he had discussed with Mary and her proposed solution, and he asked you whether you agreed with the approach Mary had recommended.

You now have a dilemma. On the one hand, you want to support Mary's newly delegated authority. On the other hand, you want to ensure that your project goes smoothly and successfully. What should you do?

The only response you can make to Joe that will support your delegation of authority to Mary is "Do whatever Mary told you to do."

What if you responded to Joe, "Yes, Mary's solution sounds good to me"? That answer won't work. By declaring that you like Mary's solution, you undercut Mary's authority to make the decision on her own! Perhaps you just wanted to tell Joe that you had full confidence in Mary's ability to develop an appropriate solution and that the one she proposed was an example of her good judgment. However, in reality, your response suggests to Joe that you are still in the approval process because you just gave your approval to Mary's *decision* rather than her *authority*.

You want to support your delegation, but you also want to ensure your project's success. So how do you deal with the following situations?

✔ **You don't agree with Mary's recommendation.** If you fear that following Mary's recommendation will have catastrophic consequences, you must suggest to Joe that he wait until you can discuss the issue with Mary. In this instance, protecting your project and your organization is more important than supporting your delegation of authority.

In all other instances, though, you should tell Joe to follow Mary's suggestion because she has the authority to make that decision. Here are several reasons to do so, even if you don't agree with her choice:

- She may know more about the situation than Joe told you.

- Maybe she's right and you're wrong.

- Suppose your approach is better than Mary's. How will she make better choices in the future if you don't explain why you disagree with her decision?

- If Mary believes that you'll jump in to save her every time she makes a bad decision, she'll be less concerned about making the correct decision the first time.

You can always ask Mary later to explain privately the rationale for her decision, and you can offer your thoughts and opinions when you feel they're necessary.

✔ **Joe's call indicates a more general problem with the team's procedures and working relationships.**

- Perhaps you weren't clear when you explained the new working procedures with Mary to your team member. Explain and reinforce the new procedures to Joe.

- Perhaps Joe didn't like Mary's answer and is trying to go behind her back to get his way. Again, you must reinforce that the decision is Mary's to make.

- Perhaps Mary wasn't clear enough in her recommendation to Joe. Suggest to Mary that she explain the reasons behind her solutions more clearly and that she probe to make sure people understand and are comfortable with the information she shares.

- Perhaps some interpersonal conflict exists between Joe and Mary. Talk with both of them to determine whether such a conflict exists and, if it does, how it came about. Work with Joe and Mary to help them address and resolve the conflict.

## Delegating to achieve results

Delegation always involves some risk — you have to live with the consequences of someone else's decisions. However, you can take the following steps to increase your comfort level and thereby improve the person's chances for successful performance:

1. **Clarify what you want to delegate.**

   Describe in unambiguous terms the work you want the other person to perform and the results you want him to achieve. If necessary, also explain what you don't want the person to do.

2. **Choose the right person.**

   Determine the skills and knowledge you feel a person must have to perform the task successfully, and don't delegate the task to a person who lacks these skills and knowledge. (See Chapter 6 for more on describing the skills and knowledge people need to do a job.)

3. **Make the delegation correctly.**

   Explain the work to be done, how much effort you expect the person to expend, and the date she should have the work completed. Put this information in writing for clarity and future reference.

4. **Be available to answer questions.**

   Maintaining contact while the person performs the task allows you to ensure that any ambiguities and unexpected situations encountered are resolved to your satisfaction. It also conveys to the person that the task is important to you.

5. **Monitor performance.**

   Set up frequent, well-defined checkpoints at which you can monitor performance. Then keep that schedule.

# Sharing responsibility

The decision to delegate authority is unilateral; it doesn't require the agreement of both parties. You can choose to give someone the authority to make a decision whether or not he wants it. After you give your authority to another person, he is free to pass it on to someone else (if you haven't specifically told him not to).

Responsibility, however, is a two-way agreement. You ask me to respond to a customer inquiry, and I agree that I will. Because you and I agree that I will handle the inquiry, I can't decide to give the assignment to someone else and then not worry about whether he will handle it. I committed to you that the inquiry would be addressed; the only way I can free myself from this responsibility is to ask you to agree to change our original understanding.

Suppose Alice, your boss, asks you to prepare a report highlighting the latest sales figures for your organization. You figure that you can prepare the text of the report in Microsoft Word and any necessary graphics in Microsoft PowerPoint. You know where to get the raw sales data, and you know how to use Word, but you don't know how to use PowerPoint. However, Bill, a member of your staff, does know how to use PowerPoint. So you accept Alice's assignment, figuring that you can ask Bill to prepare any graphics. When you ask Bill whether he'll help you, he says that he will.

A week later, Alice asks how you're doing on the report. You tell her that you've completed the text, but Bill hasn't finished the graphics. You suggest that she check with Bill to find out how he's doing and when he'll be finished. How do you think Alice will respond to your suggestion?

After a moment's silence, Alice reminds you that you agreed to prepare the report and, therefore, ensuring that all parts of the work are complete is your responsibility, not hers. In other words, because you accepted the responsibility for completing the report, you can't choose unilaterally to give away part of that responsibility to someone else.

By the way, Alice was correct in refusing to deal directly with Bill for a couple of other reasons:

- ✔ If Alice had agreed to check directly with Bill, she would have been doing you a disservice. She would have tacitly been telling Bill that whenever you give him assignments in the future, he should be concerned about satisfying her rather than you. In other words, she would have undermined your leadership position.

- ✔ It would have been difficult for Alice to follow up with Bill, even if she had wanted to, because she didn't know exactly what you asked him to do or when you asked him to have it done.

The only way you can relieve yourself of some or all of the responsibility you accepted is to ask Alice whether she will agree to a revised plan.

## Holding people accountable when they don't report to you

People who make promises, fail to keep their promises, and then suffer no consequences create some of the worst frustrations in a project environment. Encourage reliable performance by observing the following guidelines:

- ✔ **If you're responsible, you should be held accountable.** In other words, if you make a promise, you should always experience consequences based on how well you honor your promise.

- ✔ **If you're not responsible, you shouldn't be held accountable.** When something goes wrong but you weren't responsible for ensuring that it was handled correctly, you shouldn't face negative consequences. (Of course, you shouldn't receive positive accolades when it goes well.)

  Holding people accountable when they aren't responsible is called *scapegoating*. When you assign blame to the closest person, you only encourage people to avoid dealing with you in the future.

However, when a person who doesn't report to you administratively promises to do something for you, holding her accountable can be a touchy issue. You may not try to hold her accountable because you think it's inappropriate (after all, you're not her boss) or because you don't know how. But remember: Holding people accountable is appropriate and necessary when they've accepted a responsibility. Accountability helps people know that they're on the right track, and it enables you to formally acknowledge when they have completed the promised assignments. You don't need authority to hold people accountable; they just must accept the responsibility.

Use the following approaches to hold people accountable when you have no direct authority over them:

- ✔ **Find out who does have direct authority over the person and bring that supervisor into the process.** Consider soliciting the approval of the person's boss. When you do this correctly and at the right time, you can improve the chances for success. If a person's boss is unaware that his staffer agreed to perform a task for you, your chances of getting the boss's help when the person fails to perform as promised are small. However, if the boss supported his staffer's offer to help you when it was made, neither the boss nor his staffer should be surprised if you solicit the boss's help when the staffer doesn't do the task.

✔ **Put it in writing.** Have you ever noticed how strangely people react when you put an informal agreement in writing? All of a sudden, they act as if you don't trust them. Put your agreement in writing to formalize it, to clarify the terms, and to serve as a reminder. If they ask, explain that writing the agreement has nothing to do with lack of trust. If you didn't trust them, you wouldn't work with them at all!

✔ **Be specific.** The clearer you make your request, the easier it is for the person to estimate the effort she needs to respond to the request and to produce the right result the first time.

You may be uncomfortable being too specific because you feel that giving the person *orders* is inappropriate (after all, you have no direct authority over her). But your specifics make the task easier to perform.

✔ **Follow up.** Negotiate a schedule to monitor the person's performance and to address any issues or questions that arise. Be sure to

- Negotiate a follow-up schedule at the outset. If you call unannounced at random times, you appear to be checking up because you don't trust the person.

- Base your follow-up schedule on when the person plans to achieve certain intermediate milestones; this timeline gives you more objective criteria for an assessment.

✔ **Make the person accountable to the team.** Your most valuable professional asset is your reputation. When a person promises to do something for you, let others on your team know about the promise. When the person lives up to that promise, acknowledge it in front of her colleagues. If the person fails to live up to the promise, let her know that you'll share that information with others too.

✔ **Get commitment.** When a person indicates that she will help you out, be sure to get a firm, specific commitment that the desired result will be achieved by a specific time and for a specific cost. Beware of declarations like "I'll give it my best effort" or "You can count on me."

✔ **Create a sense of urgency and importance.** You may want to minimize any pressure the person feels by offering to *understand* if she can't perform to your expectations because of one reason or another. Unfortunately, this approach suggests that the work you're asking her to do isn't really that important and actually increases the chance that she won't complete it. Instead, let the person know how her work influences other activities and people on the project. Let her know why she needs to perform to expectations and what the consequences will be — to the project and the organization — if she isn't successful.

Check out the sidebar "Hold the line when he drops the ball" in this chapter for a good example of holding someone accountable when he isn't your direct report.

# Illustrating Relationships with a Linear Responsibility Chart

Defining and sharing team roles and responsibilities upfront can improve performance and help to identify and head off potential difficulties during a project. You can display team roles and responsibilities in a Linear Responsibility Chart (LRC) (see Figure 10-1).

**Figure 10-1:**
A Linear Responsibility Chart displays relationships.

|  | Project Manager | Task Leader | Project Staffer A | Group Director | Purchasing |
|---|---|---|---|---|---|
| **Design questionnaire** | A | S, A | P |  |  |
| **Select respondents** |  | P |  |  |  |
| **Conduct pretest** |  | P | S |  |  |
| **Print questionnaires** | A | P |  | A | A |

P = Primary responsibility    S = Secondary responsibility    A = Approval

The LRC is a matrix that depicts each project audience's (see Chapter 3) role in the performance of different project activities. As Figure 10-1 illustrates:

- Project activities are in the left-hand column.
- Project audiences are in the top row.
- The role of each audience with respect to each activity is in the intersections of the rows and columns.

Figure 10-1 illustrates a portion of the LRC for designing and conducting a customer needs survey. This chart defines three ways people can participate in project activities:

- **Primary responsibility (P):** You've committed to ensure the results are achieved.
- **Secondary responsibility (S):** You've committed to ensure some portion of the results is achieved.
- **Approval (A):** You're not actually working on the activity, but you approve what others have done.

# Hold the line when he drops the ball

Suppose you recently began working on a project to develop and implement an upgraded inventory control system. You just found out that your friend Eric had been working on this project until a month ago, so you call him to discuss his experiences.

After a few minutes, you ask him whether he'll do you a favor. You explain that you and three other team members are developing a users' manual for the new system. You ask him whether, in view of his extensive knowledge of this project's history, he'd be willing to write a draft of Chapter 1 of that manual on the system's history and development. Today is Monday, and you explain you need the draft by a week from Friday. Eric agrees, and you both hang up.

Unfortunately, you never receive the draft of Chapter 1 from Eric. He never calls you to explain why he didn't submit the draft, and you never check with him to see what's happening.

Does this situation sound familiar? You probably make and receive requests like this several times each day. Unfortunately, too many times people promise to help you out but don't deliver. What can you do? The answer is you must find ways to hold people accountable when they make an agreement to complete an assignment for you.

Of course, you can only hold people accountable if they accept a responsibility in the first place. Therefore, in our illustration, the first question is: After your phone call, did Eric assume the responsibility to write a draft of Chapter 1 for you and your colleagues?

Very simply, the answer is *yes*. Why? Because he said he would. I'm not suggesting that Eric is responsible for preparing the draft of Chapter 1 and that you and your colleagues are off the hook. Your responsibility to prepare the users' manual hasn't changed, but Eric did accept the responsibility to prepare this draft for you. Whether Eric no longer works on the project or that he doesn't report to your boss isn't the question. He's responsible because he said he would be.

Eric may argue that he has a personal obligation to complete the draft (because he said he would) but no organizational obligation because the agreement wasn't in writing and he wasn't formally on your project team. That argument doesn't hold up. Personal and organizational commitments are the same. If he didn't want to accept the obligation, he only had to say *no*.

The second question is: Did you hold Eric accountable for his failure to keep his promise? The answer is *no*. You did nothing in response to his failure to deliver a draft of Chapter 1.

If the reason you didn't receive the draft is because Eric never sent it, what messages does your behavior (or, in this case, your lack of behavior) send to Eric?

- ✔ **The assignment wasn't that important.** What a terrible message! You asked Eric to take time from his busy day to do something for you, and you didn't even care whether he completed the task? He's probably happy that he decided not to spend time on the task because apparently it wouldn't have made any difference anyway.

- ✔ **Eric's behavior was okay.** This message is even worse! It confirms that making promises and then not performing and not even explaining your reason for not performing is okay. Situations may have arisen that made it impossible for Eric to honor the commitment, but does that justify not calling to tell you about the situation? Unfortunately, this type of behavior, multiplied many times every day, defines an organizational environment where promises mean little and breaking them becomes an accepted part of business as usual.

Most likely, these messages aren't the ones you intended to convey. You probably figured that Eric was busy, and you didn't want to make a big deal because he agreed to go out of his way to help you. Unfortunately, he can't know what's in your mind because you didn't tell him.

Maybe he didn't ignore his promise to prepare the draft. Consider some other possibilities:

✔ **He sent you the draft but it got lost in the delivery system.** Unfortunately, most people figure that no news is good news. When Eric didn't get a call from you, he probably assumed that you'd received the draft and found it acceptable. Certainly, he reasoned, you would've called if you had any questions!

✔ **He misunderstood you initially; he thought you needed the draft by a month (rather than a week) from Friday.** Maybe he's still working on the draft and plans to give it to you on the date he thought you needed it.

Accountability is a management control process. Responding to a person's actions lets the person know whether he's on target or whether he needs to make a correction. Not responding to unacceptable performance unfortunately increases the likelihood that it will occur again.

The LRC is just a format; for each project, you define and assign the roles you feel are appropriate. You may, for example, decide to use the following roles in addition to the three already defined:

> ✔ **Review (R):** You review and comment on the results of an activity, but your formal approval is not required.

> ✔ **Output (O):** You receive products from the activity.

> ✔ **Input (I):** You provide input for the activity work.

This section helps you read an LRC, develop your own chart, and improve your chart to meet your own needs. Your only limit is your creativity!

## Reading an LRC

To illustrate how you read the LRC, consider the activity *Design questionnaire* in Figure 10-1. The chart suggests that three people work together on this activity as follows:

> ✔ Staffer A has primary responsibility for the questionnaire's content, format, and layout. On this project, Staffer A reports to the task leader who, in turn, reports to the project manager.

> ✔ The task leader performs selected parts of the questionnaire design under the general coordination of Staffer A. The task leader must approve all aspects of the questionnaire design before work can proceed to the next step.

> ✔ The project manager must approve the entire questionnaire, even though she isn't doing any of the actual design and layout herself.

Analyze this chart vertically by audience and horizontally by activity for situations that may give rise to problems. After you identify these situations, you can decide how to address them. Table 10-1 notes some observations about the assignments displayed in Figure 10-1 and issues they may suggest.

| Table 10-1 | Situations and Issues Suggested in Figure 10-1 |
|---|---|
| *Situation* | *Possible Issues* |
| The task leader is heavily committed. | The task leader won't have enough time to handle all these duties. The task leader is making all key decisions. What if the task leader leaves during the project? |
| The group director doesn't get involved until he is asked to approve the funds for printing the questionnaires. | The group director will slow down the approval process by asking questions about the purpose of the project, the use of the results, and so on. |
| The project manager has no direct responsibilities for individual project activities. | Will the project manager fully under stand the substance and status of the project work? |
| The task leader is the only person involved in selecting the respondents. | Do you want a key decision (that can determine the value of the entire pretest) made by only one person? |
| The activity called *print questionnaires* requires three approvals. | Does anyone else have to approve the questionnaire before it can be used? |
| | Are too many people approving the questionnaire? Would it be acceptable to notify just one or two of these people? The activity may take longer than estimated because this approval process is out of your control. |

After you identify a potential issue, you can choose how to deal with it. Possibilities include

- ✔ **Ignoring the issue.** As an example, you may decide that three approvals are necessary, even though the number is high.

- ✔ **Taking simple steps to minimize the risk of a problem.** For example, you may ask the task leader to thoroughly document all important information in case he leaves the project unexpectedly.

- ✔ **Addressing the issue further in a formal risk-management plan.** See Chapter 8 for a discussion of how to analyze and plan to manage risks.

## Developing an LRC

Having the people who play a part in your project participate in developing the LRC increases its accuracy, as well as the people's buy-in. However, although the information included in the LRC is straightforward, getting everyone to agree on people's roles can be time-consuming.

The following steps can help you get people's input and approval with the least time and effort:

1. **Identify all people who'll participate in or support your project.**

   See the discussion of audiences in Chapter 3 for details.

2. **Develop a complete list of activities for your project.**

   See the discussion of a Work Breakdown Structure in Chapter 4 for details.

3. **Discuss with all team members how they'll each support the different project activities.**

   For each of their assigned activities, discuss the level of their responsibility and authority, as well as the specific work they will perform. Also discuss with them any involvement that others will have on their activities. If specific people haven't been identified for certain activities, consult with people who have done those types of activities before.

4. **Prepare an initial draft of your LRC.**

   Draw the table for your chart, and then enter your project's activities in the left-hand column and the people who will support the activities in the first row. In the cells formed by the intersection of each row and column, enter the roles you discussed with each person they would have.

5. **Ask the people whom you consulted in Step 3 to review and approve your draft chart.**

If people agree with the chart, ask them to indicate their agreement in writing. If they express concerns about some aspects, ask them to note their concerns in a memo or an e-mail.

6. **If some of those people don't approve the draft chart, incorporate their recommended changes into a second draft and again ask all people who gave input to review and approve the chart.**

If you make any changes to the draft LRC, have everyone review and approve the revised chart, even if they had previously seen and approved the prior version.

7. **Go back to Step 5 and continue the process, until everyone you consulted in Step 3 approves the chart.**

## *Ensuring your chart is accurate*

For complex projects, the LRC can be quite large. Also, keeping the chart current and consulting throughout the project with all the people identified can be time-consuming. However, having a chart with incorrect information can result in duplicated efforts and overlooked activities.

The following suggestions can help you keep your LRC accurate and current:

✔ **Develop a hierarchy of charts for larger projects.** Including 50 or more activities on the same LRC can be cumbersome. Consider developing a series of nested charts for larger projects. Prepare a high-level chart that identifies responsibilities for work assignments or tasks in your Work Breakdown Structure, and then develop separate charts for individual work assignments or tasks that detail responsibilities for associated lower-level activities. (See Chapter 4 for the definition of work assignments, tasks, and lower-level activities in a Work Breakdown Structure.)

Figure 10-2 illustrates a simple example. Suppose you're planning a project to design and implement an information system. Prepare a high-level LRC that details the roles for major work assignments, such as *finalize requirements, design system,* and *test system.* Display in a second chart the roles of the team leader and his group on the lower-level activities that comprise *finalize requirements.*

✔ **Involve the entire team when developing your chart to ensure accuracy and buy-in.** The project manager doesn't know exactly how experts and technical representatives from different groups should perform tasks in their areas of specialty, so they need to tell him how they'll approach their assignments. And, even if he did know, people have a greater commitment to a plan if they participate in developing it.

### Design and Conduct a Customer Needs Survey

| People ╲ Activities | Project Manager | Team Leader A | Team Leader B | Team Leader C |
|---|---|---|---|---|
| Finalize requirements | A | P | | |
| Design system | A | | P | S |
| Test system | A | S | S | P |

### Finalize Requirements

| People ╲ Activities | Team Leader A | Staffer A | Staffer B | Staffer C |
|---|---|---|---|---|
| Review literatrure | A | P | S | |
| Conduct focus groups | P | S | | S |
| Prepare report | A | S | S | |

**Figure 10-2:**
A hierarchy of Linear Responsibility Charts.

✔ **Put your chart in writing.** You may feel you're saving time by not putting the chart in writing because people all know what it should say anyway. But, putting the chart in writing is essential for two reasons:

- You can identify possible problems that you may not have caught if you were considering pieces of information separately.

  Refer to the LRC in Figure 10-1. Before preparing the chart, the task leader knew that he was primarily responsible for selecting respondents to pretest the questionnaire. Other team members knew they weren't involved in that activity but probably assumed that someone in addition to the task leader was. Writing down this information in the table highlights that the task leader is, in fact, the only one involved in the activity.

- You ensure that people have a common understanding of their roles and relationships.

> ✔ **Review and update your chart throughout your project.** The longer your project, the more likely that activities will be added or deleted, that people will leave the team, and that new people will join the team. Periodically reviewing and updating your LRC enables you to
>
>   • Assess whether the current assignments are working out and, if not, where changes may be needed.
>
>   • Clarify the roles and responsibilities for new activities.
>
>   • Clarify the roles and responsibilities for people who join the team.
>
>   • Clarify how you'll handle the roles and responsibilities of someone who leaves the team.

If you join a project and find that no LRC exists, develop one. You can develop a chart at any time during a project. If the project is already underway, develop a chart to clarify the roles and responsibilities from the current point forward.

# Dealing with Micromanagement

*Micromanagement* is a person's excessive, inappropriate, and unnecessary involvement in the details of a task that he asks another person to perform. Whatever the reasons for micromanagement, it can lead to inefficient use of personal time and energy, as well as to tension and low morale among staff.

Micromanagement can be debilitating both to the micromanager and to the person she micromanages because they spend time and energy in unproductive activities that don't contribute to project success. In this section I help you look at the causes for micromanagement, give you some tips on ways to gain your micromanager's trust and confidence, and suggest how to work with a micromanager.

## Understanding why a person micromanages

No objective criteria can really describe when a person is micromanaging, rather than providing close guidance and support. Whether you're being micromanaged is a subjective judgment; it depends upon whether you feel that your boss is spending too much time looking over your shoulder. The first step in dealing with a micromanager is to let the person know you feel that his oversight is a bit excessive. Try to give him some objective indicators to explain why you feel as you do.

Occasionally, the micromanager will be surprised at your reaction and change her undesirable behavior. If not, then consider whether one or more of the following reasons may be the cause:

- ✔ **The person is interested in and enjoys the work.** Set up times to discuss interesting technical issues with the person.

- ✔ **The person is a technical expert and feels that he can do the job best.** Review your technical work frequently with that person; give the person opportunities to share his technical insights with you.

- ✔ **The person may feel that he didn't explain the assignment clearly or that unexpected situations may crop up.** Set up a schedule to discuss and review your progress frequently so that the micromanager can promptly uncover any mistakes and help you correct them.

- ✔ **The person is looking for ways to stay involved with you and the team.** Set up scheduled times to discuss project activities. Provide the micromanager with periodic reports of project progress, and make a point to stop by and say *hello* periodically.

- ✔ **The person feels threatened because you have more technical knowledge than he does.** When talking about your project in front of others, always credit the micromanager for his guidance and insights. Share key technical information with the person on a regular basis.

- ✔ **The person doesn't have a clear understanding of how he should be spending his time.** Discuss with the person the roles he would like you to assume on project activities. Explain how the person can provide useful support as you perform the work.

- ✔ **The person feels that he has to stay up on the work you're doing in case anyone else asks about it.** Discuss with the person what type of information he needs and how frequently he needs it. Develop a schedule to provide progress reports that include this information.

## Helping a micromanager gain confidence in you

Your boss may be micromanaging you because he doesn't yet have full confidence in your ability to perform. Instead of being angry or resentful, take the following steps to help the person develop that confidence:

- ✔ **Don't be defensive or resentful when the person asks you questions.** Doing so makes you appear as though you're hiding something, which only makes the person worry even more. Instead, willingly provide all information asked for.

✔ **Thank the micromanager for his interest, time, and technical guidance.** Complaining about what you perceive to be excessive oversight only strains your relationship, increases the person's fears and insecurities, and most likely causes the person to micromicromanage you. After you explain that you value his input and will take it into account, you can try to develop a more acceptable working relationship.

✔ **Offer to explain how you approach your tasks.** Explain the techniques and approaches you use and how you ensure you meet established product requirements, schedules, and budgets. Seeing that you perform your work using appropriate, high-quality techniques will increase your manager's confidence that you'll successfully complete the assignment he gave you.

✔ **Work with the person to develop a scheme for sharing progress and accomplishments.** Develop meaningful and frequent checkpoints. Frequent monitoring early in your work reassures you both that you're successfully performing the assignments.

## Working with a micromanager

You can reduce or even eliminate most micromanagement by improving your communication and strengthening your interpersonal relationships. Consider taking the following steps:

✔ **Don't assume.** Don't jump to conclusions. Examine the situation, get to know the person who's micromanaging you, and try to understand his motivations. Expect that you can develop a working relationship that you're both comfortable with.

✔ **Listen.** Listen to the micromanager's questions and comments; see if patterns emerge. Try to understand his real interests and concerns.

✔ **Observe the person's behavior with others.** If the person micromanages others, then the micromanagement likely stems from his feelings rather than from your actions. Try to figure ways to address the person's real interests and concerns.

✔ **If at first you don't succeed, try, try again.** Draw your first conclusion and take steps to address the situation. If that approach doesn't work, reassess the situation and develop an alternative strategy. Keep at it until you succeed.

# Chapter 11

# Starting Your Team Off on the Right Foot

A fter intense work on a tight schedule, you submit your project plan for review and approval. A few days later, your boss comes to you and says,

> "I have some good news and some bad news. Which would you like to hear first?"
>
> "Tell me the good news," you respond.
>
> "Your plan's been approved."
>
> "So, what's the bad news?"
>
> "Now you have to do the project!"

Starting your project off correctly is a key to ultimate success. Your project plan describes what you'll produce, the work you'll do, how you'll do it, when you'll do it, and the resources you'll need. You based your plan on the information you had at the time, and, if information wasn't available, you made assumptions. The more time between your plan's completion and its approval, the more changes you're going to find in your plan's assumptions.

As you prepare to start your project, you need to reconfirm or update the information in your plan, determine or reaffirm which people will play a role in your project, and prepare the systems and procedures that will support your project's performance. This chapter tells you how to accomplish these tasks and get your project off to a strong start.

# Finalizing Your Project's Participants

A *project audience* is a person or group that supports, is affected by, or is interested in your project. (See Chapter 3 for a detailed discussion of how to identify project audiences.) In your project plan, you describe the roles you anticipate people to play and the amount of effort you expect team members to invest. You identify the people by name, by title or position, or by the skills and knowledge they need.

This section shows you how to reaffirm who you'll involve in your project. This section also helps you make sure everyone's still on board — and tells you what to do if some people aren't.

## Confirming your team members' participation

As you start your project, confirm the identities of the people who'll work to support your project by verifying that specific people are still able to uphold their promised commitments and, if needed, recruiting and select new people to fill the remaining needs.

Contact all people who will support your project to

1. **Inform them that your project has been approved and when work will start.**

   Not all project plans are approved. You rarely know in advance how long the approval process will take or how soon your project can start. Inform team members as soon as possible so they can schedule the necessary time.

2. **Confirm that they're still able to support your project.**

   People's workloads and other commitments may change between the time you prepare your plan and your project's approval. If a person is no longer able to provide the promised support, recruit a replacement as soon as possible.

3. **Explain what you'll do to develop the project team and start the project work.**

   Provide a list of all team members and others who will support the project. Also mention the steps you'll take to introduce members and kick off the project.

**4. Reconfirm the work you expect them to perform, when they're to do it, and the amount of time you expect them to spend on it.**

Clarify specific activities and the nature of the work. Depending on the size and formality of your project, you can use any format from a quick e-mail to a formal *work-order agreement.*

As Figure 11-1 illustrates, a typical work-order agreement includes the following information:

| **Work-Order Agreement** | | |
|---|---|---|
| Project name: | Project number: | |
| Activity name: | Work Breakdown Structure code: | |
| Description of work to be performed: | | |
| Start date | End date | Number of hours to be spent |
| **Approvals** | | |
| Project manager: | Team member: | Team member's supervisor: |
| Name　　　　Date | Name　　　　Date | Name　　　　Date |

**Figure 11-1:**
A typical work-order agreement.

✔ **Identifiers:** Include project name, project number, activity name, and Work Breakdown Structure (WBS) code. (For more information about the WBS, see Chapter 4.) The project name and number confirm that your project is now official. You use the activity name and WBS code number to record work progress as well as time and resource charges.

✔ **Work to be performed:** Describe the different activities and procedures as well as outputs of the project.

✔ **Activity start date, end date, and number of hours to be spent:** Including this information reaffirms

  • The importance of doing the work within the schedule and budget

  • The person's acknowledgement that he expects to do the described work within these time and resource constraints

  • The criteria you'll use to assess the person's performance

✔ **Written approvals from the person who'll do the work, his supervisor, and the project manager:** Including these written approvals increases the likelihood that these people have read and understood its elements and commit to support it.

Be sure you specify all of this information when reconfirming a person's commitment to your project. The longer you wait to specify any of this information, the greater the chances are that a person won't provide the support you had hoped for.

If you choose not to use a formal work order, be sure to write down all key information that clarifies your agreement and get signed approvals from the team member and his supervisor. Asking for signed approvals encourages people to consider carefully before they make any commitments and serves as a reference and reminder of exactly what was promised.

## Assuring that others are on board

Others may also play a role in your project's success, even though they may not officially be members of your project team. Two such groups are *drivers,* people who have a say in defining the results of your project, and *supporters,* people who will perform a service or provide resources for your team.

A special audience is your *project champion,* a person in a high position in the organization who strongly supports your project; who will advocate for your project in disputes, planning meetings, and review sessions; and who will take necessary actions to help ensure your project's success. (See Chapter 3 for a detailed discussion of these different types of project audiences.)

Contact your project champion and all other drivers and supporters to

- ✔ Inform them your project has been approved and when work will start

- ✔ Reaffirm your project's objectives

- ✔ Confirm with identified drivers that the project's planned results still address their needs

- ✔ Clarify with supporters exactly how you want them to help your project

- ✔ Develop specific plans for involving each audience throughout the project and keeping them informed of progress

In addition, some people will be interested in your project but won't define its planned results or directly support your efforts. As you identify these observers, choose those individuals you want to keep informed of your progress throughout the project and plan how you will do it. (See Chapter 3 for a discussion of how to identify project observers and Chapter 13 for different ways to keep people informed about your progress.)

## *Filling in the blanks*

If your plan identifies proposed project team members by job title, position description, or skills and knowledge, you have to find actual people to fill the specified roles. You can fill the roles by assigning this responsibility to someone already on your organization's staff, by recruiting a person from outside your organization, or by contracting with an external organization.

Whichever method you choose, prepare a written description of the activities you want each person to perform. This description can range from a simple memo for informal projects to a written job description for more formal ones.

Write down your needs for each category of personnel separately. At a minimum, include the following information in your description:

- ✔ Project name, number, and start date
- ✔ Necessary skills and knowledge
- ✔ Activities to be performed and start and end dates
- ✔ Anticipated level of effort

If you plan to look inside your organization, do the following:

- ✔ Identify potential candidates by working with your human resources (HR) department and area managers.
- ✔ Meet with the candidates to discuss your project, describe the work, and assess their qualifications.
- ✔ Choose the best candidates and ask them to join your team.
- ✔ Document the agreement.

If you're looking outside the organization, consult with your organization's HR to identify potential resources. Provide your HR with a detailed description of the qualifications, skills, and knowledge needed, the expected tasks, and the level of effort. Sit in on the interview and assessment process.

Also, if you plan to obtain the support of external consultants, work with your organization's contracts office. Provide the contracts office with the same information that you would provide your HR office. Review the contract document before your contracting officer signs it.

In addition, work with people in key organizational units to identify people, other than team members, who will support your project. After you identify these people:

✔ Meet with them to clarify your project's goals and anticipated outputs and the ways in which they will support your performance.

✔ Develop plans for involving them and keeping them informed of progress throughout your project.

# Developing Your Team

Merely assigning people to tasks doesn't create a project team. A *team* is a collection of people who are committed to common goals and who depend on one other to do their jobs. Project teams consist of members who can and must make a valuable and unique contribution to the project.

A team is different from other associations of people who work together. For example,

✔ A *group* consists of people who work individually to accomplish their particular assignments on a common task.

✔ A *committee* consists of people who come together to review and critique issues, propose recommendations for action, and, on occasion, implement those recommendations.

As soon as you identify your project team members, take steps to define and establish your team's identity as well as its operating practices. Develop these elements, making sure your team understands and accepts them:

✔ **Goals:** What the team as a whole and members individually hopes to accomplish

✔ **Roles:** Each member's assignments

✔ **Processes:** The techniques that team members will use to perform their project tasks

✔ **Relationships:** The attitudes and behaviors of team members toward each other

This section discusses how to help begin creating your team's identity by having members review and discuss the plan, examine overall team and individual team member goals, agree on everyone's roles, and start to establish productive working relationships.

## Reviewing the approved project plan

As soon as people join the team, have them review the approved project plan to reinforce the project's goals, clarify the work planned, confirm the feasibility of time and resource estimates, and identify any potential problems. Meet as a group to discuss people's thoughts and reactions, after they've reviewed the plan.

Team members who contributed to the proposal can remind themselves of the project's background and purpose, their planned roles, and the work to be done. They can also identify situations and circumstances that may have changed since the proposal was prepared and then review and reassess project risks and risk-management plans.

New team members can understand the project's background and purpose, find out about their roles and assignments, raise concerns about time frames and budgets, and identify issues that may affect the project's success.

## Developing team and individual goals

Team members commit to your project when they believe their participation can help them achieve worthwhile professional and personal goals. Help team members develop and buy into a shared sense of the project goals by

- ✔ Discussing the reasons for the project, its supporters, and the impact of its results. (See Chapter 2 for a discussion of how to identify the needs your project will address.)
- ✔ Clarifying how the results may benefit the organization's clients.
- ✔ Emphasizing how the results may support your organization's growth and viability.
- ✔ Exploring how the results may impact each team member's job.

Encourage people to think about how their participation may help them achieve personal goals, such as acquiring new skills and knowledge, meeting new people, increasing their visibility in the organization, and enhancing their opportunities for job advancement. Obviously, projects aren't only about helping team members achieve personal benefits. However, when team members can realize personal benefits while performing valued services for the organization, the members' motivation and commitment to project success will be greater. (See Chapter 14 for more on how to create and sustain team member motivation.)

## Defining team member roles

Nothing causes disillusionment and frustration faster than bringing motivated people together and then giving them no guidance on working with each other. Two or more people may start doing the same activity independently, and other activities may be overlooked entirely. Eventually, these people find tasks that don't require coordination, or they gradually withdraw from the project to work on more rewarding assignments.

To prevent this frustration, work with team members to define the activities that each member works on and the nature of their roles. Possible roles include the following:

- ✔ **Primary responsibility:** Has the overall obligation to complete an activity
- ✔ **Secondary or supporting responsibility:** Has the obligation to complete part of an activity
- ✔ **Approval:** Must approve the results of an activity before work can proceed
- ✔ **Available for consultation:** Can provide expert guidance and support if needed
- ✔ **Must receive output:** Receives either a physical product from an activity or a report of an activity

If you prepared a Linear Responsibility Chart as part of your project plan, use it to start your discussions of project roles with your team members (see Chapter 10 for more on how to use a Linear Responsibility Chart). However, encourage questions and concerns from team members until they're comfortable that the roles are feasible and appropriate.

## Defining your team's operating processes

Develop the procedures that you and your team will use to support your day-to-day work. Having these procedures in place allows people to effectively and efficiently perform their tasks, as well as contribute to a positive team atmosphere. At a minimum, develop procedures for the following:

- ✔ **Communication:** Sharing project-related information in writing and through face-to-face interactions. Such procedures may include
  - • When and how to use e-mail to share project information
  - • Which types of information should be in writing
  - • When and how to document informal discussions

- How to set up regularly scheduled reports and meetings to record and review progress

- How to address special issues that arise

✔ **Conflict resolution:** Resolving differences of opinion between team members regarding project work. You can develop

- *Standard approaches* (normal steps that you take to encourage people to develop a mutually agreeable solution)

- *Escalation procedures* (steps you take if the people involved can't readily resolve their differences.)

✔ **Decision making:** Deciding among alternative approaches and actions. Develop guidelines for choosing the most appropriate choice for the situation, including consensus, majority rule, unanimous agreement, and decision by technical expert. Also develop *escalation procedures* — steps you take if the normal decision-making approaches get bogged down.

## Supporting the development of team member relationships

On high-performance project teams, members trust each other and have cordial, coordinated working relationships. But, developing trust and effective work practices takes time and concerted effort. Help your team members get to know and be comfortable with one other as soon as your project starts by encouraging them to

✔ Work through conflicts together

✔ Brainstorm challenging technical and administrative issues

✔ Spend informal personal time together, such as having lunch or participating in non-work-related activities after hours

## Helping your team to become a smooth-functioning unit

When team members trust each other, have confidence in each other's abilities, can count on each other's promises, and communicate openly, all of their efforts can be devoted to performing their project work instead of dealing with interpersonal frustrations.

Help your team achieve this high performance level of functioning by guiding them through the following stages:

- ✔ **Forming:** Identifying and meeting team members; politely discussing project objectives, work assignments, and so forth. Share the project plan, introduce people to each other, and discuss each person's background, organizational responsibilities, and areas of expertise.

- ✔ **Storming:** Raising and resolving personal conflicts about the project or other team members.

  - Encourage people to discuss any concerns they have about the project plan's feasibility, and be sure you address those concerns.

  - Encourage people to discuss any reservations they may have about other team members or team members' abilities.

  - Focus these discussions on ways to ensure successful task performance — you don't want the talks to turn into unproductive personal attacks.

  - You can initially speak privately with people about issues you're uncomfortable bringing up in front of the entire team. Eventually, though, you must discuss their concerns with the entire team, in order to achieve a sense of mutual honesty and trust.

- ✔ **Norming:** Developing the standards and operating guidelines that govern team-member behavior. Encourage members to establish these team norms instead of relying on the procedures and practices they use in their functional areas. Examples of these norms include the following:

  - **How people present and discuss different points of view:** Some people present points of view politely, while others aggressively debate their opponents in an attempt to prove their point.

  - **Timeliness of meeting attendance:** Some people always show up for meetings on time, while others are habitually 15 minutes late.

  - **Participation in meetings:** Some people sit back and observe, while others actively participate and share their ideas.

  At a team meeting, encourage people to discuss how team members should behave in different situations. Address concerns people may express and encourage the group to adopt team norms.

- ✔ **Performing:** Doing project work, monitoring schedules and budgets, making needed changes, and keeping people informed.

Keep the following in mind as you guide your team through its developmental phases:

- **If everything goes smoothly on your project, it doesn't matter whether the team has successfully gone through the forming, storming, and norming stages.** But when the project hits problems, your team may become dysfunctional if it hasn't progressed through every stage. Suppose, for example, that the team misses a major project deadline. If team members haven't developed mutual trust for one another, they're more likely to spend time searching for someone to blame than working together to fix the situation.

- **On occasion, you may have to revisit a stage you thought the team had completed.** For example, a new person may join the team, or a major aspect of the project plan may change.

- **Your team won't automatically pass through these stages; you have to guide them.** Left on their own, teams often fail to move beyond the forming stage. Many people don't like to confront thorny interpersonal issues, so they ignore them.

- **Periodically assess how the team feels it's performing; decide which, if any, issues the team needs to work through.** Managing your team is a project itself!

# Laying the Groundwork for Controlling Your Project

Controlling your project throughout its performance requires that you collect appropriate information, evaluate your performance compared with your plan, and share your findings with your project's audiences. This section highlights the steps you take to prepare to collect, analyze, and share this information.

## Selecting and preparing your tracking systems

Effective project control requires accurate and timely information to help you identify problems promptly and take effective corrective action. This section highlights the information you'll need and how to get it.

Throughout your project, you'll track performance in terms of the following:

- ✔ **Schedule achievement:** How well you're meeting established dates

- ✔ **Personnel resource use:** The levels of effort people are spending on their assignments

- ✔ **Financial expenditures:** Funds you're spending for project resources

See Chapter 12 for a detailed discussion of the information systems you can use to track your project's progress.

If you use existing systems to track your project's schedule performance and resource use, set up your project on these systems as follows:

- ✔ **Obtain your official project number.** Your *project number* is the official company identifier for your project. All products, activities, and resources related to your project are assigned that number. Check with your organization's finance department or project office to find out your project's number and check with your finance or information technology department to determine the steps you must take to set up your project on the organization's financial tracking system labor recording system and/or activity tracking system.

- ✔ **Finalize your project's Work Breakdown Structure (WBS).** Have team members review your project's WBS and make any necessary changes or additions. Assign identifier codes to all WBS elements. (Check out Chapter 4 for a complete explanation of the WBS.)

- ✔ **Set up charge codes for your project on the organization's labor tracking system.** If team members record their labor hours by projects, set up charge codes for all WBS activities. This allows you to monitor the progress of individual WBS elements, as well as the total project.

  Also, if your organization's system can limit the number of hours for each activity, enter those limits. Doing so ensures that people don't mistakenly charge more hours to activities than your plan allows.

- ✔ **Set up charge codes for your project on your organization's financial system.** If your organization tracks expenditures by project, set up the codes for all WBS activities that have expenditures. If the system can limit expenditures for each activity, enter those limits.

## Establishing schedules for reports and meetings

To be sure you satisfy your information needs and those of your project's audiences, set up a schedule of reports you'll prepare and meetings you'll hold during the project. Planning your communications in advance with your audiences helps ensure you adequately meet their individual needs and allows them to reserve time on their calendars to attend the meetings.

Meet with project audiences and team members to develop a schedule for regular project meetings and progress reports. Confirm these details:

- ✔ Reports that will be issued
- ✔ Meetings that will be held and their specific purposes
- ✔ When reports will be issued and when meetings will be held
- ✔ Who will receive the reports and attend the meetings
- ✔ The formats and content of the reports and meetings

See Chapter 13 for a discussion of the reports and meetings you can use to support ongoing project communications.

## Setting your project's baseline

The project *baseline* is the version of the plan that guides your project activities and provides the comparative basis for your performance assessments. At the beginning of your project, use the plan that was approved at the end of the *definition* phase, modified by any approved changes made during the *start* phase, as your baseline. During the project, use as your baseline the most recent approved version of the project plan. (See Chapter 12 for more discussion on setting and updating your project's baseline.)

# Announcing Your Project

After you've notified your key project audiences (that is, team members, drivers, and supporters) that the project has been approved and when it'll start, introduce it to others who may be interested (see Chapter 3 for a discussion how to identify the *observers* in your project's audience). Consider one or more of the following approaches to announce your project to these people:

✔ An e-mail to selected individuals or departments in your organization

✔ An announcement in your organization's newsletter

✔ A flyer on a prominent bulletin board

✔ A formal kickoff meeting (if your project is large or will have broad organizational impact)

In each instance, tell people the purpose and scope of your project, your intended outcomes and results, and the key dates. Tell them how they can get in touch with you if they have questions or would like detailed information.

# Laying the Groundwork for Your Post-Project Evaluation

A *post-project evaluation* is a meeting in which you

✔ Review the experience you have gained from the project.

✔ Recognize people for their achievements.

✔ Plan to ensure that good practices will be repeated on future projects.

✔ Plans to head off problems on future projects you encountered on this one. (See Chapter 15 for more about a post-project evaluation.)

Start laying groundwork as soon as your project begins to ensure you capture all relevant information and observations about the project to discuss at the post-project evaluation meeting. Do this as follows:

✔ Tell the team you'll hold a post-project review when the project ends.

✔ Encourage team members to keep records of problems, ideas, and suggestions throughout the project. When you prepare the final agenda for the post-project evaluation session, you'll ask people to review these records and notes to find topics to discuss.

✔ Clarify the criteria that define your project's success by reviewing the latest version of your project's objectives with team members.

✔ Describe the details of the situation before you began the project (if the project was designed to change or improve a situation). Doing so enables you to assess the changes in these details from beginning to end.

✔ Maintain your own *project log* (a narrative record of project issues and occurrences) and encourage other team members to do the same.

# Part IV

# Steering the Ship: Managing Your Project to Success

The 5th Wave          By Rich Tennant

You ever get the feeling some of the deputies are beginning to lose focus?

# In this part . . .

The further ahead you try to plan, the more likely conditions are to change. So, successful project management requires that you start off strong, keep moving in the right direction, and make necessary changes to your plan in a timely manner.

In this part, I discuss different information systems you can use to monitor your project's performance and expenditures. I show you ways to track, analyze, and report on project activities; and I discuss techniques to sustain team members' focus and commitment. I then suggest steps to bring your project to a successful close and ways to plan and conduct a post-project evaluation.

# Chapter 12

# Tracking Progress and Maintaining Control

## In This Chapter

▶ Keeping on course: The project plan versus actual performance

▶ Utilizing systems to track scheduling, labor hours, and expenditures

▶ Formulating and taking corrective actions

▶ Managing changes

*A* sad reality of projects is that they're often born amid high hopes and expectations and die in frustration and disappointment. Your project plans represent visions that you believe will work; however, those plans don't implement themselves automatically, and they can't predict the future with certainty.

Successful projects require continued care and management to ensure that the project follows the plans correctly and, as a result, leads to the desired results. When unexpected situations occur, you must react promptly to adjust your efforts and keep your project on track.

This chapter discusses the steps in the project control process and focuses on the systems and techniques for collecting, analyzing, and reporting on schedule performance, labor hours, and expenditures, and taking corrective actions when needed.

# Controlling Your Project

*Project control* entails the following activities you perform throughout your project to ensure that your project proceeds according to plan and produces the desired results (see Appendix B for a float chart illustrating the cyclical nature of project control):

✔ **Reconfirming the plan:** At the beginning of each *performance period* (the time interval at which you regularly review and assess project performance), reaffirm with team members the following project responsibilities and commitments they made for the coming period:

- Activities they agreed to perform

- Dates they will start and end these activities

- Amount of person-effort they agreed they would need to perform these activities

✔ **Assessing performance:** During the performance period, have team members record information on completed products, successful acceptance tests, dates they reached milestones, dates they started and ended activities, number of hours they worked on each activity, amount of resources they used for each activity, and expenditures they made for each activity. Collect this information at the end of the performance period, compare your team's performance with the plan, and determine the reasons for any differences.

✔ **Taking corrective action:** If necessary, take steps to bring your project's performance back into conformance with your plans, or if that's not possible, change the existing plans to reflect a new set of expectations.

✔ **Keeping people informed:** Share your achievements, problems, and future plans with your project's audiences. (See Chapter 13 for suggestions on how to share progress information with your project's audiences.)

Choose the time period for monitoring your project's performance based on the overall length of the project, the risk of unexpected occurrences, and your proximity to major project milestones. Although you may choose to monitor select project activities on a daily basis in certain situations, plan to assess your project's overall performance at least once a month to identify promptly any unexpected occurrences or performance problems that must be addressed.

When a person reaffirms her existing commitments for the upcoming performance period, the chances are greater that she will perform her assignments successfully, on time, and within budget. If she is unable to honor the commitments she made previously (for example, if she has unexpectedly been assigned to work on another high-priority effort during the same time period), you can work with her to develop new plans for how and when she will complete her assignment for your project.

Initially, you may be uncomfortable reconfirming commitments that people have made for an upcoming performance period because you feel that it

✔ **Suggests that you don't trust the person.** After all, the person has made a commitment to do the specified work; wouldn't she tell you if she were unable to live up to that commitment?

✔ **Increases the likelihood that she'll say she can't live up to the original promise.** You're concerned that raising the topic may actually encourage her to say she can't honor her commitments.

In most cases, though, neither situation proves to be true. First, raising the issue doesn't suggest a lack of trust; if you didn't trust the person, you wouldn't be talking with her at all! On the contrary, checking in with her reflects your appreciation that she may not have had a chance to tell you about new circumstances that make it difficult to honor her commitments. Second, raising the issue doesn't increase the chances that she'll opt out of a commitment — it buys you time. If the person can't perform, you'll find that out at the end of the performance period anyway, when she hasn't finished the work. So taking time to reconfirm actually provides an entire performance period to develop alternative ways of dealing with her new restrictions.

# Establishing Project Management Information Systems

A *project management information system* (PMIS) is a set of procedures, equipment, and other resources for collecting, analyzing, storing, and reporting information that describes project performance. To support your ongoing management and control of the project, you need to collect and maintain information about schedule performance, work effort, and expenditures. This section tells you how to collect, analyze, and report on these three parts of your project's performance.

## Identifying the three parts of a PMIS

A project management information system contains the following three parts:

✔ **Inputs:** Raw data that describe select aspects of project performance

✔ **Processes:** Storage and analysis of the data to compare actual performance with planned performance

✔ **Outputs:** Reports presenting the results of the analyses

In addition to defining the data items, designing a PMIS requires that you specify how to collect the data, who collects it, when they collect it, and how they enter the data into the system. All of these factors can affect the timeliness and accuracy of the data and, therefore, of your project performance assessments.

Many information systems have the technical support of computers, scanners, printers, and plotters. However, an information system can consist of manual processes and physical storage devices as well. For example, you can record project activities in your notebook calendar and keep records of project budgets in your file cabinet. But you still need to monitor your procedures for collecting, storing, analyzing, and reporting your information because those procedures also affect the accuracy and timeliness of your project performance assessments.

## Monitoring schedule performance

Regularly monitoring your project's schedule performance can provide early indications of possible activity-coordination problems, resource conflicts, and cost overruns that may occur in the future. The following sections show you what information you need to monitor schedule performance, how to collect and evaluate it, and how to ensure its accuracy.

### Defining the data to collect

You can describe an activity's status either by noting whether it's started, in progress, or finished, or by indicating the portion of the activity that's been completed.

Be careful if you decide to use *percent completed* to indicate an activity's progress. Most often, this measure represents only a guess because you have no clear way to determine this percentage. For example, saying that your new product design is 30 percent complete is virtually meaningless because you can't determine *how much* of the thinking and creating is actually done.

Suggesting that you have completed 30 percent of your design because you have expended 30 of the 100 hours budgeted for the task or because three of the ten days allotted for its performance have passed is equally incorrect. The first indicator is a measure of *resource* use, and the second is a measure of *time* elapsed. Neither measure indicates the amount of substantive *work* completed.

On the other hand, if your activity has clear segments that take roughly the same amount of time and effort, you may be able to determine an accurate measure of percent complete. For example, if you planned to conduct telephone interviews with 20 different people and you have completed 10, you can argue that the activity is 50 percent complete.

If you choose to describe your project's schedule performance by noting the status of individual activities, collect either or both of the following pieces of data to support your analyses:

✔ The start and end dates for each lowest-level activity in your project's Work Breakdown Structure (WBS)

✔ The dates key events (such as *contract signed, materials received,* or *environmental test completed*) are reached

See Chapter 4 for a discussion of the WBS and Chapter 5 for the definitions of an activity and an event.

### Analyzing schedule performance

Assess your project's schedule status by comparing actual activity start/end dates and actual key-event dates to their planned dates. Figures 12-1 and 12-2 present formats that support ready comparisons of these data.

Figure 12-1 depicts a combined activities and key-events report. The following information in this report comes from your project plan:

✔ The activity or key event identifier and description

✔ The person responsible for ensuring that the activity or event occurs

✔ The dates the activity should start and end or the event should occur

These data describe performance during the period of the report:

✔ The dates the activity actually starts and ends or the event actually occurs

✔ Relevant comments about the event

| Activity | Person Responsible | Start Date | | End Date | | Comments |
|---|---|---|---|---|---|---|
| | | Planned | Actual | Planned | Actual | |
| 2.1.1. Design questionnaire | F. Smith | Feb 14 | Feb 15 | Feb 28 | Feb 28 | |
| KE 2.1.1. Questionnaire design approved | F. Smith | - | - | Feb 28 | Feb 28 | |
| 2.2.2. Pilot test questionnaire | F. Smith | Apr 20 | Apr 21 | Apr 30 | Apr 25 | Critical Path |

**Figure 12-1:** A combined activities and key-events report.

Figure 12-2 illustrates a *progress Gantt chart.* You shade an appropriate portion of each bar to represent activity progress. This sample chart presents project performance as of June 30. According to the chart, the design phase is complete, the develop phase is one month behind schedule, and the conduct test phase is one month ahead of schedule.

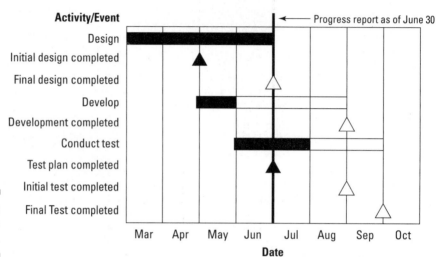

**Figure 12-2:**
A progress
Gantt chart.

The most meaningful way to assess activity progress is to consider the activity's intermediate events that you've achieved to date. The progress Gantt chart in Figure 12-2 really says that on June 30 you achieved all the intermediate events of Task 2 that you had planned to reach by May 31 or, as noted in the previous paragraph, that Task 2 is one month ahead of schedule.

*Note:* You may think I violated my own guideline by reporting on four-month activities. (I suggest in Chapter 4 that your lowest-level activities should last no more than two weeks.) However, you can prepare these reports with any level of detail you choose, depending on your audiences' interests and needs. This high-level report presents information for four-month activities, but the detailed plan would break these activities into subelements of two weeks or less.

Not everyone interprets a progress Gantt chart the same way. I intended the chart to suggest that Task 2 is one month behind schedule. However, some. people have told me that they interpret the report to mean Task 2 is 25 percent complete because one of the four segments for Task 2 is shaded. And one person said that the chart indicated Task 2 actually ended on June 30, although I've never figured out how he justified that interpretation. The message is: Be sure you include a legend with your graph that explains clearly how you want people to interpret it.

## Collecting schedule performance data

In order to collect the schedule performance data, develop a standard format and process for recording your work accomplishments. Standard formats and processes improve the accuracy of your information and take less time. I frequently use the combined activities report and key-events report format.

Consider the following factors when you schedule activity monitoring.

✔ **Is the activity on a critical path?** Delayed activities on a critical path will delay your overall project schedule (see Chapter 5 for a detailed discussion of critical paths). Therefore, consider monitoring critical-path activities more often to identify potential problems as soon as possible and minimize their effect on the project schedule.

✔ **Is the activity on a path that's close to being critical?** Activities on non-critical paths can have some delays before their path becomes critical. The maximum delay for noncritical activities is called *slack time* or *float* (see Chapter 5). If an activity's slack time is very short, a small delay can cause the path to become critical. Therefore, consider monitoring activities that have very small slack times more often (again to identify potential problems as soon as possible).

✔ **Is the activity risk high?** If you feel that an activity is very likely to encounter problems, consider monitoring it more frequently to identify those problems as soon as they occur.

✔ **Have you already encountered problems with this activity?** Consider monitoring activities more frequently if you've already had problems with them. All things being equal, past problems increase the chances of future problems.

At the beginning of a performance period, I print separate reports for each team member that include their activities and events for the period. I ask team members to record actual activity start and end dates and actual key-event dates in the appropriate columns, along with any comments they want to share. I ask them to send me a copy of the completed report on the first business day after the performance period.

Recording and reporting on progress this way has several advantages:

✔ Recording achievements at the time they occur increases the likelihood that the data are accurate.

✔ The agreed-upon schedule for submitting information to me reduces the chance that I'll surprise people with unexpected requests for progress data.

✔ Having people continuously review their proposed schedules and record their accomplishments heightens their awareness of goals and increases the chances that they'll meet their commitments.

✔ The purpose of control is to encourage people to perform according to your plan, not just to collect data. The more aware the team members are of their work in relation to the overall schedule, the greater the likelihood that they'll hit the schedule. If they don't know or care about the target date, they're unlikely to hit it.

I also use the combined activities and key-events report format to reaffirm people's commitments at the start of a performance period. When I give them the report detailing their activities and events for the coming period, I ask them to verify the information and reaffirm their commitments. We discuss and resolve any issues that they identify.

Monitor schedule performance at least once a month. Experience has shown that waiting longer does the following:

✔ Allows people to lose focus and commitment to the activity and increases the chances that the activity won't end on schedule

✔ Provides more time for small problems to go undetected and thus evolve into bigger problems

### Improving the accuracy of your schedule performance data

Collecting the right data items is the first requirement for effectively controlling your project's schedule. However, your analyses will be meaningless unless the data are correct.

Do the following to improve the accuracy of your schedule performance data:

✔ **Tell the team members how you plan to use their schedule performance data.** People are always more motivated to perform a task if they understand the reasons for it.

✔ **Provide schedule performance reports to the people who give you the data.** People are even more motivated to perform a task if they get direct benefits from it.

✔ **Publicly acknowledge those people who give you timely and accurate data.** Positive reinforcement of desired behavior confirms to people that they're meeting your expectations; it also emphasizes that desirable behavior to other people.

✔ **Clearly define activities and events.** Clear definitions help you determine when a milestone does or doesn't occur, and when an activity does or doesn't take place.

✔ **Use all the data that you collect and don't collect more data than you'll use.** Collect only the data that you know you'll use to assess schedule performance.

### *Choosing a vehicle to support your schedule tracking system*

Check to see whether your organization uses an enterprise-wide project planning and tracking system. The best places to look for this information are your organization's Project Management Office (PMO), Information Technology Department, and Finance Department (see Chapter 17 for different types of software used to support project management and Chapter 18 for more on a PMO). If the organization does have such a system, check to see whether you can use it to monitor your project, whether it provides the information you need, and whether its information is timely and accurate.

If your organization doesn't have an existing system you can use, you will have to develop your own. You can use either a manual system or a computer-based system; both offer advantages and disadvantages.

Manual systems include day planners, personal calendars, and handwritten project logs. If you use any of these systems to record your activities and achievements, you don't need special computers or software, which may save you money.

However, manual systems have these disadvantages:

✔ Storing your data requires space. The more data you have, the more space you need.

✔ Comparing and analyzing the data by hand can be time-consuming, and the chances for errors creeping in are greater.

✔ Preparing reports by hand is time-consuming.

A computer-based PMIS can be supported by the following:

✔ Integrated project management software, such as Microsoft Project

✔ Database software, such as Microsoft Access

✔ Spreadsheet software, such as Microsoft Excel

✔ Word processing software, such as Microsoft Word

These systems offer the advantages of faster processing, more efficient data storage, and professionally designed reports. However, they're also more difficult to learn to use, more difficult to maintain, and more expensive.

Many manufacturers offer software packages in these categories. However, more than 80 percent of the organizations that I've worked with use Microsoft software for these functions (thus my examples of Microsoft software packages in the previous bullets). Check to see whether this software available on your organization's local area network (LAN).

## Monitoring work effort

Comparing work effort expended with work effort planned can highlight when people are incorrectly expanding or reducing the scope of an activity, are more or less qualified than you anticipated, are encountering unexpected difficulties performing the work, and warn of the possibility of using up allocated work effort before your project ends.

Monitoring work effort requires you to collect the actual effort spent on each lowest-level WBS activity. (See Chapter 4 for a discussion of the WBS.)

### Analyzing work effort expended

Evaluate your project's work effort expenditures by comparing the actual expenditures with those in your plan. Figure 12-3 depicts a typical labor report that describes the work effort by each team member on each lowest-level project activity. The following information in this report comes from your project plan:

- An activity identifier and description
- The total hours budgeted for each team member to spend on each activity
- The hours budgeted for each team member to spend on each activity every week

You obtain or derive the following information from data during the period covered by the report:

- The actual number of hours spent by each team member on each activity
- The total number of remaining hours for each team member on each activity
- The running difference between the total number of hours in the plan and the number each team member actually spent on each activity

| WBS Code | Description | Employee | | Budget | Work Effort Expended (Person-hours) | | | | |
|---|---|---|---|---|---|---|---|---|---|
| | | | | | Week 1 | Week 2 | Week 3 | Week 4 | ... |
| 3.1.2 | Design questionnaire | H. Jones | Planned | 130 | 20 | 40 | 50 | 30 | ... |
| | | | Actual | 0 | 10 | 30 | 35 | 25 | ... |
| | | | Remaining | 130 | 120 | 90 | 55 | 30 | ... |
| | | | Difference | 0 | +10 | +20 | +35 | +40 | ... |
| | | F. Smith | Planned | 70 | 0 | 20 | 20 | 15 | ... |
| | | | Actual | 0 | 0 | 25 | 10 | 15 | ... |
| | | | Remaining | 70 | 70 | 45 | 35 | 20 | ... |
| | | | Difference | 0 | 0 | -5 | +5 | +5 | ... |

**Figure 12-3:** A labor report.

Actual labor expenditures rarely agree 100 percent with the planned amounts. (In fact, if the number of hours for each task each month is identical to the number in your plan for several months, you may wonder whether people are copying the numbers from the plan onto their time sheets!) Typically, variances of 10 percent above or below the expected numbers in any month are normal.

Consider the charges for two team members in the labor report in Figure 12-3. Smith appears to be working in accordance with the plan. He charged more hours in Week 2 than planned, fewer in Week 3, and the same as planned in Week 4. Jones's situation is very different. Each week, Jones is spending less time on the project than planned, and the total shortfall of hours is building steadily. Whether or not this shortfall indicates a problem is not clear, but the systematic undercharging does point to a situation that needs further investigation.

### Collecting work effort data

Having people fill out time sheets is the most effective way to collect work effort expenditure data. Figure 12-4 illustrates a typical time sheet.

A time sheet includes the following data:

✔ The number of hours a team member worked on each activity each day

✔ The member's signature verifying that the information is correct

✔ An approval signature (typically the project manager or someone she designates) verifying that the time charges are valid and appropriate

| Employee: Name | Signature | | From _____ to _____ | | Approval: Name | | Signature | |
| --- | --- | --- | --- | --- | --- | --- | --- | --- |

| Activity | | | Sun | Mon | Tue | Wed | Thu | Fri | Sat | Total |
| --- | --- | --- | --- | --- | --- | --- | --- | --- | --- | --- |
| Project No. | WBS Code | Description | Apr 3 | Apr 4 | Apr 4 | Apr 6 | Apr 7 | Apr 9 | Apr 9 | |
| | | | | | | | | | | |
| | | | | | | | | | | |
| | | | | | | | | | | |
| | | | | | | | | | | |
| | | | | | | | | | | |
| | | | | | | | | | | |
| | | | | | | | | | | |
| | | | | | | | | | | |
| **Total Hours** | | | | | | | | | | |

**Figure 12-4:**
A typical weekly time sheet.

In most instances, recording work on an activity to the nearest half-hour is sufficient.

*Note:* Some people may record their time in intervals smaller than half an hour. Lawyers, for example, often allocate their time in six-minute segments. Their clients would have it no other way — given that a lawyer may charge $300 or more per hour!

A *time log* is a form that breaks the day into intervals and enables a team member to record the specific activity that he worked on in each interval. For example, to record time in half-hour intervals for a member who begins work at 8:30 a.m., the first interval on the log is 8:30 to 9 a.m., the second is 9 to 9:30 a.m., and so on.

If team members fill out time logs conscientiously, they provide more-accurate data because the log allows them to account for every segment of the day. However, maintaining a time log is far more time-consuming than filling out a time sheet. Normally, detailing on a time sheet the total time a person spends working on his different activities each day is sufficient.

### Improving the accuracy of your work effort expenditure data

Just as with schedule performance data, the more accurate your labor hour expenditure information is, the more meaningful your analyses will be. Take the following steps to increase the accuracy of the work effort expenditure data that you collect:

✔ **Explain to people that you're using their labor effort expenditures to help you determine when you may need to change aspects of the plan.** When you ask people to detail the hours they spend on specific assignments, they often fear that you'll criticize them for not spending time exactly in accordance with the plan — no matter what the reason — or for not spending enough hours on project work as opposed to other administrative duties. Unfortunately, if they believe these are your motives, they'll allocate their work hours among activities to reflect what they think you want to see instead of what they're really doing.

✔ **Encourage people to record the actual hours they work instead of making their total hours equal 40 hours per week.** If people must record a total of 40 hours per week and they work overtime, they'll omit hours or try to reduce them proportionately. You want workers to record accurate data.

✔ **Include categories for time on nonproject activities, such as *unallocated, administrative overhead,* and so on.** If you want people to record their time expenditures honestly, you must provide them with appropriate categories.

✔ **Encourage people to fill out their own time sheets.** Some people ask a third person, such as a secretary, to fill out time sheets for them. But people have a hard enough time remembering themselves what they did the past day or the past week; expecting someone else to accurately remember it for them is totally unrealistic.

✔ **Collect time sheets weekly if possible, or at least once every two weeks.** No matter how often you ask people to fill out their time sheets, many people wait until the sheet is due to complete it. If you collect sheets once a month, those people will be sitting there at the end of the month trying to remember what they did four weeks ago!

✔ **Don't ask people to submit their time sheet before the period is over.** On occasion, managers ask workers to submit time sheets on Thursday for the week ending on Friday. But, this practice immediately reduces the accuracy of the data because a worker can't be certain what she'll be doing tomorrow. More important, though, this practice suggests to workers that, if guessing at Friday's allocation is acceptable, maybe they don't have to be too concerned with the accuracy of the rest of the week's data either.

### Choosing a vehicle to support your work effort tracking system

Before you choose a method for tracking your work effort, check whether your organization has a time-recording system in place that can accurately record data the way you need it. When assessing an existing time-recording system, consider the following:

✔ Time-recording systems typically allocate a person's pay to regular work, vacation time, sick leave, and holiday leave. As such, the system may require exempt employees (that is, employees who aren't paid for overtime) to record no more than 40 hours per week. Additionally, these systems often lack the capability to track regular work by detailed WBS categories.

✔ People are often uncomfortable recording the hours they spend on different assignments because they aren't sure how the organization will use the information.

✔ Standard reports from the system may not present information in the ways you need it to support your work-effort tracking.

If you decide to create your work-effort recording and storage capability, you can consider developing a manual or computer-based system. Manual systems typically involve having people note in their daily calendars or personal diaries the hours they spent on different activities. Unfortunately, data recorded this way are often incomplete and inaccurate. In addition, you'll have difficulty pulling the data together to perform organized assessments and prepare meaningful reports.

You can support a computer-based system with the following software:

✔ Project-management software, such as Microsoft Project

✔ Database software, such as Microsoft Access

✔ Spreadsheet software such, as Microsoft Excel

See Chapter 17 for a discussion of the potential uses and benefits of software to support project management.

## Monitoring expenditures

You monitor your project's financial expenditures to verify that they're in accordance with the project plan and, if they're not, to determine how to address any deviations. You may think that you can determine project funds used to date and funds remaining by just reading the balance in your project's financial account (the project's *checkbook*). However, spending project funds entails several steps before you actually pay for an item. As you complete each step, you have a better sense of whether you will incur the expenditure and, if you do, its exact amount.

The process leading up to the disbursement of funds for goods and services includes the following steps:

1. **You include a rough estimate of the item's cost in your project's budget.**

   You can develop this rough estimate from your prior experience, by checking with others who have purchased similar items in the past, or by checking with your procurement department. Usually, you don't check with specific vendors or supplies when developing this rough estimate.

2. **You submit a written, approved request for the item to your procurement department.**

   This request should specify the rough estimate of the cost included in your project budget and any upper limit that the actual cost can't exceed. The project manager or his designee approves it and anyone else who controls the expenditure of project funds (such as the finance department) approves it.

3. **Your procurement department selects a vendor and submits a purchase order.**

   The purchase order formally requests the vendor to furnish you the item and specifies the procurement department's most recent estimate of the price.

4. **The vendor agrees to provide the item you requested.**

   The vendor provides you written confirmation that he will sell you the item, together with the item's price and applicable taxes and shipping and handling charges and projected delivery date.

5. **You receive and accept the item but aren't yet billed for it.**

   You receive the item and verify that it meets the agreed specifications. If you don't accept the item after the vendor makes repeated attempts to fix any problems you have with it, your procurement department cancels the purchase order and you begin looking for a different vendor or a different item that will meet your needs.

6. **You or your finance department receives a bill for the item.**

   This bill details the item's final cost, together with associated discounts, taxes, and shipping and handling charges.

7. **Your finance department disburses funds to pay for the item.**

   The bill for your item is paid with money from your project's funds.

As you proceed from the first step to the last in this list, your estimate of the item's price becomes more accurate, and the likelihood that you'll actually make the purchase increases.

This list identifies every step in the procurement process. Depending on the size of your purchase and the size and formality of your organization, you may handle some of these stages informally for some purchases.

Responsive project monitoring requires you to have a clear idea of available project funds at each stage of the process. To do so, you typically want to monitor purchase requisitions, purchase orders, commitments (that is, purchase orders or contracts that you and the contractor or vendor agreed to), accounts payable, and expenditures. (Check out the sidebar "Following a purchase through the process" for an example on how to recognize the different steps in an actual procurement.)

### Analyzing expenditures

You evaluate your project's financial performance by comparing the actual expenditures with those you planned. Figure 12-5 depicts a typical cost report that presents expenditures for the current performance period and from the beginning of the project for different levels of WBS activities. The following information in this report comes from your project plan:

✔ Activity identifiers and descriptions

✔ The total funds budgeted for each activity in the performance period

✔ The cumulative funds budgeted to date for each activity

✔ The total budget for each activity

| WBS Code | Activity | Performance Period Budget | Performance Period Actual | To Date Budget | To Date Actual | Total Budget |
|----------|----------|--------|--------|--------|--------|--------|
| | Total | $8,500 | $8,200 | $15,500 | $15,100 | $200,000 |
| 1.0 | Finalize requirements | 5,000 | 4,400 | 12,300 | 11,400 | 45,000 |
| 1.1 | Conduct focus groups | 3,000 | 2,900 | 7,500 | 7,100 | 10,000 |
| 1.2 | Review documents | 1,500 | 1,200 | 4,000 | 3,800 | 5,000 |
| 1.3 | Prepare report | 500 | 300 | 800 | 500 | 4,000 |
| | ⋮ | | | | | |

**Figure 12-5:** A cost report.

## Following a purchase through the process

Suppose you identified in your plan that you need to buy a new computer as soon as possible after your project starts. Based on your prior experience and your familiarity with the marketplace, you budgeted $2,000 to purchase this computer. As soon as your project starts, you write a purchase requisition for the computer and send it to the procurement department. You describe the characteristics the computer should have and put down an estimated price of $2,000. At this point, you have $2,000 less to spend on other purchases because, as far as you know, you will have to pay this $2,000 to a computer vendor at some point in the future.

After receiving your purchase request, your procurement department checks with different vendors, selects one, and issues a purchase order for $1,920 (which includes the vendor's confirmed cost for the computer as well as associated taxes and estimated shipping charges). At this point, the procurement department has confirmed that a vendor has agreed to

fill your request and has improved the accuracy of your estimated cost for the computer.

As a result, you have more confidence that you'll receive the computer and a better sense of its actual cost. When the vendor signs the purchase order, he is confirming the intent to deliver and the computer's total cost.

After you receive the computer and check it out, you have virtually erased all doubts about receiving the computer, and when you receive the bill for the computer, you know the cost. Although the computer may malfunction or a hidden cost may crop up, the likelihood is very low.

Finally, after you pay the bill for the computer, you're almost certain that no portion of those funds will be available for other purchases. You may choose to return the computer at some point in the future and receive a partial refund, but the chances of that happening are slight.

The actual numbers for the period come from the data you obtain during that period. *Actual* in this illustration may mean the value of purchase requisitions, purchase orders, commitments, accounts payable, and/or expenditures.

*Earned Value Management* (EVM) is a method of determining — from resource expenditures alone — whether you're over or under budget and whether you're ahead of or behind schedule. On complex projects, EVM is a useful way to identify areas you should investigate for possible current problems or potential future problems. See Chapter 19 for further discussion of Earned Value Management.

### Collecting expenditure data and improving its accuracy

Typically, you obtain your expenditure data from purchase requisitions, purchase orders, vendor bills, and written checks. You normally see all purchase requisitions because you probably have to approve them. The procurement department typically prepares purchase orders, and you may be able to get copies. Vendor bills usually go directly to the accounts payable group in the finance department, and these people pay the checks. You may be able to have the finance department send copies of bills to you to verify the amounts and so forth, and you can request reports of all checks from your project fund if the finance department tracks expenditures by project code.

The following can increase the accuracy of your project's expenditure data:

- ✔ To avoid double-counting an expenditure, be sure that you remove purchase orders from your totals after you receive the bill (or verify that payment has been made).

- ✔ Be sure to include the correct WBS charge code on each purchase requisition.

- ✔ Verify that the purchase order also includes the correct WBS charge code.

- ✔ Periodically remove void or cancelled purchase requisitions and purchase orders from your lists of outstanding purchase requisitions and purchase orders.

### Choosing a vehicle to support your expenditure tracking system

Before developing your own system to monitor your project's expenditures, first check the nature and capabilities of your organization's financial tracking system. Most organizations have a financial system that maintains records of all expenditures. Often the system also maintains records of accounts payable. Unfortunately, many financial systems categorize expenses by cost center but don't have the capacity to classify expenses by project or activity within a project.

If you have to develop your own system for tracking project expenditures, consider using the following types of software:

- ✔ Integrated project-management package, such as Microsoft Project

- ✔ Accounting package, such as QuickBooks

- ✔ Database package, such as Microsoft Access

- ✔ Spreadsheet package, such as Microsoft Excel

See Chapter 17 for more information on the potential uses and benefits of software to support project management.

Even if your organization's financial system can classify expenditures by activity within a project, you probably have to develop your own system for tracking purchase requisitions and purchase orders. Consider using a spreadsheet program or database software to support this tracking.

# Putting Your Control Process into Action

The previous sections tell you how to set up the systems that provide you the necessary information to guide your project. This section tells you how to systematically use those systems to consistently monitor and guide your project's performance.

## Heading off problems before they occur

Great project plans often fall by the wayside when well-intentioned people try on their own to achieve the best possible results. They may spend more hours than the plan allowed, hoping the additional work can produce better results. They may ask people who weren't in the original plan to work on the project, hoping these people's expertise can improve the quality of the project results. Or they may spend more money for an item than the budget allowed, believing the new choice to be of higher quality.

If possible, set up procedures at the start of your project that prevent people from exceeding established budgets without prior approval. For example, if people record the number of hours they spend on each project activity:

✔ Confirm with them the number of hours they may charge to each activity before they start it.

✔ Arrange for the time-recording system to reject attempts to charge more hours than planned for an activity unless the person has your prior written approval.

✔ Arrange for the time-recording system to reject any project hours by unauthorized people.

For purchases of equipment, materials, supplies, and services:

- ✔ Confirm anticipated purchases, the upper limits for cost of individual items (if any), and the upper limit on the total expenditures.
- ✔ Arrange for the procurement office or financial system to reject attempts to overspend these limits without your prior written approval.

A change to your project's budget may be necessary and desirable. However, you want to make that decision with full awareness of the change's effect on other aspects of the project.

## Formalizing your control process

To guide your project throughout its performance, establish procedures to collect and submit the required information, to assess work and results, to take corrective actions when needed, and to keep audiences informed of your project's status. Follow these procedures throughout your project's life.

1. **At the start of a performance period, reconfirm with people their commitments and your expectations.**

   (See the earlier section "Controlling your project".)

2. **During the period, have people record schedule performance data, work effort, and purchase requisitions and purchase orders they issue.**

   (See the earlier sections "Collecting schedule performance data," "Collecting work effort data," and "Collecting expenditure data and improving its accuracy" for more details.)

3. **At agreed-upon intervals during or at the end of the period, have people submit their activity performance, expenditure, and work-effort data either to all relevant organizational systems or to systems specially maintained for your project.**

4. **At the end of the period, enter people's tracking data into the appropriate PMIS, compare actual performance for the period with planned performance, identify any problems, formulate and take corrective actions, and keep people informed.**

   (See the sections "Getting back on track: Rebaselining," "Identifying possible causes of delays and variances," and "Identifying possible corrective actions" for more details.)

5. **At the beginning of the next performance period, start the cycle again.**

Monitoring project performance doesn't identify problems; it identifies symptoms. When you identify a symptom, you must investigate the situation to determine the nature of any underlying problems, the reasons for the problems, and how to fix them.

But you can't get an accurate picture of where your project stands by monitoring only one or two aspects of your project. You must consider your project's performance in all three of its dimensions — outcomes produced, activity time frames, and resources used — together to determine the reasons for any inconsistencies you identify.

Suppose a member of your project team spent half as much time working on a project activity during the period as you had planned for it. Does this mean you have a problem? You really can't tell. If he accomplished all his planned events and the quality of his products met the established standards, then perhaps not.

If he didn't accomplish some events or the quality of his products was subpar, a problem may exist. You must consider product quality and schedule achievement together with the discrepancy between planned and actual work hours to determine whether your project actually has a problem.

## *Identifying possible causes of delays and variances*

After you confirm that a problem exists, bringing your project back on track requires that you first understand what caused the problem. The following circumstances may cause schedule delays:

- ✔ People spent less time during the performance period on the activity than they agreed to.
- ✔ The activity is requiring more work effort than you figured.
- ✔ People are expanding the scope of the activity.
- ✔ Steps you hadn't identified are necessary to complete the activity.
- ✔ The people working on the activity have less experience with similar activities than you anticipated.

The following situations may result in people charging more or less time to activities than you planned:

- ✔ The person performing the work is more or less productive than you assumed when you developed the plan (see Chapter 6 for a discussion of productivity).

- ✔ You allowed insufficient time for becoming familiar with the activity before starting to work on it.

- ✔ The person is more or less efficient than you considered (see Chapter 6 for a discussion of efficiency).

- ✔ The activity is requiring more or less work than you anticipated.

You may spend more or less on your project activities than you planned for the following reasons:

- ✔ You received the bills for goods or services later than you planned, so they're paid later than you planned.

- ✔ You prepaid for certain items to receive special discounts.

- ✔ You didn't need certain goods or services that you had budgeted for in your plan.

- ✔ You needed goods or services that you hadn't budgeted for in your plan.

## Identifying possible corrective actions

When your project's performance deviates from your plan, first try to bring your project back in accordance with the existing plan, and second, if necessary, investigate formally changing some of the commitments in the existing plan to create a new plan.

Consider the following approaches for bringing a project back in line with its existing plan:

- ✔ **If the variance results from a one-time occurrence, see whether it will disappear on its own.** Suppose you had planned to spend 40 person-hours to buy a piece of equipment but you actually spent 10 person-hours. You figured you'd have to visit four stores before you found the equipment, but you found exactly what you wanted for the price you wanted to pay at the first store. Don't immediately change your plan to reallocate the 30 person-hours you saved on this activity. Most likely you'll wind up overspending slightly on some future activities and the work effort expenditures will tend to even each other out.

✔ **If the variance suggests a situation that will lead to similar variances in the future, consider changing your plan to prevent the future variances from occurring.** Suppose a team member required twice the allotted work effort to finish her assignment because she's less experienced than the plan anticipated. If her lack of experience will continue to cause her to be less productive on future assignments, revise the plan to increase the amount of effort you plan for her to spend on those assignments. (See Chapter 5 for information on how to reduce the time to complete a project and Chapter 6 for a discussion of how to modify personnel assignments.)

## Getting back on track: Rebaselining

A *baseline* is the current version of your project plan that guides project performance and provides a standard for comparing your actual project performance. *Rebaselining* is officially adopting a new project plan to guide activities and serve as the comparative basis for future performance assessments.

If you feel that revising your plan and adopting a new baseline is necessary,

✔ Consult with key project audiences to explain why the changes are necessary and to solicit the audiences' approval and support.

✔ Make sure all key project audiences know about the new baseline.

✔ Keep a copy of your original plan and all subsequent modifications to support your final performance assessment when the project is over.

Rebaselining is a last resort when project work isn't going according to plan. Exhaust all possible strategies and approaches to get back on track before you attempt to change the plan itself. (Check out Chapter 5 for information about changing the order and durations of activities to make up for unexpected delays and Chapter 6 for details on reallocating work effort to activities.)

# Reacting Responsibly When Changes Are Requested

No matter how carefully you plan, occurrences you hadn't anticipated will most likely happen during your project. Perhaps an activity turns out to be more involved than you figured, client needs and desires change, or new technology evolves. When situations such as these arise, you may need to change some aspects of your project to respond to these new conditions.

Even though change is necessary and desirable, it always comes at a price. Furthermore, different people may have different opinions about which changes are important and how to implement them.

This section helps you manage changes in your project. It provides some helpful steps to follow when considering and acting upon a change request. It also looks at *scope creep* and how you can avoid it.

## Responding to change requests

On large projects, formal change-control systems govern how you can assess and act on requests for changes. Whether you handle change requests formally or informally, however, always follow these steps:

1. **When you receive a request for change to some aspect of your project, clarify exactly what the request is asking you to do.**

2. **If possible, ask for the request in writing or confirm your understanding of the request by writing it down yourself.**

   (In a formal change-control system, people must submit all requests for changes on a change-request form.)

3. **Determine the potential effect of the change on all aspects of your project.**

   Also consider what may happen if you don't make the change.

4. **Decide whether you'll implement the change.**

   If this change affects other people, involve them in the decision too.

5. **If you decide not to make the change, tell the requester and explain the reason(s).**

6. **If you decide to make the change, write down the necessary steps to implement the change.**

   (In a formal change-control system, all aspects of a change are detailed in a written change order.)

7. **Update your project's plan to reflect any changes in schedules, outcomes, or resource budgets as a result.**

8. **Tell team members and appropriate audiences about the change and the effect you expect it to have on your project.**

Observe the following guidelines to ensure that you can smoothly incorporate changes into your project:

✔ **Don't use the possibility of changes as an excuse for not being thorough and detailed in your original planning.** Be as accurate and complete as possible when you prepare your project plan to save time and money in the future.

✔ **Remember that change always has a cost.** Don't ignore that cost, figuring you have to make the change no matter what the cost is. Determine the cost of the change so you can plan for it and, if possible, minimize it.

✔ **Assess the effect of change on all aspects of your project.** Maintain a broad perspective — a change early in your project may affect your project from beginning to end.

# Creeping away from scope creep

*Scope creep* is the gradual expansion of project work *without* formal acknowledgment and acceptance of these changes or their associated costs and effects. Scope creep can occur due to the following:

✔ Lack of clarity and detail in the original description of project scope, objectives, and work

✔ Willingness to make small changes to a project without formal review and approval

✔ Allowing the people who don't do the work associated with the changes to decide whether to make changes

✔ Feeling that you should never say "No" to a client

✔ Personal pride that encourages you to believe you can do anything

Control scope creep by the following:

✔ Identifying all project objectives in your project plan and describing them in sufficient detail

✔ Always assessing the effect of requested changes on project products, schedules, and resources

✔ Sharing your true feelings about whether you can implement the requested changes

✔ Developing positive, mutually trusting relationships with your clients so they're more receptive when you raise issues associated with the requested changes

# Chapter 13

# Keeping Everyone Informed

. . . . . . . . . . . . . . . . . . . . . . . . . . . . . . . . . . . . . . . . . . . . . . .

## In This Chapter

▶ Choosing how to share the news: Writing or meeting?

▶ Authoring your project progress report

▶ Managing an assortment of meeting styles

. . . . . . . . . . . . . . . . . . . . . . . . . . . . . . . . . . . . . . . . . . . . . . .

*I*magine standing at one end of a large room filled with assorted sofas, chairs, and tables. You've accepted a challenge to walk to the other end without bumping into any of the furniture. But, as you set off on your excursion, the lights go off, and you now have to complete your trip in total darkness, with only your memory of the room's layout to guide you.

Sounds like a pretty tough assignment, doesn't it? How much easier it would be if the lights went on every few seconds — you could see exactly where you were, where you had to go, and where the furniture got in the way. The walk would still be challenging but much more successful than in total darkness.

Surprisingly, many projects are just like that walk across the room. People plan how they'll perform the project — who will do what, by when, and for how much — and they share this information with the team members and other people who will support the project. But as soon as the project work begins, people receive no information about their progress, the work remaining, or obstacles that may lie ahead.

Effective communication is a key to successful projects — sharing the right messages with the right people in a timely manner. Informative communications support the following:

✔ Continued buy-in and support from key audiences and team members

✔ Prompt problem identification and decision-making

✔ A clear project focus

✔ Ongoing recognition of project achievements

✔ Productive working relationships among team members

Planning your project communications upfront enables you to choose the appropriate media for sharing different messages. This chapter can help you keep everyone in the loop so they know your project's status.

# Choosing the Appropriate Medium

When deciding how to communicate with your team and your project's audiences (check out Chapter 3 for a detailed discussion of these audiences), choosing the right medium is as important as deciding what information to share. This choice ensures that people get the information they need when they need it.

Project communications come in two forms:

- **Formal** communications are preplanned, conducted in a standard format in accordance with an established schedule. Examples include weekly team meetings and monthly progress reports.

- **Informal** communications occur as people think of information they want to share. Informal communications occur continuously in the normal course of business. Examples include brief conversations by the water cooler and e-mails you dash off during a day.

 Take care not to rely on informal interchanges to share important information about your project because they often involve only a small number of the people who should hear what you have to say. To minimize the chances for misunderstandings and hurt feelings:

- Confirm in writing any important information that you share in informal discussions.

- Avoid having an informal discussion with only some of the people who are involved in the topic.

Both formal and informal communications can be written or oral. The following sections suggest when to use each format and how to make it most effective.

## Just the facts: Written reports

Written reports enable you to present factual data more efficiently, choose your words to minimize misunderstandings, provide a historical record of the information you share, and share the same message with a wide audience.

However, written reports do have drawbacks. They don't allow your audience to ask questions to clarify the content, meaning, and implication of your message. With written reports, you can't verify that your audience received and interpreted your message as you intended. In addition, reports don't enable you to pick up nonverbal signals that suggest your audience's reactions to the message, and they don't support interactive discussion and brainstorming about your message. Most important, you may never know whether your audience even read the report!

Keep the following pointers in mind to improve the chances that people read and understand your written reports:

- **Prepare regularly scheduled reports in a standard format.** This consistency helps your audience find specific types of information quickly.

- **Stay focused.** Preparing several short reports to address different topics is better than combining several topics into one long report. People are more likely to pick up the important information about each topic.

- **Minimize the use of technical jargon and acronyms.** If a person is unfamiliar with the language in your report, she'll miss at least some of your messages.

- **Use written reports to share facts, and be sure to identify a person or people to contact for clarification or further discussion of any information in those reports.** Written reports present hard data with a minimum of subjective interpretation, and they provide a useful, permanent reference. A contact person can address any questions a recipient has about the information or the reasons for sharing it.

- **Clearly describe any actions you want people to take based on information in the report.** The more specifically you explain what you want people to do, the more likely they'll do it.

- **Use novel approaches to emphasize key information.** For example, print key sections in a different color or on colored paper, or mention particularly relevant or important sections in a cover memo. This additional effort increases the chances that your audience will see the report *and* read it.

- **After you send your report, discuss one or two key points that you addressed in the report with people who received it.** This follow-up conversation can quickly tell you whether they've read it.

- **Keep your reports to one page if possible.** If not, include a short summary (one page or less) at the beginning of the report (check out the nearby sidebar "Keep it short, and that means you!").

## Keep it short, and that means you!

Be careful of the *"yes, but"* syndrome — where you think an idea sounds great for others, but your *special* situation requires a different approach. In a training program a number of years ago, I shared my suggestion to keep project reports to one page or less. Most people agreed that doing so made sense, but one participant rejected the notion. He proceeded to explain that his project was so important and so complex that he sent his boss monthly project reports that were a minimum of ten pages in length. "And," he added, "my boss reads every word."

I had the opportunity to speak with this participant's boss a few weeks after the training session about a totally unrelated matter. In the course of our conversation, he happened to mention his frustration with a person on his staff who felt his project was so important that he had to submit monthly progress reports no less than ten pages long. He said that he usually read the first paragraph, but he rarely had time to review them thoroughly. He added that he hoped this person had listened carefully when I suggested that reports should be one page or less!

Refer to "Preparing a Written Project-Progress Report" later in this chapter for specifics on writing this special type of communication.

## *Move it along: Meetings that work*

Few words elicit the same reactions of anger and frustration that the word *meeting* can provoke. People consider meetings to be everything from the last vestige of interpersonal contact in an increasingly technical society to the biggest time-waster in business today.

You've probably been in meetings where you wanted to bang your head against the wall. Ever been to a meeting that didn't start on time? How about a meeting that didn't have an agenda or didn't stick to the agenda it did have? Or how about a meeting where people discussed issues you thought were resolved at a previous meeting?

Meetings don't have to be painful experiences. If you plan and manage them well, meetings can be effective. They can help you find out about other team members' backgrounds, experiences, and styles; stimulate brainstorming, problem analysis, and decision-making; and provide a forum to explore the reasons and interpretations of a message.

You can improve your meetings by using the suggestions in the following sections.

### Planning for a successful meeting

In order to have a good meeting, you need to do some preplanning. Keep these pointers in mind:

- ✔ **Clarify the purpose of the meeting.** This step helps ensure that you invite the right people and allows attendees to prepare for the meeting.

- ✔ **Decide who needs to attend and why.** If you need information, decide who has it. If you want to make decisions at the meeting, decide who has the necessary authority and make sure that person attends.

- ✔ **Give plenty of advance notice of the meeting.** This step increases the chances that the people you want to attend will be available.

- ✔ **Let the people who should attend the meeting know its purpose.** People are more likely to attend a meeting if they understand why their attendance is important.

- ✔ **Prepare a written agenda that includes topics and their allotted times.** This document helps people see why attending the meeting is in their interests. The agenda is also your guideline for running the meeting.

- ✔ **Circulate the written agenda and any background material in advance.** This gives everyone time to suggest changes to the agenda and to plan for the meeting.

- ✔ **Keep meetings to one hour or less.** You can force people to sit in a room for hours, but you can't force them to keep their minds on the activities and information. If necessary, schedule several meetings of one hour or less to discuss complex issues or multiple topics.

### Conducting an efficient meeting

How you conduct the meeting can make or break it. The following are essentials for conducting a productive meeting:

- ✔ **Start on time, even if people are absent.** After people see that you wait for latecomers, everyone will come late!

- ✔ **Assign a timekeeper.** This person reminds the group when a topic has exceeded its allotted time.

- ✔ **Take written minutes of who attended, the items you discussed, and the decisions and assignments the group made.** This procedure allows people to review and clarify the information and serves as a reminder of actions to be taken after the meeting.

- ✔ **Keep a list of action items that need further exploration, and assign one person to be responsible for each entry.** This step helps ensure that when you meet to discuss these issues again, you have the right information and people present to resolve them.

- ✔ **If you don't have the right information or the right people to resolve an issue, stop your discussion and put it on the action item list.** Discussing an issue without having the necessary information or the right people present is just wasting people's time.

- ✔ **End on time.** Your meeting attendees may have other commitments that begin when your meeting is supposed to end. Not ending on time causes these people to be late for their next commitments or to leave your meeting before it's over.

### Following up with the last details

Your meeting may be over, but your work isn't done. Make sure you complete the following tasks to get the greatest benefit from the session.

- ✔ **Promptly distribute meeting minutes to all attendees**. These minutes allow people to reaffirm the information when it's still fresh in their minds, and minutes quickly remind people of their follow-up tasks.

- ✔ **Monitor the status of all action items that are performed after the meeting.** Because each action is itself a miniproject, monitoring its progress will increase the chances that people successfully complete it.

- ✔ **Don't just talk about these suggestions.** *Discussing* these ideas can't improve your meetings. Act on them!

# Preparing a Written Project-Progress Report

The *project-progress report* is a project's most common written communication. The report reviews activities performed during a performance period, describes problems encountered and the corrective actions planned and taken, and previews plans for the next period.

This section helps you identify the audience for your project-progress report, provides pointers on report contents, and suggests improvements for that content so it doesn't put your team to sleep.

## *Making a list (of names), checking it twice*

A project-progress report is a convenient way to keep key audiences involved in your project and informed of their responsibilities. Decide who should get regularly scheduled project-progress reports by answering the following questions:

✔ Who needs to know about your project?

✔ Who wants to know about your project?

✔ Whom do you want to know about your project?

At a minimum, consider providing project-progress reports to your supervisor, upper management, client or customer, project team members, and other people who will be helping you on the project, as well as to people who are interested in or will be affected by the project's results.

## *Knowing what's hot, what's not in your report*

Preparing the report gives you an opportunity to step back and review all aspects of your project so you can recognize accomplishments and identify situations that may require your early intervention. Be sure to include some or all of the following information in your project-progress report:

✔ **Performance highlights:** Always begin your report with a summary of highlights. (Keep it to one page!)

✔ **Performance details:** Describe the activities, outcomes, milestones, labor hours, and resource expenditures in detail.

✔ **Problems and issues:** Highlight special issues or problems that you encountered during the period and propose any necessary corrective actions.

✔ **Approved changes to the plan:** Report all approved changes to the existing project plan.

✔ **Risk-management status:** Update your project risk assessment by reporting on changes in project assumptions, the likelihood of these updated assumptions occurring, and the effect of those updated assumptions on existing project plans.

✔ **Plans for the next period:** Summarize major work and accomplishments that you have planned for the next performance period.

## Earning a Pulitzer, or at least writing an interesting report

When writing your report, remember that you don't want it to end up as a bird-cage liner. Write the report so it's interesting and tells the appropriate people what they need to know. Use the following tips to improve the quality of your project-progress reports:

- ✔ **Tailor your reports to the interests and needs of your audiences.** Provide only the information that your audience wants and needs. If necessary, prepare separate reports for different audiences.

- ✔ **If you're preparing different progress reports for different audiences, prepare the most detailed one first and extract information from that report to produce the others.** This approach ensures consistency among the reports and reduces the likelihood that you'll perform the same work more than once.

- ✔ **Produce a project-progress report at least once a month, no matter what your audience's request.** Monitoring and sharing information about project progress less often than once per month significantly increases the chances of major damage resulting from an unidentified problem.

- ✔ **Make sure that all product, schedule, and resource information in your report is for the same time period.** Accomplishing this may not be easy if you depend on different organization systems for your raw performance data.

If you track project schedule performance on a system that you maintain yourself, you may be able to produce a status report by the end of the first week after the performance period. However, your organization's financial system, which you use to track project expenditures, may not generate performance reports for the same period until a month later.

Address this issue in your project's start-up phase (see Chapter 11 for suggested start-up activities.). Determine your sources for status data, the dates your updated data is available from each source, and the time periods that those data apply to. Then schedule your combined analysis and reporting so that all data describe the same time period.

- ✔ **Always compare actual performance with respect to the performance plan.** Presenting the information in this format highlights issues that you need to address.

- ✔ **Include no surprises.** If an element requires prompt action during the period (like a key person unexpectedly leaving the project team), immediately tell all the people involved and work to address the problem. However, be sure to mention the occurrence and any corrective actions in the progress report to provide a written record.

> ✔ **Use your regularly scheduled team meetings to discuss issues and problems that you raise in the project-progress report.** Discuss any questions people have about the information in the project-progress report. (However, don't read verbatim to people from the written report that they've already received!)

# Holding Key Project Meetings

Active, ongoing support from all major project audiences gives you the greatest chance for achieving project success. Continually reinforce your project's vision and how you're progressing toward it, and help your project's audiences understand when and how they can most effectively support your efforts. This section looks more closely at the three types of meetings you may hold during your project.

## Regularly scheduled team meetings

Regularly scheduled team meetings give members an opportunity to share progress and issues and to sustain productive and trusting interpersonal relationships. These meetings also provide an opportunity to reaffirm the project's focus and to keep members abreast of activities within and outside the project that affect their work and the project's ultimate success. Recognizing that most people work on several projects at the same time, these meetings can reinforce the team's identity and working relationships.

Consult with team members to develop a meeting schedule that's convenient for as many people as possible. If some people can't attend in person, try to have them participate in a conference call. (See Chapter 17 for more about how you can use technology to support your project.)

In addition to the suggestions for productive meetings in the "Move it along: Meetings that work" section earlier in this chapter, observe the following guidelines when planning and conducting team meetings:

> ✔ Even though the meetings are regularly held, always prepare a specific agenda, distribute it beforehand, and solicit comments and suggestions before the meeting.

> ✔ Before the meeting, distribute the progress report (take a look at the previous section, "Preparing a Written Project-Progress Report," for details of this report) for the most recent performance period.

✔ Distribute beforehand any other background information related to topics on the agenda.

✔ Limit discussions that require more in-depth consideration; deal with them in other forums.

✔ Start on time and end on time (there, I said it again!).

✔ Prepare and distribute brief minutes of the meeting.

# Using a project dashboard

To make your written project-progress reports most effective, you want to include the greatest amount of information in the least amount of space. A *project dashboard* is an information display that depicts key indicators of project performance in a format that resembles an instrument panel on a dashboard This format can convey the project's overall progress and highlight particular problems that require further attention.

When designing a dashboard for your project, take the following steps:

1. **Select the major categories of information.**

2. **Choose specific indicators for each information category.**

3. **Select the format for each indicator.**

Typical information categories that reflect important aspects of project performance include

✔ **Results:** Desired products your team has produced to date

✔ **Performance to schedule:** Dates that your team achieved milestones and started and completed activities compared with the schedule plan for milestones and activities

✔ **Performance to resource budgets:** Labor hours, funds, and other resources your team has used to date compared with their budgeted amounts

✔ **Risk management:** Current status of factors that may unexpectedly impede project performance

Choose specific indicators for each category in conjunction with the project's drivers and supporters.

As an example, a project that develops an operations manual for a piece of equipment may have the following indicators:

**Results:** The number of manual chapters written or the number of obtained approvals for the final manual

**Performance to schedule:** The number of milestone dates you've met and the number you've missed

**Performance to resource budgets:** The ratio of actual funds expended to those budgeted for all completed activities

**Management of risk:** The number of original risks that may still occur or the number of new risks you've identified during the project

You can display indicators in a table, bar graph, pie chart, or speedometer format. See the following figure that illustrates the types of displays in a project dashboard.

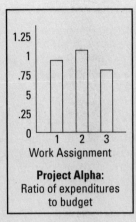

**Project Alpha:**
Ratio of expenditures
to budget

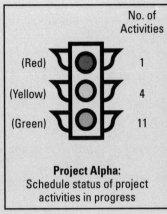

**Project Alpha:**
Schedule status of project
activities in progress

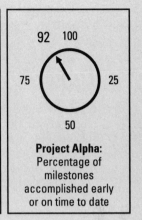

**Project Alpha:**
Percentage of
milestones
accomplished early
or on time to date

In addition, indicators often have a traffic light format:

> **Green light:** The element is proceeding according to plan.
>
> **Yellow light:** One or more minor problems exist.
>
> **Red light:** One or more serious situations require immediate attention.

Determine the specific criteria for green-, yellow-, and red-light status for each indicator in consultation with the project's drivers and supporters.

When creating a dashboard for your project, be sure to

✔ Work with the intended audiences of a report to select the categories, indicators, and their display formats.

✔ Always present *actual* indicator values alongside *planned* values.

✔ Keep the project dashboard report to one page or less.

## Ad hoc team meetings

Hold ad hoc team meetings to address specific issues that arise during your project. An ad hoc meeting may involve some or all of your team's members, depending on the topic. Because issues often arise unexpectedly, do the following:

✔ Clarify the issue and what you hope to achieve at your meeting.

✔ Identify and invite all people who may be interested in, affected by, or working on the issue.

✔ Clearly explain the meeting's purpose to all invitees.

✔ Carefully document all action items that the attendees develop at the meeting and assign responsibility for their completion.

> ✔ Be sure to share the results of an ad hoc meeting with all team members who may be affected by the results, who have an interest in them, and whose support you need to implement them.

## Upper-management progress reviews

An upper-management progress review is usually presided over by a senior manager, run by a project manager, and attended by team members and representatives of all functional areas. This review allows you to tell upper management about your project's status, its major accomplishments, and issues that require their help. The review is also an opportunity for you to note ways to keep the project in line with major organization initiatives.

Take every opportunity to help upper management remember why your project is important to them. They may have approved your project only months ago, but chances are your project's now just one of many activities in your busy organization.

Make your upper-management progress review effective by observing the following tips:

- ✔ Identify the interests of your audience and explain how your project is meeting those interests.

- ✔ Keep your presentation short; choose a few key messages and emphasize them.

- ✔ Highlight your key information, but be prepared to go into more detail on issues if they ask you to do so.

- ✔ Allow time for questions.

- ✔ Present updated information on project risks and how you're addressing them.

- ✔ Distribute a brief handout at the meeting that summarizes the key points of your presentation.

- ✔ After the meeting, distribute notes that highlight issues raised and actions that you agreed on at the session.

# Chapter 14

# Encouraging Peak Performance by Providing Effective Leadership

*In This Chapter*

▶ Clarifying the difference between management and leadership

▶ Tapping into the different sources of power

▶ Developing and maintaining motivation

*L*eadership is one of the most important issues facing organizations today because of the rapid changes that are occurring in every facet of our lives. As a result, a large body of literature has emerged that explores how to guide people to achieve common goals in a wide variety of settings.

When working in a matrix environment (see Chapter 9 for more specifics about the matrix structure), your project's success depends on your ability to organize, coordinate, and support a diverse team that's working toward a common goal. Often these people come from different areas of your organization, have different operating styles, and don't report to you administratively. Successfully guiding such a group of people requires both vision and structure.

This chapter discusses tips for aligning, focusing, and motivating the people supporting your project to maximize the chances for your project's success.

## Practicing Management and Leadership

Leadership and management are two related but distinct sets of behaviors for guiding and supporting people through the stages of a project. *Management* focuses on creating plans and assessing performance; *leadership* emphasizes defining a vision and encouraging other people to help make that vision a reality. Management focuses on systems, procedures, and information; leadership focuses on people. Management creates order and predictability; leadership facilitates change.

When planning your project, explore the *why* of the project (a leadership issue) to help elicit people's buy-in and commitment. Also explore the *what, when,* and *how* (management issues) to develop a feasible approach for successfully achieving the project's goals. When organizing your project, clarify who will support the different project activities (a management task) and help them get excited about doing it (a leadership task).

Continually let people know how the project is progressing and deal with any problems you encounter along the way (management tasks); and remind people of the project's benefits and acknowledge their contributions to the project's success (leadership tasks). Table 14-1 illustrates leadership and management approaches to support the key stages of a project.

| Table 14-1 | Comparison of Leadership and Management Approaches to Project Activities | |
| --- | --- | --- |
| **Activity** | **Leadership** | **Management** |
| Planning | Creating and sharing visions and strategies | Specifying objectives, schedules, and budgets |
| Organizing | Eliciting commitments from members | Assigning people to the team and defining their roles |
| Performing | Motivating team members | Monitoring and reporting on progress and dealing with problems |

# Developing Personal Power and Influence

*Power* is the ability to influence the actions of others. Establishing effective bases of power enhances your ability to coordinate your team and other key audiences. In this section, I tell you how to develop your personal power bases and how to use the power you can derive from these bases to energize and motivate people throughout the life of your project.

# *Understanding why people will do what you ask*

Because personal power is the ability to influence and guide the actions of others, the first step in developing this power is to understand the different reasons people may choose to do what you ask.

People respond to your requests and directions for different reasons:

- ✔ **Rewards:** People do what you ask because they want the benefits you can give them. Examples of rewards include raises and recognition.

- ✔ **Punishments:** People do what you ask because they *don't* want what you can give them. Examples of punishments include poor performance appraisals and undesirable job assignments.

- ✔ **Your position:** People take your requests more seriously because they feel the project manager should direct team members. You can lose this power if you behave inappropriately, but you have it initially.

- ✔ **What you stand for:** People do what you ask because they agree with your goals. They know that your requests and actions are attempts to achieve the same results that they want.

- ✔ **Who you are:** People listen to you because they appreciate and respect who you are, as reflected by your sensitivity, your loyalty to others, your sense of humor, or other characteristics of your behavior.

- ✔ **Your expertise:** People listen to you because they respect the skills and knowledge that you bring to your job. They listen to you because they believe you're probably right.

You don't have to be the technical expert on your project to command the respect of your team members. But you do need to be an expert in the skills and knowledge that your job demands on the project. Because you're the project manager, these skills and knowledge include your ability to plan and control the project, encourage effective communication, encourage a positive and productive work environment, and understand the political environment in your overall organization.

Being both the technical expert and the project manager on your project can work against you. If you're not careful, you can discourage others from accepting responsibilities and performing their work independently because

✔ They feel that their work can never be as good as yours.

✔ You keep the challenging and important assignments for yourself because you like the work and think you can do it best.

✔ You resist approaches that differ from the ones you normally take.

✔ You tend to micromanage people to ensure that they're performing assignments just as you would.

Of course, your technical expertise can be a significant asset if you use it correctly. Your praise for a job well done means a lot more than praise from someone who is less qualified to assess the work.

Although many factors can contribute to your ability to influence people, your power over other people is generally

✔ **Ascribed:** Someone gives you authority to reward and punish others.

✔ **Achieved:** You earn the respect and allegiance of other people.

Achieved power is far more effective than ascribed power. People who act in response to your ascribed power usually do the least necessary to get the rewards they want or to avoid the consequences they fear. On the other hand, people motivated by your achieved power will work to accomplish the highest possible quality of results because they've decided that doing so is in their best interests.

Whether you recognize and acknowledge it, you have considerable opportunity to develop and use achieved power. You can *choose* how you want to influence people's behavior, or you can *inadvertently* influence their behavior. But either way, your actions do influence people's behavior.

## Establishing the bases of your power

You can get a sense of the power you have over someone by the willingness with which she agrees to do and then does what you request. If you already get all the cooperation from others that you need, just keep doing what you're doing. However, if you feel frustrated by people's resistance and lack of cooperation when you ask for their help, take steps to improve the power you have over them.

Successfully influencing the behavior of others requires that you first understand the different power that you potentially have over them and second, that you effectively use that power. Your ascribed power over people depends, in part, on people's perceptions of the specific authority you and others whom you can influence have over them. Your achieved power is based upon people's perceptions of what you know, who you are, and what you stand for.

## Getting what you asked for

People tend to believe what we say when they don't have a good reason to disbelieve. Unfortunately, we often say exactly what we don't want people to believe or do — and then we're surprised when they listen to us.

When I was in high school, my social life wasn't all that great. Years later, I thought about my experiences — the frustrations and disappointments. The more I thought about it, the more convinced I was that my approach was a major reason for my lack of success. Here's an example of a typical phone conversation when I called a girl to ask her out on a date:

"Hi, this is Stan Portny."

"Hi, Stan."

"Say, I don't suppose you'd want to go out with me Saturday night, would you?"

"I hadn't thought about it, but I guess you're right. I don't."

I'd hang up the phone, depressed and convinced that I'd never be able to get a girl to go out with me. In retrospect, although I didn't realize it, I had actually succeeded in getting the girl to do the very thing I had suggested!

I related this story to a friend a while back, and my friend immediately agreed with my observation. He then asked the key question: "Why do we say the very things we don't want people to hear?" After much discussion, we agreed that the reason is either fear of success (what would I say if I were alone on a date with her for three hours?) or fear of failure (trying to minimize the pain of being rejected). Unfortunately, by trying to minimize the pain of failure, we wind up essentially guaranteeing that we'll experience it.

This behavior is frequent in project management. On a new project, the project manager immediately gives all the reasons why the project may not work and, even if the team completes it, why the results won't be as great as everyone thinks. Then he wonders why the project team doesn't commit to the project's success! If you want to succeed, you have to be willing to declare your commitment to your goal and devote all of your efforts to achieving it, even though there's always a chance that you won't reach it.

---

Take the following steps to improve your ability to influence your team members and other people in your project environment:

- ✔ **Determine the authority you have over the people you want to influence.** Common types of authority include the ability to give salary increases and promotions, complete performance appraisals, and assign people to future jobs.

- ✔ **Find out who else has authority over the people you want to influence.** If you don't make the decision about whether and how much to increase a person's salary but you can influence the individual who does, the person will react to you as if you, too, had some measure of ascribed power over him.

✔ **Clarify for yourself why the project's successful completion is in your organization's interest, and share those reasons with other.** You'll be in a better position to help another person see why it would be in her best interest to help you complete your project, if you know all the benefits your project is designed to yield.

✔ **Get to know the people you want to influence; understand, appreciate, and acknowledge their special talents and strengths.** Getting to know other people helps you understand the types of rewards and recognition they would appreciate most. It also tells them you care for them as people, not just as technical resources for your project.

✔ **Let these people get to know your good side.** Your achieved power over others is based on their perceptions of your character and abilities.

✔ **Don't condemn or complain, but do give feedback when necessary.** Condemning is making negative judgments about others, and complaining is criticizing people or things without doing anything to improve them. Both entail sharing negative opinions rather than facts, which demoralizes and demotivates people, while doing little to achieve high-quality results. Constructive feedback, however, entails sharing factual information to improve people's performance. People respect others who they feel are interested in helping them succeed.

✔ **Become proficient in the tasks you have to perform.** People listen to you more seriously if they feel you know what you're talking about.

You must reestablish your bases of power for each new project you perform because you're dealing with different people and your power bases depend heavily on the specific details of the project itself. Further, your bases of power can diminish over time if you don't consistently reinforce them. Meeting with team members at the start of your project can help them appreciate your style and recognize that all of you want to accomplish similar goals. However, if you don't have contact with those members for six months, their initial positive impressions can fade — right along with your ability to influence their commitment and performance.

# Creating and Sustaining Team-Member Motivation

Efficient processes and smooth relationships at work create the opportunity for successful projects. And having team members personally commit to your project's success gives you the greatest chance of achieving it. Therefore, your major task as a project manager is to encourage every member to be motivated and committed to the project's success.

Motivation is a personal choice — the only person you can motivate directly is yourself. You can create the *opportunity* for other people to become motivated, but you can't make the decision for them. Four factors encourage a person to become and remain motivated to achieve a goal:

- ✔ **Desirability:** The value of achieving the goal
- ✔ **Feasibility:** The likelihood that you can achieve the goal
- ✔ **Progress:** Your accomplishments as you work to reach your goal
- ✔ **Reward:** The payoff when you reach the goal

When your project meets people's professional and personal needs in each of these four areas, you strengthen their commitment to help the project succeed. In this section, I show you specific ways to meet these needs.

## Increasing commitment by clarifying your project's benefits

Although some people commit to completing an assignment because someone tells them to do so, you get a much more serious commitment when a person recognizes and appreciates a project's benefits. When discussing your project's benefits with your team, consider ones that are important to your organization, its employees, and its clients, such as the following:

- ✔ Improved products and services
- ✔ Increased sales
- ✔ Improved productivity
- ✔ Better work environment

Also consider potential benefits to each team member, such as the following:

- ✔ Acquiring new skills and knowledge
- ✔ Working in an enjoyable environment
- ✔ Expanding business contacts
- ✔ Enhancing career potential

When you help people realize their personal benefits from participating in a project, you increase their commitment to the project and, therefore, the chances that the project will succeed.

Occasionally someone reminds me that his staff receives salaries for doing their jobs. In other words, he's suggesting that he doesn't have to worry about people realizing personal benefits from their assigned tasks. As far as he's concerned, people will perform their assignments because they want to receive their paychecks. Unfortunately, this type of reward power encourages people to do the least work necessary to ensure their next paycheck rather than to work toward the highest-quality results.

I'm not suggesting your main concerns on a project are your team members' personal benefits. However, people are more committed if they feel they can accomplish personal goals while helping their organization achieve its goals.

Help your team to understand and appreciate the benefits that your project can achieve for the organization by

- ✔ Identifying the situation that led to your project
- ✔ Identifying your project's key drivers and clarifying their hopes for the project (see Chapter 3 for the definition of *project drivers*)
- ✔ Encouraging team members to discuss the expected benefits and the value of those benefits

Also encourage your team members to identify personal benefits that they may realize from participating in your project by

- ✔ Discussing their personal interests and career goals and relating those interests and goals to aspects of the project
- ✔ Discussing past projects they've enjoyed and the reasons they've enjoyed them
- ✔ Discussing some of the benefits that you and other people hope to realize by working on this project

## Encouraging persistence by demonstrating project feasibility

A project is *feasible* if it's possible to accomplish it. No matter how desirable you may feel a project is, you'll give up more easily when you encounter any difficulties if you're convinced that nothing you do can cause it to succeed. You don't need a guarantee of success, but you must believe that you have a chance.

Of course, feasibility is a subjective assessment. What seems impossible to one person can appear feasible to another. Your assessment of feasibility can become a self-fulfilling prophecy. If you think that an assignment is feasible, you work hard to complete it; if you encounter problems, you try to work them out. However, if you really believe that you have no chance of succeeding, you give up at the first sign of difficulty. Any problems just confirm what you already knew — the project was doomed from the start. Of course, as soon as you give up, you have no chance of succeeding, so your initial belief that the project wasn't feasible has been confirmed!

Help people to believe a project is feasible by working with them to define what the team will produce, when, and how. Specifically, do the following:

- ✔ Involve team members in the planning process.
- ✔ Encourage them to identify potential concerns, so you can address them.
- ✔ Explain why you feel that your targets and plans are feasible.
- ✔ Develop responsive risk-management plans (see Chapter 8).

## Letting people know how they're doing

Appreciating your project's value and feasibility helps to motivate people initially. However, if the project lasts longer than a couple of weeks, the team's initial motivation can die out without continual reinforcement. People need to know how they're doing over time for three reasons:

- ✔ Achieving intermediate milestones provides personal satisfaction.
- ✔ Recognizing their successes confirms they're on the right track.
- ✔ Successfully completing intermediate steps reinforces their belief that they can accomplish the final goals.

Have you ever seen a 12-month project where all the major milestones occurred in months 11 and 12? When do you think people got serious about this project? Months 10, 11, and 12 (if they were still around by then)! Do the following to help to keep people on track and excited about your project:

- ✔ Establish meaningful and frequent intermediate milestones.
- ✔ Continually assess how people are doing.
- ✔ Frequently share information with people about their performance.
- ✔ Continually reinforce the project's potential benefits.

See Chapter 13 for ways to inform people of your project's progress.

# Providing rewards for work well done

Rewarding people at a project's conclusion for their effort and accomplishments confirms to them that they accomplished the desired results and met the audience's needs and that team members and managers recognize and appreciate their contributions. This recognition, in turn, makes it more likely that they will welcome the opportunity to participate in future projects.

Rewards can take several forms, including the following:

- ✔ You talk with the person and express your appreciation for her help.
- ✔ You express your appreciation in a written note or e-mail to the person.
- ✔ You express your appreciation in writing to the person's supervisor.
- ✔ You formally submit input to the person's performance appraisal.
- ✔ You nominate the person for a future assignment she particularly wants.
- ✔ You nominate the person for a cash award.
- ✔ You issue the person a certificate of appreciation.
- ✔ You take the person out to lunch.

Rather than guessing which form of reward the person will appreciate most, ask him directly.

Do the following, to make the rewards most effective:

- ✔ Be sure your acknowledgment and appreciation is honest and sincere.
- ✔ Note the specific contribution the reward recognizes.
- ✔ Respect the person's personal style and preferences when giving the reward:
  - • Some people enjoy receiving acknowledgements in front of their co-workers, while others prefer receiving them in private.
  - • Some people appreciate receiving an individual award; others appreciate receiving an award presented to the entire team.

# Chapter 15

# Bringing Your Project to Closure

. . . . . . . . . . . . . . . . . . . . . . . . . . . . . . . . . . . . . . . .

## In This Chapter

▶ Planning for a successful project termination

▶ Crossing those t's and dotting those i's: The remaining administrative issues

▶ Helping your team through closure

▶ Producing a value beyond the project: The post-project evaluation

. . . . . . . . . . . . . . . . . . . . . . . . . . . . . . . . . . . . . . . .

*O*ne characteristic that distinguishes a project from other work assignments is its distinct end, a point at which all work is complete and the results are achieved. However, with the intense demands pulling you on to your next assignment, completed projects can languish and eventually fade away instead of clearly ending with an announcement, recognition of the results, and a thank-you to the people who made them possible.

Unfortunately, this demise hurts both the organization and the people who performed the work. When you don't assess the extent to which your project achieved the desired outcomes, you can't determine whether you conceived, planned, or performed the project well. Furthermore, team members don't have the chance to experience closure, achievement, and a job well done.

This chapter shows you how to bring your project to a close by finishing all substantive work, performing the final administrative tasks, and helping team members complete their association with your project and move on. In addition, this chapter helps you announce your project's end and conduct a post-project evaluation.

## Staying the Course to Completion

Following your project all the way through to completion helps ensure that everyone gets the maximum benefits from your project's results. It also allows you to determine all of these benefits and compare them with the costs incurred, to confirm the company's return on investment, and validate its process for selecting projects.

Bringing a project to an end typically entails wrapping up a multitude of small details and open issues. Dealing with these numerous assignments can be frustrating under the best of circumstances. However, the following situations can make the end of a project even more difficult:

✔ Often you don't have a detailed, written list of all the activities you must perform.

✔ Some team members may have transferred to new assignments, making it necessary for the remaining members to assume new responsibilities in addition to their original ones.

✔ The project staff may lose motivation as general interest in the project wanes and people look forward to new assignments.

✔ The project staff may want the project to continue because they don't want to end the personal and professional relationships they've developed or they're not excited about their next assignment.

✔ Your customer (internal or external) may not be very interested in completing the final details of the project.

Reduce the impact of difficult situations such as these and increase the chances for your project's success by planning for closure at the outset of your project, identifying and attending to all closure details and tasks, and refocusing your team.

## Plan ahead for concluding your project

If you wait until the end of your project to start thinking in detail about closure, you may be too late to gather the necessary information and resources. Start thinking about closure as you plan your project as follows:

✔ **Start laying the groundwork for closure when you prepare your project plan.** Ensure that you describe your project objectives completely and clearly and identify all relevant objective measures and specifications. If one of the project objectives is to change an existing condition, describe that situation before you begin your project so you have a comparative basis for assessment at the end of your project.

✔ **Include project closure activities in your project plan.** Specify in your project's Work Breakdown Structure (WBS — see Chapter 4 for more on this project-planning tool) all activities you'll have to perform to close out your project, and then plan sufficient time and resources to perform these activities.

## Update your plans as you prepare closure activities

View termination (the *close* phase — see Chapter 1) as a separate project. When you think you've accomplished the intended project results, update the preliminary closure plans from your initial project plan.

Gather your remaining team members and specify everything that must happen before the project can end, and then identify all activities you'll perform, including:

- ✔ Completing any unfinished project activities
- ✔ Obtaining all necessary acceptances and approvals
- ✔ Assessing the extent to which project results met expectations

You can then assign responsibilities and resources for each activity. Finally, develop a project-closure checklist that specifies each activity and the person responsible.

## Charge up your team for the sprint to the finish line

As team members work hard to fulfill project obligations, their focus often shifts from accomplishing the project's overall objectives to completing their individual assignments. In addition, other audiences who were initially very interested in the project's results may become involved with other priorities and activities as the project continues. Yet successful project completion requires a coordinated effort by all key participants.

In order to reinforce your team's focus and interest, do the following:

- ✔ **Remind people of the value and importance of the project's final products.** Frequently discuss the benefits the organization will realize from your project's final results as well as the individual benefits that team members will gain. People are more likely to work hard to successfully complete a project when they realize the benefits that they'll achieve.

- ✔ **Call your team together and reaffirm your mutual commitment to bring the project to successful completion.** Discuss your personal commitment to completing your project successfully and why you feel it's important. Encourage other people to make similar commitments. People overcome obstacles and perform difficult assignments more effectively when they're committed to succeed.

✔ **Monitor final activities closely and give frequent feedback on performance to each team member.** Set up frequent milestones and progress reporting times with team members. Staying in close touch with team members provides you and them with up-to-date info on how near you are to final closure; it also provides the opportunity to identify and deal with any issues and problems that may arise.

✔ **Be accessible to team members.** Make yourself available when team members want to confer with you. Consider having lunch periodically with team members and letting them see you around their office area. Being accessible demonstrates your interest in and the importance of their work. It's another way to ensure that you deal promptly with any problems.

# Handling the Administrative Issues

Just as you must have authorization for people to legally spend time, effort, and resources to perform work on a project, this authorization must be rescinded when you close the project — to ensure that people won't continue to spend time, effort, or resources on it in the future. Officially terminate this authorization by doing the following:

✔ **Obtain all required approvals.** Obtain written approval that your project has passed all performance tests and followed standards and certifications. In addition, be sure you have obtained customer or client acceptances. This step confirms that no additional work is necessary on the project.

✔ **Reconcile outstanding transactions.** If you've made project purchases from outside sources, resolve any disputes with vendors and suppliers and pay all outstanding bills. Make sure that any project work effort or expenditures that were posted to incorrect accounts are adjusted.

✔ **Close out charge categories.** Get official confirmation that no future charges can be made to your project accounts.

# Providing a Good Transition for Team Members

Help project team members complete their project responsibilities and move on to their next assignments. Handling this transition in an orderly and agreed-upon fashion allows people to focus their energies on completing their tasks on your project instead of wondering where and when their next assignment will be. In particular, do the following:

✔ **Acknowledge and document team members' contributions.** Express your appreciation to people for their assistance on your project and share with them your assessment of their performance. Also take a moment to thank their supervisors for making these workers available to your project, and provide the supervisors with an assessment of their employees' performance.

Share positive feedback in public; share constructive criticisms and suggestions for improvement in private. In both cases, be sure to share your comments with team members personally and follow up your conversation in writing.

✔ **Help people plan for their transition to new assignments.** If appropriate, help people find their next project assignment. Help them develop a schedule for winding down their involvement with your project while ensuring that they fulfill remaining obligations.

Consider holding a final project meeting or lunch to provide people closure on their work and project relationships.

✔ **Announce to the organization that your project is complete.** You have three important reasons to make this announcement:

   • To alert people in your organization that the planned outcomes of your project are now available

   • To confirm to people who supported your project that their efforts led to a successful result

   • To let people know they can no longer charge time or resources to your project

✔ **Take a moment to let team members and others who supported your project know the true results of the work they invested.** Nothing can provide stronger motivation to jump into the next assignment and provide continued high-quality support.

Check out the "Using a novel approach to announce your project's closure" sidebar in this chapter to see one person's unusual way for letting people know his project was over.

# Conducting a Post-Project Evaluation

Lay the groundwork for repeating good practices and experiences and avoiding the same mistakes in the future by conducting a post-project evaluation.

A *post-project evaluation* is an assessment of project results, activities, and processes to

## Using a novel approach to announce your project's closure

If your project was small, chances are that all participants know it's over and they're aware of the results. But if the project took a long time (six months or more) and involved many groups in your organization, people who participated early may never see the actual results of their efforts.

A while back, a client of mine had just completed a one-year project that entailed the design, development, production, and introduction of a small piece of equipment for an aircraft cockpit. At the official end of his project, he reflected on the many different people who had helped from all areas of his organization. In addition to the engineers who completed the final installation and testing of the equipment, contract officers, procurement specialists, financial managers, human resource specialists, test lab personnel, logisticians, and others had all helped.

He realized that, if past experience was any indicator, the vast majority of these support people would never see the final result of their efforts. So he decided to do something that his organization had never done; he put together a small display in his workplace that illustrated the birth, evolution, and fruition of his project.

He included everything from the signed contract document and purchase orders to the initial design model and engineering drawings to the pictures of the device in an airplane, pictures of a pilot who would use it, and photos of the maintenance people who would support it. He then sent messages to the people who had worked on the project, announcing the display and inviting them to come by to visit.

The response was overwhelming. He estimated that more than 100 people came by to look at the display. He overheard comments by people throughout the organization about how they had performed individual tasks large and small that contributed to the success of this equipment — equipment that they now could see would affect people's lives. The most poignant comment he received was from a technician who worked in the test laboratory. The technician told him this was the first time in his 11 years at the organization that he had ever seen the final results of an item he had tested.

My client estimated that he spent several hours assembling the display. Yet the positive results he and his organization received from this sharing were immeasurable.

- ✔ Recognize project achievements and acknowledge people's contributions.
- ✔ Identify techniques and approaches that worked and devise steps to ensure they're used in the future.
- ✔ Identify techniques and approaches that didn't work and devise steps to ensure they aren't used again in the future.

A *project postmortem* is another term for *post-project evaluation*. I avoid using the former term, however, because it conjures up the image of an autopsy to determine the cause of death! I prefer to leave people with a more positive memory of their experience with a project.

This section helps you conduct a post-project evaluation, from preparing for it, to conducting it, to following up.

## Preparing for the meeting throughout the project

Your project evolves through five stages (conceive, define, start, perform, and close) as it goes from an idea to a completed effort (see Chapter 1 for definitions of each stage). Take steps in each stage to lay the groundwork for your post-project evaluation:

✔ **Conceive phase:**

- Determine the benefits that your project's *drivers* wanted to realize when they authorized your project. (See Chapter 3 for definition and discussion of drivers and the other types of project audiences.)

- If your project is designed to change an existing situation, take *before* measures that describe the situation to compare with *after* measures taken when the project is completed.

✔ **Define phase:**

- Ascertain any additional project drivers that you didn't identify in the concept phase. The expectations of your project's drivers serve as the criteria for defining your project's success, so you want to know who they all are.

- Develop clear and detailed descriptions of all project objectives.

- Include the activity *Conduct a post-project evaluation* in your Work Breakdown Structure (WBS) and allow time and resources to perform it. (See Chapter 4 for a discussion of a WBS.)

✔ **Start phase:**

- Tell team members that the project will have a post-project evaluation.

- Encourage team members to record issues, problems, and successes throughout their project involvement in a handwritten or computerized project log. Review the log when proposing topics for discussion at the post-project evaluation.

✔ **Perform phase:**

- Maintain files of cost, labor-hour charges, and schedule performance reports throughout the project. (See Chapter 12 for details on how to track and report resource expenditures and schedule performance.)

- Encourage team members to continue making entries in their project logs.

✔ **Close phase:**

- If changing an existing situation was a project objective, take *after* measures of that situation's key characteristics.

- Obtain final cost, labor-hour, and schedule performance reports for the project.

- Hold a post-project evaluation session.

- Distribute minutes from the post-project evaluation session.

## Setting the stage for the post-project evaluation meeting

A post-project evaluation is only as good as the information it's based on concerning results, expenditures, and performance. The information must be complete, detailed, and accurate. Prepare for your post-project evaluation meeting by collecting information on the following:

✔ Results

✔ Schedule performance

✔ Resource expenditures

✔ Problems that arose during the project

✔ Changes during the project in objectives, schedules, and budgets

✔ Unanticipated occurrences or changes in the environment during the project

✔ Customers' satisfaction with the project results

✔ Management's satisfaction with the project results

Collect this information from the following sources:

- Progress reports
- Project logs
- Cost reports
- Schedule reports
- Project memos, correspondence, and meeting minutes
- Customer opinions
- Management opinions
- Team member opinions

Prepare a detailed agenda for the post-project evaluation meeting that includes the times when topic discussions will start and end. Consider including the following topics:

- Statement of the meeting's purpose
- Specific outcomes to be accomplished
- Highlights of project performance
  - Results, schedules, and resources
  - Approaches to project planning
  - Project tracking-systems and procedures
  - Project communications
  - Project-team practices and effectiveness
- Discussion and recognition of special achievements
- Review of customer and management reactions to the project
- Discussion of problems and issues
- Discussion of how to reflect experiences from this project in future efforts

Circulate a draft of the agenda, all related background materials, and a list of attendees to all expected attendees at least one week before the meeting. This advance notice gives people time to suggest additions, deletions, and changes. Revise the agenda to address these suggestions, and distribute the final agenda to all meeting participants.

## Conducting the post-project evaluation meeting

A successful post-project evaluation meeting requires that you address the right topics and that people share their project thoughts and experiences openly and honestly.

At the post-project evaluation meeting, explore the following issues:

✔ Did you accomplish the project objectives?

✔ Did you meet the project schedule?

✔ Did you complete the project within budget?

✔ With regard to problems during the project

- Could you have anticipated and planned for them in advance? If so, how?

- Did you handle them effectively and efficiently?

✔ Did you use the organization's project-management systems and procedures effectively?

Do the following, to ensure you get the most accurate information and the best recommendations for future actions:

✔ **Invite the right people.** Invite all people who participated in your project at all points throughout its life. If the list of potential invitees is too long, consider meeting separately with selected subgroups and then holding a general session where everyone reviews the results of the smaller meetings and you solicit final comments and suggestions.

✔ **Declare at the beginning of the session that this is to be a learning experience rather than a finger-pointing session.**

As project manager, you run the post-project evaluation meeting and declare at the outset that the session is to be a time for self-examination and suggestions for ensuring the success of future projects. If people start to attack or criticize other participants, you can immediately bring the discussion back on track by asking the following questions of the participants:

- What can you yourself do in the future to deal more effectively with such situations?

- What can you do in the future to prevent such situations from occurring?

If people resist your attempts to redirect their conversations, you can mention actions that you, as project manager, can take in the future to head off or deal with similar situations more effectively and then ask people to share additional ideas.

- ✔ **Encourage people to**
  - Identify what other people did well.
  - Examine their own performance and see how they could have handled situations differently.
- ✔ **Consider holding the session away from your office.** People often feel more comfortable critiquing existing practices and discussing new approaches when they're away from their normal work environment.

Be sure to assign a person to take notes during the post-project evaluation meeting. In addition to a list of attendees and highlights of information, the notes should list all agreed-upon activities to implement the lessons learned from the meeting and the people responsible for those activities.

## Following up on the post-project evaluation

Often your busy schedule pulls you to new projects before you've analyzed and benefited from the previous experiences. However, even when people do take a few moments to review experiences, they seldom incorporate the advice in future operating practices.

As soon as possible after your post-project evaluation session, the project manager should prepare and distribute a report that's based on the meeting minutes and addresses the following topics:

- ✔ Practices to incorporate in future projects
- ✔ Steps to take that encourage these practices
- ✔ Practices to avoid on future projects
- ✔ Steps to be taken to avoid these practices

Consider this report as you plan future projects to make sure you apply the lessons you've learned. The sidebar "Déjà vu: Avoiding the same mistakes" in this chapter shows a good example of why a written report is important.

# Déjà vu: Avoiding the same mistakes

A participant at one of my training sessions shared her frustration about a situation back at her job. A month earlier, she had attended a full-day post-project evaluation for a year-long project. The project had achieved most of the desired results, but this success came at the cost of budget overruns, schedule slips, and team members' emotional and physical exhaustion from the pressure of working in a continual crisis mode. People spent most of the evaluation day exploring how to handle future efforts more smoothly and efficiently.

Now in a new assignment, she was noticing that the people who participated in that post-project evaluation were all making the same mistakes they had made on the previous project! She wondered why they were totally ignoring the lessons from the previous experience.

I asked how the other team members had reacted to the report of recommendations from the post-project evaluation. She appeared stunned and admitted that no one had taken any notes at the session or prepared a report of the session. More than ten mid- and high-level managers had spent an entire day discussing plans and approaches to improve their organization's operations, but no one had put those ideas down on paper. No wonder nothing had changed — no one knew specifically what changes to make or how to make them happen.

# Part V

# Taking Your Project Management to the Next Level

The 5th Wave                    By Rich Tennant

"The new technology has really helped me become organized. I keep my project reports under the PC, budgets under my laptop, and memos under my pager."

# In this part . . .

You become a truly skilled project manager by continuing to increase your knowledge and refine your practices, and by effectively using tools and resources from start to finish.

In this part, I discuss how to use the techniques in this book to manage multiple projects. I also suggest ways to use new technologies and, just as important, ways to avoid some of their pitfalls. I then offer tips for introducing the tools and techniques in this book at your job. Finally, I walk you through an advanced method for assessing project schedule and cost performance that can provide early warning signs of potential problems on larger projects.

# Chapter 16

# Managing Multiple Projects

● ● ● ● ● ● ● ● ● ● ● ● ● ● ● ● ● ● ● ● ● ● ● ● ● ● ● ● ● ● ● ● ● ● ● ● ● ● ● ● ● ● ● ● ● ●

### In This Chapter

▶ Describing a multiple-project environment

▶ Planning to address the special challenges of a multiple-project environment

▶ Getting off to a good start in a multiple-project environment

▶ Maintaining focus in a multiple-project environment

▶ Getting more for your money in a multiple-project environment

● ● ● ● ● ● ● ● ● ● ● ● ● ● ● ● ● ● ● ● ● ● ● ● ● ● ● ● ● ● ● ● ● ● ● ● ● ● ● ● ● ● ● ● ● ●

*A* journey of a thousand miles begins with a single step. Managing the most-complex, multiple-project environments begins with effectively planning and controlling each project individually. However, when separate projects interrelate, challenges as well as opportunities can arise. Anticipating and addressing the challenges can improve the chances for project success. And taking advantage of opportunities can lead to higher-quality products in less time and with fewer resources.

The tools for identifying and analyzing these challenges and opportunities are the same as those used to plan and control a single project. This chapter discusses the special aspects of a multiple-project environment and what you can do to succeed.

## Defining a Multiple-Project Environment

A *multiple-project environment* is more than just a setting where many projects take place at the same time. Instead, some or all of the projects share common elements. For example, they may

　✔ Have some of the same team members.

　✔ Use some of the same organizational support services.

　✔ Have the same client or sponsor.

✔ Have some of the same audiences.

✔ Include some of the same activities.

✔ Use some of the same resources (in addition to personnel).

✔ Be part of a single, overarching initiative.

In other words, they may produce one of the products or services required to accomplish an overall business objective, or they may be one of several phases that all lead to a final result.

Achieving the greatest cumulative benefit from these interrelated projects requires that you

✔ Decide whether to perform projects based on the benefits they generate as well as the benefits they offer other projects that depend on their support.

✔ Address in each project's plan requirements, dependencies, and constraints arising from other projects.

✔ Resolve conflicting demands for resources based on clear and consistent priorities that reflect the anticipated *net* benefits (the excess of benefits over costs) of all projects.

✔ Clearly and completely document the commitments to provide the resources for each project.

✔ Ensure that each project's team is focused, energized, and prepared to work effectively and efficiently.

✔ Monitor and report on project performance succinctly and in a timely manner, and address promptly all performance issues identified.

*Project Portfolio Management* is the coordinated process of selecting, planning, organizing, performing, and controlling groups of projects to achieve an organization's business objectives. When you consider projects as a group instead of individually, you ensure that you

✔ Undertake all necessary work to achieve the desired objective

✔ Provide the necessary resources for all projects authorized

✔ Set and maintain activity priorities within and among projects

Project Portfolio Management requires

✔ A well-established planning and budgeting process

✔ Effective project management processes, procedures, and practices

✔ Accurate and timely reporting of work-hours and dollars spent on individual projects

✔ A centralized point of coordination and oversight for planning, controlling, and supporting the projects

The remainder of this chapter presents suggestions for addressing the special issues and situations you may encounter when planning, starting, and performing multiple projects. (See Chapter 1 for to see how identifying and comparatively analyzing projected benefits and costs can support the project selection process.)

# Planning in a Multiple-Project Environment

You use the same tools, techniques, and processes to create a plan in a multi-project environment as you do for a stand-alone project. However, this section helps you identify and address the special situations that may occur in a multiple-project environment.

## Identifying project audiences

An essential part of planning any project is identifying the different audiences that will support, influence, or be affected by the project. (See Chapter 3 for more on project audiences.)

When identifying people who will be affected by, interested in, or needed to support your project, do the following:

✔ **If the same person is involved in two or more projects, be sure to specify whether the audience is a driver, supporter, or observer on each of the projects.** A person may be a driver on one of your projects and a supporter on another. Depending on the role the person plays, you will seek and share different information with him and expect different kinds of support.

✔ **Be sure your project's Audience List includes the managers and team members of all other projects that depend on or support yours.** Doing so can help ensure timely and accurate information sharing among related projects.

# Preparing the Statement of Work

Check out Chapter 2 for information on the *Statement of Work* (SOW). When describing the background, planned outcomes, restrictions, and assumptions for your project, do the following:

- ✔ If the results of a project are used in other projects or if the project depends on the outputs from other projects, identify these projects and their effects on each other in the Background section of the Purpose Statement.

- ✔ If one person will be involved in several related projects:

  - Describe in the Strategy section of each project's Purpose Statement why the person is involved and specifically how his roles on the projects will differ.

  - Identify in the Constraints section all requirements and restrictions that will affect each project as a result of the person's involvement in other related projects.

    For example, the person may be unavailable to work on Project A for a particular three-week period this summer because he must work on Project B during that same time period.

# Developing the Work Breakdown Structure

When developing the Work Breakdown Structure (WBS — refer to Chapter 4 for more on this information item), identify and detail sufficiently all activities that people assigned to multiple projects will work on. This detailing allows you to be more realistic when discussing the amount and timing of effort those people should plan for each project.

# Differentiating people's roles

Clarifying people's roles on projects is especially important when they may be doing similar work on more than one project at the same time. The Linear Responsibility Chart (LRC) is a tabular display of each person's particular role and responsibilities on a project. (See Chapter 10 for more information about the LRC.)

Plan to involve people consistently throughout each project they work on to help maintain their focus and commitment. Also explain how you expect people to support each activity on their different projects so you can have accurate estimates of work effort and understand when these people are available.

## Identifying cross-project dependencies

Dependencies among activities and products on different projects often aren't identified, when project teams keep mostly to themselves. Consider carefully the work on other projects related to your own to identify and document all such relationships and to minimize the chances of unplanned delays.

## Heading off conflicting resource demands

When different projects require the same people and resources during the same time period, the resources often wind up being overcommitted. Sometimes these overcommitments occur because people on one project are unaware that people on other projects have similar resource needs; other times they happen when each project manager stubbornly feels his project is the most important. In both cases, communicating early and often can help resolve or even avoid such situations.

Keep the following in mind when managing the personnel in a multiple-project environment:

- ✔ Lobby to keep the records of time commitments and charges for all people working on multiple projects in a single database to make identifying and resolving conflicting assignments easier.

- ✔ Develop the personnel resource assignments for all projects at the same time so project managers can readily identify all conflicts and resolve them according to the correct priorities.

- ✔ Take into account the effect that switching between projects may have on a person's productivity.

- ✔ Where possible, assign people to projects for contiguous periods of time instead of switching them frequently from one project to another. Recognize that a person's productivity and efficiency drop when she frequently moves between assignments.

Do the following, when planning the use of resources other than people:

- ✔ Consult with people on other projects who are doing work similar to yours to see whether they need any of the same resources during the same time periods. If you find that some people will, work together to prepare a schedule for using the resource that provides both of you the support you need, while not scheduling the resource for more hours than it has available.

- ✔ If you find out that other projects need a particular resource in the same time period that you do, see if you can take advantage of *economies of scale* (lowering costs by increasing volume) (check out "Making use of economies of scale" later in this chapter for more info).

## Addressing risks in a multiple-project environment

Preparing effectively for any type of project requires that you anticipate things that may not go according to plan so you can be prepared to deal with them promptly and effectively if they occur (see Chapter 8 for information on managing risks). However, some aspects of a multiple-project environment are more likely than others to cause unexpected occurrences in your project. You should always consider their potential impact in your risk-management assessment.

A *risk factor* is a situation that may give rise to one or more project risks. Consider the following possible risk factors when considering potential risks in a multiple-project environment:

- ✔ The number of your team members that are working on more than one project during the same time period

- ✔ The number of different projects your team members are working on

- ✔ The number of projects you are performing for the same client

- ✔ The resources (other than personnel) that are being used by different projects during the same time period

- ✔ The number of projects using each resource

- ✔ The number of other projects your project audiences are involved with

- ✔ The number of other projects that are part of the same overarching initiative yours is

- ✔ The number of dependencies between your project's activities and those of other projects

# *Starting a Project in a Multiple-Project Setting*

You have the opportunity to set your project apart in the minds of its team members and its project audiences, as soon as it officially begins. This section suggests how you can reconfirm and formalize your team's personnel assignments, create your project team's identity, and focus and announce your project to the organization.

## *Formalizing resource commitments*

When a person serves as a team member on two or more projects, she has greater competition for her time both initially and whenever unexpected events occur. If the projects have different managers, the competition can be more intense because each manager is most concerned with his own project. These situations require managers and team members from the different projects to maintain collaborative, professional relationships and to consider the needs of all projects when resource conflicts arise to reach resolutions that provide the greatest cumulative benefit for the organization.

Preparing written Work-Order Agreements for all team members can clarify the level and timing of their commitments and can highlight any existing conflicts. (See Chapter 11 for more information on preparing Work-Order Agreements.)

To encourage the appropriate people to read and commit to these agreements, include the following signatures on them:

- ✔ The person who is committing the time
- ✔ That person's immediate functional supervisor
- ✔ The project manager
- ✔ Anyone else who may be involved in personnel-allocation decisions

When you're contemplating changes for a person's commitment on your project, be sure to coordinate with the managers of all her other projects. When you make the changes, update the existing Work-Order Agreement and share it with all people involved.

## Creating the project team

Chapter 11 notes the following four issues that a project manager should address when forming a new project team:

- ✔ Goals
- ✔ Roles
- ✔ Processes
- ✔ Relationships

If people have worked together previously, they may feel they don't have to revisit some of these issues. However, to be effective, the team must consider each of them in the present context.

Pay special attention to the following when addressing these issues:

- ✔ **Clearly identify the individual goals of each project on which the people are working.** If the projects are part of a common initiative, describe the special and unique aspects of each project and how the combined efforts help achieve the overall goals.

- ✔ **Encourage team members to consider how each project can specifically help them to achieve their personal goals.** Because part of the audiences and/or work is certain to be different for each project, each project likely offers special and unique opportunities.

- ✔ **Clarify the specific roles each person plays on the different projects.** Even if some of the work is similar, the person may not necessarily support that work in the same way on all projects.

- ✔ **Design communication, decision-making, and conflict resolution processes that allow for collaboration with people from other related projects.** Encouraging people on different projects to share information with each other can help to avoid potential disagreements before they occur and lead to better and faster solutions to problems when they do arise.

- ✔ **For each project, establish escalation procedures for handling conflicts that team members can't resolve themselves.** Having established procedures to follow when people on different projects can't resolve a disagreement by themselves can lead to faster solutions with less chance of residual personal animosity.

## Introducing the project to the organization

Often, when several projects with overlapping team memberships kick off at the same time, the distinction between them becomes blurred in the eyes of the team members and the organization.

Do the following to establish individual identities for multiple projects that have similar or overlapping components:

- ✔ **Introduce each project separately, either in separate meetings, in distinct, self-contained parts of the same meeting, or in different written announcements.** First, discuss all aspects of the project and then identify its relationships with any other projects.

- ✔ **Communicate separately with each audience that's participating in more than one project and emphasize the importance of their contributions to each project.** Identify any areas of overlap or dependency between the different projects and explain how they'll be coordinated. Also emphasize why it's important that the audiences treat the projects as separate entities, instead of one multifaceted effort.

# Performing the Project(s) — Putting the Plan into Action

Planning and preparing for a project sets the stage for project success, but you realize actual success only by putting the plans into action. This section looks at three activities that you must perform effectively and consistently as you work on all of your projects.

## Detailing for successful daily activities

As you develop a project's schedule, you decide the particular time periods for each activity (see Chapter 5). However, to optimize your chances of completing all the activities that are slated for the same time period, you must specify each day's activities and schedule in detail.

In a multiple-project environment, where more independent forces are pulling people and resources in different directions, consider the following items in more detail than you would for a single project when setting your daily priorities:

- ✔ **Lower-level activity dependencies:** The order in which you perform the subparts of an activity

- ✔ **Availability of personnel:** Other commitments of the people who will work with you on an activity

- ✔ **Availability of other resources:** Times during the day that the facilities, equipment, or other resources that you need in your work are reserved for other jobs

- ✔ **Project risks:** The chances that the activity may take longer, require more or different resources, or not produce the desired results

In addition, minimize unnecessary *activity-jumping* (switching from one activity to another for short periods of time), a practice that increases the total time to complete an activity.

Prepare the following items each day to support your work planning:

- ✔ **A to-do list:** A list of the activities you want to perform arranged from highest to lowest priority

- ✔ **A daily calendar:** A record of the specific times to start and end each activity on the list

You can keep these lists on your computer, on written sheets of paper, or in whatever you find convenient. Just be sure to update them every day and follow them religiously.

## Reporting on progress

As projects unfold, people often become lost in the particular priorities of the moment and lose sight of how all the pieces are fitting together. Periodic progress reporting is especially important in a multiple-project environment to remind people of their team's goals and to keep people on related projects updated on the progress and any changes on projects they depend on or support. (Refer to Chapter 12 for a general discussion of project assessment and progress reporting.)

When dependencies and linkages exist between separate projects, follow these guidelines for project progress reporting:

- ✔ Share information on each activity's progress with all projects that are dependent on that activity's results.

- ✔ Obtain and share with your team any information on external project activities that affect your project.

- ✔ Reinforce with your team the unique results of your project and the special work it entails.

- ✔ If your project is part of a larger initiative, continually discuss how the other parts are proceeding and how your project supports or depends on those other projects.

## Managing changes

Evaluating the impact of proposed changes and informing the appropriate people when changes are made can be a time-consuming task on any project. It's particularly challenging in a multiple-project environment because more people are involved, and it may be more difficult to find effective, efficient, and timely ways to involve them.

When evaluating a potential change in a multiple-project environment, consider its effect on all projects that interface with it. If you decide to change some aspect of your project plan, share a written description of that change with all people responsible for related activities on other projects.

# Taking Advantage of Special Opportunities

When multiple projects entail similar activities, or require people with similar special expertise, or use similar resources, you can often save time and money and at the same time improve the overall quality of work. A little advanced planning and some ongoing coordination are all you need. This section can help.

## Planning for similar activities

If several projects include the same activity, consider coordinated planning. For example, you can hold joint sessions with representatives from each project team to detail the subelements of the activity and estimate the necessary time and resources. If feasible, develop a single plan for this activity that all related projects can then incorporate into their plans. At the very least, encourage teams to review and consider using parts of other plans for the same activity.

When you coordinate the plans for common activities, you

- ✔ Improve the quality of the plan for the current project by getting the creative input from a wider range of experienced people
- ✔ Reduce the time to prepare the plans
- ✔ Develop knowledge that improves the quality of and reduces the time for planning future projects with similar activities

## *Making use of economies of scale*

Taking advantage of *economies of scale* refers to recognizing benefits as a result of working on a larger scope. An example is paying less per item when you buy 1,000 items than when you buy 100. If 10 companies each wanted to purchase 100 of these items, each one could get its items for the cheaper price if they together placed one order for 1,000 instead of 10 separate orders for 100. In the extreme, sometimes several projects working together can procure a resource that none of them working alone could afford.

When you identify a situation where a possibility of a joint effort exists, do the following:

1. **Identify the projects that may use the resource.**

2. **Determine the difference in costs for using the resource separately and using it in a coordinated plan (see the following example).**

3. **Determine the times that each activity must use the resource.**

4. **Schedule the activities to maximize the use of the resource in the shortest time.**

5. **Assign responsibility for obtaining and coordinating the use of the resource.**

Suppose three projects require the expertise of a person who isn't currently on staff. Each project needs this person for approximately one month over a three-month calendar period (an average commitment during the three-month period of 33 percent). A project by itself would have difficulty finding a consultant or temporary staffer to work for partial days periodically during the three months. However, if the three projects coordinate their schedules, they can keep the resource occupied full time for three months (by having him spend one month on each of the three projects during the three-month period).

# Chapter 17

# Using Technology to Up Your Game

· · · · · · · · · · · · · · · · · · · · · · · · · · · · · · · · · · · · · · · · · · · · ·

### In This Chapter

▶ Recognizing software's role in project planning and control

▶ Sizing up the benefits and limitations of e-mail

▶ Using technology to support virtual teams

· · · · · · · · · · · · · · · · · · · · · · · · · · · · · · · · · · · · · · · · · · · · ·

*E*ffective project management requires systems and procedures that help people work together to achieve common goals. A major part of project management is information — getting it, storing it, analyzing it, and sharing it. However, the key to successful project management is using this information to guide and encourage people's performance.

Technological advances provide easier and more affordable ways to handle information. For example, computer software allows you to enter, store, and analyze information and then present the results in professional formats. And e-mail allows written communication with people in remote locations at all hours of the day (and night!).

However, technology alone can't encourage focused and committed team performance. In fact, excessive reliance on today's technology can actually result in poor morale, confused and disorganized team members, and lower overall performance. This chapter guides your use of technology in jobs that it handles well. For the jobs that aren't well suited for technology, I discuss other, more-appropriate means of handling people's information needs.

# Using Computer Software Effectively

Today's software for special analyses and reporting looks so good that you may be tempted to believe it's all you need to ensure your project's success. However, even though the software works effectively and efficiently, it *can't* perform the following essential tasks:

✔ **Ensure that information is appropriately defined, timely, and accurate.** In most instances, people record information to support project planning and control, and then they enter the info into a computer. You can program the software to check for correctness of format or internal consistency, but the software can't ensure the quality and integrity of the data.

Suppose you use a computer program to maintain labor hour records that team members charge to your project. You can program the computer to reject hours that are inadvertently charged with an invalid project code. However, you can't program the computer to recognize hours charged to the wrong project with a valid code.

✔ **Make decisions.** Software can help you objectively determine the results of several possible courses of action. However, software can't effectively take into account all the objective and subjective considerations that you must weigh before making a final decision.

✔ **Create and sustain dynamic interpersonal relationships.** Despite people's fascination with chat rooms, e-mail, and other types of computer-aided communication, computers don't foster close, trusting relationships between people. If anything, technology makes relationships more difficult to develop because it removes your ability to see facial expressions and body language.

This section looks at different types of software available, how software can help you manage your project, and how to introduce software into your work environment.

## Looking at your software options

When your project is sufficiently complex, you can use software for a wide variety of tasks, including storing and retrieving important information, analyzing and updating that information, and preparing presentations and reports that describe the information and results of the analyses.

The available software falls into two categories. Each type has benefits and drawbacks.

### Stand-alone, specialty software

*Stand-alone, specialty software* consists of separate packages that perform one or two functions very well. The following types of specialized software can support your project planning and performance:

- **Word processing** (Microsoft Word is an example): Useful for preparing project plans, maintaining a project log, creating progress reports, and preparing written communications.

- **Business graphics and presentation** (Microsoft PowerPoint is an example): Useful for preparing overheads and slide shows for project presentations and developing charts and artwork for written reports and publications.

- **Spreadsheet** (Microsoft Excel is an example): Useful for storing moderate amounts of data, performing repetitive calculations, and presenting information in a variety of chart formats.

- **Database** (Microsoft Access is an example): Useful for storing and retrieving large amounts of data for subsequent analysis and presentation.

- **Accounting** (Intuit QuickBooks is an example): Useful for keeping records of project income and expenses and producing a variety of descriptive and comparative reports.

- **Day planner and scheduler** (Microsoft Outlook is an example): Useful for scheduling your calendar, maintaining a to-do list, keeping your address book, and managing your e-mail activities.

Many manufacturers offer software packages in the preceding categories. However, because so many of the organizations I've worked with use Microsoft software, I've noted examples of Microsoft software packages in the different categories. You may have heard of them before, and, if you don't have them already, you can easily install them on your computer.

Initially, specialty packages performed one or two functions very well. As they've evolved, however, they've expanded to include capabilities that support their primary functions: Word-processing packages now possess some spreadsheet, business graphics, and database capabilities; spreadsheet packages now have some business-graphics and word-processing capabilities; and database packages now have some spreadsheet and word-processing capabilities.

In general, specialty packages offer the following strengths:

- **They offer powerful capability in their area of specialty.** For example, a business graphics-and-presentation package makes it relatively easy to prepare professional-quality presentations that effectively share information and stimulate your audience's interest.

✔ **You most likely have several packages already on your computer.** Having these packages already available means you can use them immediately for no additional cost.

✔ **People probably know how to use many of the common specialty packages.** As a result, people are more apt to use them and use them correctly. Also, you save time and money because people don't require special training to use them.

However, these packages pose some potential concerns:

✔ **They're likely to encourage piecemeal approaches to project planning and control, which may omit certain key steps.** You can use a business-graphics package to draw a Gantt chart (see Chapter 5). However, ensuring your schedule is feasible requires you to consider the effect of activity interdependencies when you prepare it. A business-graphics package can't perform that function for you.

✔ **They don't integrate easily.** For example, you can depict your project's schedule in a Gantt chart and display personnel hours over the duration of each task in a spreadsheet. However, if one team member is unexpectedly out for a week, you have to make separate changes by revising the person's hours in the spreadsheet and then changing the Gantt chart in the graphics package to reflect new activity start and end dates. Even though some programs can share data directly with other programs, the process is often cumbersome.

### Integrated project-management software

*Integrated project-management software* combines database, spreadsheet, graphics, and word-processing capabilities to support many of the activities normally associated with planning and performing your project. An example of an integrated package is Microsoft Project, although more than 50 such packages of all shapes and sizes are on the market today.

A typical integrated project-management package allows you to do the following:

✔ Create a hierarchical list of activities and their components

✔ Define and store key information about your project, activities, and resources

✔ Define activity interdependencies (see Chapter 5 for more information on activity interdependencies)

- ✔ Develop schedules by considering activity durations, activity interdependencies, and resource requirements and availability

- ✔ Display a schedule in Gantt-chart and table formats (see Chapter 5)

- ✔ Assign people to work on project activities for specific levels of effort at certain times

- ✔ Schedule other resources for project activities at specified times

- ✔ Determine your overall project budget

- ✔ Determine the effect of changes on the project's schedule and resources

- ✔ Monitor activity start and end dates and milestone dates

- ✔ Monitor person-hours and resource costs

- ✔ Present planning and tracking information in a wide array of graphs and tables

# Project-Portfolio Management software: Raising the bar on project management

Most integrated project-management software packages support the planning, tracking, and reporting for an individual project. Project-Portfolio Management software, however, is special because it also

- ✔ Supports the assigning and tracking of people to activities on more than one project.

- ✔ Takes into account interproject activity dependencies when determining different schedule possibilities.

- ✔ Tracks and reports the progress and accomplishments of numerous projects simultaneously.

- ✔ Supports communication throughout the organization regarding the planning and performance of different projects

Consider using Project-Portfolio Management software to support project planning and control when your organization meets these criteria: has several large, cross-departmental projects underway; staffs these projects from a common resource pool; has well-established project management and data-collection practices and procedures.

Having a wide range of capabilities in a software package doesn't guarantee that you'll use them correctly. Remember the old adage: Garbage in, garbage out. Even the most advanced software package can't help your project if people don't submit accurate and timely data.

Integrated project-management packages offer benefits as well as drawbacks. The benefits include the following:

✔ **The package's functions are linked.** For example, if you enter personnel requirements one time, the program considers them when developing schedule and resource budgets and when reporting project progress.

✔ **Packages typically have a variety of predesigned report formats.** Having predesigned report templates allows you to use formats that are proven to be effective. It also saves you time and money when preparing and distributing your reports.

---

# Choosing an integrated project-management package

If you decide to use an integrated project-management package, consider the following factors when choosing your program:

✔ **Types and formats of reports.** Choose a package that supports your reports and reporting with minimum customization.

✔ **People's general comfort and familiarity with computers and software.** Will they take the time and effort to learn and then use the package? Having a package with state-of-the-art analysis and reporting capabilities is no help if people don't learn how to use it.

✔ **Your organization's present software.** Everything being equal, choose a package that's already available and in use because team members most likely have experience with it.

✔ **Your organization's existing systems to record labor hours and expenses.** If your organization does have such systems, consider a package that can easily interface with them. If the organization doesn't have these systems, consider a package that can store the information you'll need.

✔ **The project environment in your organization.** What's the size of the human-resource pool for projects, the number and typical size of projects, and so on? Choose a package that has the necessary capacity and speed.

Check out *Microsoft Project For Dummies* by Martin Doucette (Wiley) for more information on effectively using this software's capability.

On the other hand, integrated project-management packages also have their drawbacks:

▶ **The package may not be immediately available.** If it isn't currently available, you have to devote time and money to buy and install the software before you can use it to prepare project reports.

▶ **Most people require training to become comfortable with the package.** Training takes additional time and money.

## Supporting your software

No matter which type of project-management software you choose, your project's ultimate success depends on how well you coordinate and support your project planning and control activities. Table 17-1 illustrates the activities that software can support, the types of software that can provide the support, and how you can ensure that the activity is performed correctly.

| Table 17-1 | Using Software to Help Manage Your Projects | |
|---|---|---|
| *Software Capability* | *Software to Use* | *Your Responsibilities* |
| Documents project objectives | W, IPMS | Ensure all project objectives have measures and performance targets; ensure key people approve the objectives. |
| Records project audiences | W, IPMS | Identify the audiences. |
| Stores and displays the project Work Breakdown Structure (see Chapter 4) | WP, S, BG, DB, IPMS | Identify all required activities. |
| Illustrates team roles and responsibilities | W, S, BG, IPMS | Have people agree and commit to their roles and responsibilities. |
| Develops possible schedules | IPMS | Ensure duration estimates are accurate; determine all interdependencies; ensure that project drivers and supporters buy into the schedules. |
| Displays schedule possibilities | W, S, BG, IPMS | Choose actual schedule dates from among the possibilities. |

*(continued)*

**Table 17-1** *(continued)*

| Software Capability | Software to Use | Your Responsibilities |
|---|---|---|
| Displays the personnel needed and their required levels of effort | W, S, BG, IPMS | Determine personnel needs; estimate their required levels of effort. |
| Displays planned personnel allocations over time | S, B, IPMS | Choose when people will spend their hours (over time) on task assignments; decide how to deal with resource conflicts. |
| Displays funds and other non-human-resource budgets | S, B, IPMS | Determine budgets; explain budgets to project team members. |
| Keeps records of activity and milestone dates | S, IPMS | Develop procedures for collecting and submitting schedule-performance data (see Chapter 12); ensure people submit data on time. |
| Records work hours charged to the project | S, IPMS | Create charge codes; develop procedures for recording and submitting work-hour data; ensure work hours are charged to the correct accounts; ensure data are submitted and entered on time. |
| Records funds, commitments, and expenditures | S, D, A, IPMS | Create the charge codes; ensure expenditures are charged to the correct accounts; ensure data are submitted and entered on time. |
| Prepares reports of schedule and resource performance | W, A, S, IPMS | Define report formats and timetables; select people to receive reports; interpret the reports; ensure people read the reports they receive; develop necessary corrective actions. |
| Prepares presentations of project progress | W, S, BG, IPMS | Choose information to be included; select people to receive reports or attend the presentations. |

*\* The following abbreviations represent the different types of packages available: WP: Word processing, D: Database, S: Spreadsheet, A: Accounting, BG: Business graphics, IPMS: Integrated project-management software.*

## Introducing project-management software into your operations

Before you rush out and buy any project-management software, plan how to maximize its capabilities and avoid associated pitfalls. Do the following to help you select and install your software:

- ✔ Be sure you have a firm grasp of project planning and control approaches before you consider any software.

- ✔ See what software other groups in your organization are using or have used; find out what they like, what they don't, and why.

- ✔ If possible, ask someone who already has a copy of the software whether you can spend a few minutes exploring its operation.

- ✔ After the package is on your computer, load a simple project or a small part of a larger project (that is, enter the activities, durations, interdependencies, resources, and so on).

- ✔ Use only a few of the program's capabilities at first (determine the effect of small changes on your schedule, print out some simple reports, and so on); use more capabilities as you get more comfortable and feel the need for them.

- ✔ Consider attending a formal training program after you've become comfortable accessing the software's different capabilities.

After you've undertaken these steps, you can effectively use software to support your project planning and control activities. On an ongoing basis, ensure that you obtain all updates and changes to the software and consider purchasing software upgrades that introduce significant new capabilities.

# Making Use of E-Mail

Before the advent of e-mail, people consistently told me that the two most common frustrations in their daily routine were unproductive meetings and playing telephone tag. Is it any wonder that people embraced e-mail as soon as it hit the workplace?

Because e-mail is so common, I don't devote too much time to it in this book. However, this section briefly looks at its pros and cons, its appropriate uses with your project team, and ways to use it to your advantage.

# *The pros and cons of e-mail*

E-mail is a fast and convenient means of one-way, written communication. As such, it has many desirable qualities:

- ✔ **The sender and receiver don't have to be present at the time of communication.** You can write an e-mail message whenever you want, and your recipient can read it at his convenience.

- ✔ **The sender and receiver don't have to be in the same place.** You can send your message from Iowa to Tibet.

- ✔ **Your message is delivered quickly.** Relaying your message doesn't depend on delivery schedules, work hours, or weather conditions.

- ✔ **E-mail serves as written documentation.** The receiver can read your message several times to clarify its meaning, and it serves as a reminder that you have shared the information.

- ✔ **You can store e-mail on computer hard disks, Zip disks, USB flash drives, CDs, or DVDs rather than in hard copy.** This saves you space and money and makes retrieval easier.

Unfortunately, e-mail also has the following drawbacks:

- ✔ **People may not read it.** I often meet people who receive 50 to 100 e-mails each day! They readily admit to scanning the first few lines to decide whether a message is worth reading. Some people just read the sender's name to decide whether to read any further.

- ✔ **The medium doesn't provide real-time interaction between sender and receiver.** The receiver may have difficulty correctly interpreting the message because she can't quickly ask questions, check inferences, or ask you to paraphrase the message. You can try to clarify any issues through subsequent e-mails, but people often lose interest in the process.

- ✔ **Communication is limited to the exchange of words.** The sender's non-verbal cues (such as facial expressions, body language, and tone of voice) are lost.

- ✔ **Readers can often misinterpret the content or intent.** E-mail has a growing dictionary of meanings associated with different modes of expression. (For an example, check out the nearby sidebar, "Reading between the lines of your e-mails.") Unfortunately, when people pick up these meanings informally, their e-mails may convey the wrong message.

## Reading between the lines of your e-mails

An old adage claims "It's not *what* you say — it's *how* you say it." In a face-to-face communication, people often pay more attention to the speaker's tone of voice, facial expressions, and body language than to the words. Because e-mail can't transmit nonverbal cues, people have developed a new vocabulary to share their nonverbal messages with their e-mail recipients. Unfortunately, incorrect use of this vocabulary can send the wrong message, creating misunderstandings and hard feelings.

A client told me of a time he sent an e-mail to a co-worker. To emphasize a particular message, he typed it in bold characters. But the recipient never responded and even appeared to ignore him when they passed in the hallways. After several days, my client sought the person out and asked whether there was a problem. The co-worker said he was upset and insulted that my client had yelled at him in his e-mail. My client expressed complete surprise and confusion and asked how an e-mail could suggest a person was yelling. Apparently, some people equate boldface typing to yelling. Fortunately, my client was able to discover the misunderstanding and correct it. But it makes you wonder how often such misunderstandings go unnoticed and unaddressed!

## *Using e-mail appropriately*

E-mail can be an effective component of a comprehensive communication system for your project team. For example you can use e-mail to confirm oral discussions and agreements. In these instances, you want a written message to stand on its own with no interactive discussion or explanation. If a recipient needs to ask questions, the written message hasn't documented the information clearly and accurately.

You can also use e-mail to share factual information that requires little or no clarification. Write simple messages using straightforward language. Tell recipients how they can reach you if they have any questions.

However, e-mail *can't* be the exclusive means of communication to do the following:

> ✔ **Brainstorm to analyze problems and develop new ideas.** Use e-mail to announce the brainstorming session, invite people to attend, identify the topic(s) you'll explore, and provide relevant background material for people to review before the session. Use e-mail to share a summary of the results and future actions. But conduct the actual interchange of ideas in a face-to-face session.

✔ **Build and sustain team members' trust and commitment.** Even though you use e-mail to inform team members of each other's background and experience, commitments, and accomplishments, be sure you provide sufficient opportunities for face-to-face meetings so team members become familiar and comfortable with each other.

✔ **Share an important message.** Perhaps you can share the message initially through e-mail, but follow up with phone calls and in-person meetings to discuss the message and ensure that your recipient has correctly understood its content.

## Getting the most out of your e-mail

When used correctly, e-mail can be a valuable tool for clear, timely, convenient, and inexpensive communications. Do the following to get the most from your team e-mail communications:

✔ **Be concise.** Use clear, measurable words and avoid technological jargon and acronyms when possible.

✔ **Read your e-mail before you send it.** People's impressions of you, your ideas, and your attitude are strongly affected by what you say and how you say it. Take a moment to proof your e-mail message before you hit *Send.* Make sure you've made no typos.

✔ **Anticipate miscommunications.** Put yourself in your audience's shoes. How may they misinterpret your message? What additional information may they want to have? Have you been clear about how you want them to respond to your message? In other words, minimize the need for extra e-mails back and forth to raise questions and clarify points by writing one, well-thought-out e-mail.

✔ **Be sure people have received it.** If possible, program your system to automatically let you know when your audience has opened your e-mail. Otherwise, ask the receiver to verify that he's received the message via a return e-mail, a phone call, or a quick face-to-face conversation.

✔ **Keep a copy of important e-mails.** Maintain a file of important messages you've sent. I keep computerized records of all sent e-mails on an external hard drive, and I keep paper copies of especially important e-mails. These copies confirm the information, date, and recipients. (See Chapter 13 for more info on communication with your project audience.)

# Utilizing Communication Technology to Support Virtual Teams

The globalization of today's businesses creates a greater need for people around the world to work together on projects. This lack of proximity creates unique challenges for encouraging successful team performance. This section looks at some ways that today's technology can support the communication needs of these virtual teams.

A *virtual project team* is a group of people who work together across geographic, time, and organizational boundaries to accomplish a common set of goals and objectives. Although the needs of a virtual project team are the same as those of more conventional teams, many processes and resources used by conventional teams aren't available to the virtual team. Only through the creative use of the available communication technology can virtual teams perform at peak capacity.

High-performance team members must successfully accomplish the following tasks:

✔ **Share project and team-related information in a timely and accurate manner**

✔ **Create and sustain trusting and productive interpersonal relationships**

✔ **Effectively collaborate to perform project work**

Each of these tasks requires effective and timely communication. But, as virtual teams approach these activities, they face unique challenges:

✔ **Members may never meet each other in person.** Becoming familiar with and trust each other is more difficult; the use of nonverbal signals and body language when communicating is severely limited.

✔ **Members may have different primary languages.** This communication challenge increases the chances that people may incorrectly interpret a message.

✔ **Members may come from different organizational and cultural environments.** People's work styles and communication practices may differ.

✔ **Members may be in different time zones.** People may not be available to interact with each other during certain time periods.

Table 17-2 depicts several ways that new technology can support communications on a virtual team.

| Table 17-2 | Using Communication Technology to Support Virtual Teams | |
|---|---|---|
| *Communication Need* | *Approach* | *Application* |
| Share project-related information | E-mail | Sharing factual information; confirming and recording discussions and agreements |
| | Company intranet | Storing plans; entering, storing, and reporting on progress data; storing project-management forms and procedures |
| | Videoconferencing | Discussing and clarifying issues |
| Support interpersonal relationships | Videoconferencing | Introducing new team members; acknowledging team and individual accomplishments |
| Collaborate on project activities | Interactive web conferencing | Discussing technical topics; brainstorming |
| | Videoconferencing | Discussing technical topics; brainstorming |
| | E-mail | Sharing data, reports |

Available communication technology can address a wide range of the virtual team's routine communication needs. When possible, however, people should meet in person to periodically reinforce their relationships and the team's focus and identity.

# Chapter 18

# Improving Individual and Organizational Skills and Practices

. . . . . . . . . . . . . . . . . . . . . . . . . . . . . . . . . . . . . . . . . . . . . . .

## In This Chapter

▶ Keep a good thing going: Continuing to strengthen your abilities

▶ Pass it on: Bringing improved practices to the workplace

. . . . . . . . . . . . . . . . . . . . . . . . . . . . . . . . . . . . . . . . . . . . . . .

*B*ecoming an effective project manager is an ongoing process. The more you learn, the more you realize you need to learn. Fortunately, you have many tools to help you improve your project-management skills.

This chapter discusses some of those means for honing skills and increasing knowledge. It also provides tips for bringing those improved project management practices to the workplace.

## Continuing to Improve Your Skills and Knowledge

Whether you've been a project manager for six months or six years, you probably want to become better at your job. To continue developing your skills and knowledge, you have three main choices: attend formal training, work with a mentor, and obtain professional certification. This section looks more closely at these three options.

# Attending the appropriate formal training

If you're serious about improving your skills and knowledge, formal training may be your first option, and it has many formats: face-to-face interaction with a presenter, interaction with a presenter via video teleconferencing or the Internet, prerecorded sessions by a presenter, and programmed self-instruction.

You can get formal training through the following:

- ✓ **Individual programs:** These programs typically run one to three days and address a particular set of project-management topics.

- ✓ **Certificate programs:** These programs comprise a collection of individual courses that address a range of project-management topics in depth and lead to a certificate of participation. Certificate programs typically last six months to a year.

- ✓ **Degree programs:** These college or university programs provide a curriculum of project-management-related courses that lead to a formal degree. These programs can span up to several years.

- ✓ **Short seminars at professional-society meetings:** Sessions of this kind typically last a couple of hours and explore selected topics.

Many organizations (such as consulting firms, individual consultants, universities, professional societies, and even the organization for which you work) sponsor these training programs.

To find programs in your area, check with your organization's training or human resources department. You can also do a Google search for *project management training in (your city or state),* or visit the Project Management Institute Web site at www.pmi.org (check out the section "Obtaining a professional certification" later in this chapter for more on PMI).

When deciding which program to attend, your goal is: No surprises! To assure this, consider the following factors.

### Program content

The program content is certainly the first and one of the most important considerations. Unfortunately, this information can be elusive because program titles are often ambiguous, written descriptions can be too general or sound too technical, and a description may not even be available.

To ensure you enroll in the right formal training session for you, do the following until you clearly understand the extent of the program contents:

1. **Note the exact program title and read all brief program overviews or descriptions you can find.**

2. **Obtain a copy of the program outline (the hierarchical breakout of the topics).**

3. **Obtain a copy of the program agenda (the schedule of time intervals for each topic).**

4. **Review the program materials.**

5. **If possible, speak with the program instructor or someone who has attended the program.**

If you still don't understand the content selections after taking all these steps, find another program!

### *Program presentation style and format*

In addition to the method of presentation (such as face to face with the instructor, programmed instruction, and so on), consider the following aspects of style and format:

✔ Are the sessions mostly a lecture format?

✔ Does the lecture consist mostly of the instructor reading from slides?

✔ Do you have an opportunity for questions and answers throughout the course?

✔ Is the course tailored for your field, for your company? If so, how?

✔ What types of group exercises and case work are in the program?

✔ Do you have an opportunity to ask questions about particular situations you're dealing with in your organization?

Knowing about a program's style and format can help you select a program that directly applies to your job setting and gives you plenty of opportunity to understand its benefits and applications to your specific situation.

### *Instructor's credibility*

Larger organizations often have a cadre of instructors who can present each of their training programs. As a result, they may not select the presenter until shortly before the program begins. (They want to be free to shift instructors around at the last minute to address other demands and priorities that arise.)

Despite any research you do upfront, this last-minute shuffling can leave you with an instructor who doesn't meet your needs. When you check out a program, be sure to find out the likelihood that your instructor will be the one who's listed in the information.

The most important element in your training experience is your instructor. Don't attend the program unless you know who it will be.

When investigating your instructor, consider the following:

- ✔ **Work experience:** How long has the instructor been in the project-management field? In what capacities? Has he actually used the techniques he presents in the training?

- ✔ **Training experience:** How many times has the instructor presented training sessions in the topics that he'll address? Does he specialize in project management, or is this area just one of many in which he trains?

- ✔ **Experience in your field:** How extensively has the instructor dealt with project-management issues in your particular field?

- ✔ **Educational background:** Has the instructor had formal education in project management or related areas?

- ✔ **Professional credentials:** To what professional societies does he belong? (The Project Management Institute, PMI, should certainly be one of them!) Which professional certifications does he hold (such as the Project Management Professional, PMP, which I discuss later in this chapter)?

### Instructor's style

The instructor's style can make the difference between your leaving a session with a few pieces of new information or coming away excited and committed to use the information immediately. At my training sessions, people often tell me, "I *think* this kind of stuff will work but I *know* you believe it, and that motivates me."

Speak with the instructor beforehand by phone or in person, and consider the following:

- ✔ Is the instructor standoffish or does she relate well with people?

- ✔ Is the instructor excited about the topics she addresses?

- ✔ Are you comfortable asking the instructor questions?

- ✔ Do you feel the instructor is interested in and responsive to your particular needs and situation?

If you can't speak directly with the instructor beforehand, try to speak with someone who has attended a program led by this instructor. Although getting information through someone else's eyes is better than having none at all, remember that each person looks for different qualities in an instructor and each person's perceptions are unique. You get the most-reliable information by talking with the scheduled speaker yourself.

### Organizational credentials

Be sure the information is in accordance with the best practices in the field. One way to verify this is to confirm that the organization is approved by the PMI as a Registered Education Provider (REP). You can read more about this status at the PMI Web site: www.PMI.org.

# Working with a mentor

A *mentor* is a person who'll be your coach, counselor, and ongoing source of expertise. In addition to clarifying general issues and concepts for you, your mentor can help you

- ✔ Find opportunities to apply your new skills and techniques on your job.
- ✔ Understand your organization's project-management policies, procedures, and practices.
- ✔ Help you deal with any difficulties you encounter when trying out your new techniques.
- ✔ Serve as an objective observer to assess how well you're putting your new skills into use.

In many ways, a mentor is like a personal tutor. As such, all of the considerations for choosing an instructor (see the previous section for more info) also apply when selecting a mentor. In addition, look for someone

- ✔ Whom you respect and who has successfully managed projects in your organization.
- ✔ Who understands the current project management policies, procedures, and practices in your organization.
- ✔ With whom you feel comfortable discussing difficult questions and situations.
- ✔ Who is willing and able to devote the time necessary to help you improve your project-management practices.

Working with a mentor is less structured than attending a predesigned training program. Therefore, to derive the most benefit from your relationship, agree with your mentor beforehand what topics and issues you'll address. Then develop specific indicators to describe how well you use your new tools and techniques. And finally, develop a schedule specifying the actions you'll take and the times you'll meet to review your experiences.

## Obtaining a professional certification

Attending a training program and working with a mentor can directly improve your project management skills, knowledge, and practices. However, professional certification goes one step further because it confirms your abilities to clients, employers, co-workers, and colleagues.

The most widely known and accepted credential in this field is the PMP certification awarded by the PMI. This credential confirms that you: have demonstrated a knowledge of project best-management practices (as described in the *Project Management Body of Knowledge* published by PMI); have attained a certain level of education and actual experience working in the field of project management; are committed to abide by the PMI professional code of conduct; and are committed to continued participation and learning in the field. You can find out more information about the PMP and other certifications that the PMI offers at www.PMI.org.

Although the credential signifies a certain level of achievement in the field, the real benefit comes through the knowledge you gain and the work you do to qualify for the certification.

# Bringing Improved Project Management Practices to the Workplace

*Knowing* best practices isn't the same as actually *using* them. To improve your project management in the workplace, you must first recognize situations where you can apply new techniques and approaches and be totally familiar with how to apply them. You also need to be willing to help others understand how to adopt the new practices, and you have to *unlearn* the ineffective practices you've been using.

This section can help you prepare an action plan to change your own practices and help other people improve theirs. The section also helps you recognize resources that can help you accomplish this plan.

# Using your new skills and knowledge

The key to incorporating your new skills and techniques into your normal work process is to use them early and often. Keep the following points in mind as you choose opportunities to use your new tools:

- ✔ **Choose one or two skills or techniques you want to begin using.** You may want to start using several techniques, so choosing only one can seem uncomfortable. Unfortunately, experience shows that making numerous changes in your work methods all at once only increases the chances that none of them will stick. Use the new skill until it's second nature to you. Then choose one or two more new skills and repeat the process.

- ✔ **Commit to using these skills or techniques in *every* situation that presents itself.** Your aim is to make these techniques a habit, a reflex action that you perform naturally. Therefore, remove the choice about whether to use them. Practice makes perfect when developing a new skill or technique. (Do I sound just like your old piano teacher?)

- ✔ **Begin with work activities that are small in scope and aren't in crisis mode.** Trying a new technique is difficult enough; don't initiate it when people are already in a panic, jumping down your throat and demanding immediate results.

- ✔ **Use your new techniques on any work assignment, even one that's not formally designated a *project*.** These techniques work on any work activity that has to produce a particular result in a specified time with set resources. You're looking for all opportunities where you can use your new approach.

- ✔ **Apply your techniques to new projects as well as projects in progress.** When you choose a project in progress, prepare a plan that takes you from today to your destination. Don't spend time critiquing what you should have done on the completed portion of your project.

- ✔ **Use your new techniques even if your organization has no formal project-management processes and procedures in place.** Remember, you're using these techniques to guide your approach to your assignments, not to change the entire organization's approach.

- ✔ **Use your skills and knowledge whether you're a team member or a project leader.** Just be sure to clearly define the boundaries of the assignment you address.

- ✔ **Don't worry about having permission to use these new tools.** As long as you don't directly violate existing organizational procedures and guidelines, people are more interested in the results you produce than the methods you use.

Prepare a written *action plan* detailing specific steps to use your new skills and knowledge and when to take them. Because adopting your new techniques is a project in itself, include the same information in your action plan as in your project plan.

When developing your action plan, be sure you describe the exact behaviors you want to adopt. For example, suppose writing your project objectives clearly and unambiguously is the behavior you want to adopt. You can describe this desired behavior in two ways:

> **Not specific:** "Describe desired outcomes clearly."

> **Better:** "For every project objective statement, develop one or more measures to assess the extent of the objective's achievement. For every measure, develop one or more performance specifications that represent success."

The second alternative provides a much clearer picture of the exact behaviors you want to adopt.

In addition, identify one or more people who agree to observe your performance and provide objective and honest feedback. Specify the dates you'll meet with them to discuss their assessments.

## Sharing your new skills and knowledge

As you become more comfortable with your new abilities and can see your improved performance, you may want to share your new skills with other people. Unfortunately, if you tell your team members to use this wonderful, new technique, they'll probably respond with skepticism and resistance. Remember, you needed some time to understand and recognize the potential value of these tools before you were willing to try them out.

The following suggestions can help you be most effective in sharing your new skills and knowledge:

✔ **Show people that a technique works and how to use it instead of trying to convince them.** In other words, use the techniques yourself and let people see your process and its effects. People are always interested in techniques they believe will help achieve their goals.

✔ **Don't use technical jargon or acronyms.** Let the tool or technique speak for itself. Instead of telling people how a Linear Responsibility Chart helps you clarify team-member roles, just mention (if someone asks you) that you use a simple table that displays how each resource relates to each project activity.

> ✔ **Focus on the results you achieved with the tool, rather than the ways to use the tool.** People adopt a practice because they think it helps them achieve their goals, not because someone else told them it was a good idea. When people see you succeeding at your assignments, they'll ask whether you're using any special techniques.

### Through your organization's intranet

As you look for ways to share your information with a wider audience, consider establishing a location on the organization's intranet that's dedicated to general and organization-specific project-management issues and information. Items may include

> ✔ Current versions of the organization's project-management-related policies and procedures.
>
> ✔ All announcements, memos, and written materials addressing project-management issues and activities in the organization.
>
> ✔ Examples of well-prepared planning and control documents from actual organization projects.
>
> ✔ Professional and technical articles on project-management topics.

### Through informal means

Another way to share the information is to hold informal sessions during lunch or after work where the group addresses selected topics. Consider asking speakers from inside and outside the organization to discuss general techniques and approaches and organization-specific issues and practices.

### Through your organization's project management office

You can also offer to work with the organization's Project Management Office (PMO) to help improve project-management practices; if one doesn't exist, you can suggest that the organization create one.

A PMO serves as a central point for an organization's project-management-related activities. Typically, PMOs fall in one of two categories:

> ✔ A relatively small group of people who do some or all of the following tasks:
>
>   • Develop, distribute, and maintain organization project-management-related policies, procedures, and forms
>
>   • Help develop staff project-management capabilities through mentoring or by providing more formal training
>
>   • Maintain a central file of information about ongoing or completed organization projects

- Consolidate information and prepare periodic progress reports for organization projects

- Maintain a library of general project-management-related information

- Maintain the project-management portion of the organization's intranet

- Perform or help other people perform selected project-management activities in ongoing projects

✔ The organizational unit to which all project managers are functionally assigned. In addition to performing the preceding activities, select managers in this unit manage the organization's more complex efforts.

# Chapter 19

# Monitoring Project Performance with Earned Value Management

*B*ecause you're reading this chapter, I assume you're looking for a way to assess your ongoing project performance. *Earned Value Management (EVM),* formerly called *Earned Value Analysis (EVA)* is a technique that helps determine your project's schedule status and cost status from your resource expenditures alone. EVM is particularly useful for identifying potential problems on larger projects.

To get the most from this chapter, you should have some prior experience or knowledge in project management. This chapter helps you better understand EVM by defining it, discussing how to determine and interpret variances, and showing you how to use it in your project.

## Defining Earned Value Management (EVM)

Monitoring your project's performance entails determining whether you're ahead or behind schedule and over or under budget. However, just *comparing* your actual expenditures with your budget normally can't tell you whether you're over or under budget. With EVM, you can *assess* your project's schedule and expenditures based on your expenditures to date.

In this section, I explain many of the terms you may encounter when you do an EVM analysis.

# Understanding the EVM formulas

Suppose you're three months into your project and you've spent $50,000. According to your plan, you shouldn't have spent $50,000 until the end of the fourth month of your project. You appear to be over budget at this point, but you can't tell for sure. Either of the following situations may have produced these results:

- You may have performed all the scheduled work, but you paid more than you expected to — this means you're on schedule but over budget.

- You may have performed more work than you scheduled, but you paid exactly what you expected — this means you're on budget and ahead of schedule.

Of course, many other situations can produce these same results. However, when you use EVM, you get a more accurate picture of the true reasons for this behavior.

With EVM, you determine

- **Cost variance:** The difference between what you planned to spend by a certain date and what you really spent that represents a true cost savings or a loss.

- **Schedule variance:** The difference between what you planned to spend by a certain date and what you really spent that's due to being ahead of or behind schedule.

- **Estimate at completion:** The total amount you'll spend to perform this task if your present spending pattern continues to the end of the task.

Figure 19-1 depicts the key information in an EVM analysis. As illustrated, the difference between *planned* and *actual* expenditures on the date of the report is due to the combined effects of a schedule delay and a cost savings.

You can calculate cost and schedule variances as well as the estimate at completion from the following information:

- **Planned Value (PV)** is the approved budget to complete a particular Work Breakdown Structure (WBS) element, also referred to as the *Budgeted Cost of Work Scheduled (BCWS)*. See a complete discussion of the WBS in Chapter 4.

- **Actual Cost (AC)** is the total costs actually incurred for work done during a specified time period on a particular WBS element, also referred to as the *Actual Cost of Work Performed (ACWP)*.

- **Earned Value (EV)** is the approved budget for work done during a specified period for a particular WBS element, also referred to as the *Budgeted Cost of Work Performed (BCWP)*.

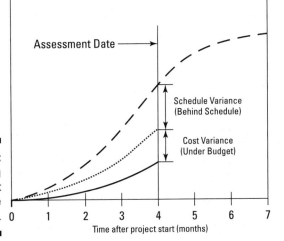

Planned Value
(PV)

— — —

Earned Value
(EV)

...............

Actual Cost
(AC)

——

**Figure 19-1:**
Monitoring
project
performance
using EVM.

Cost and schedule variances are defined mathematically as follows:

$$\text{Cost variance (CV)} = \text{EV} - \text{AC}$$

$$\text{Schedule variance (SV)} = \text{EV} - \text{PV}$$

In other words, the cost variance for a specified date is the difference between the *budgeted amount* for the work that you've actually completed and the *actual amount* you've spent. The schedule variance is the difference between the *budgeted amount* for what you *planned to do* and the *budgeted amount* for what you *actually did*.

You can determine the *cost variance percentage* (*CVP*) and the *schedule variance percentage* (*SVP*) using the following formulas:

$$\text{CVP} = \text{CV} \div \text{EV} \times 100$$

$$\text{SVP} = \text{SV} \div \text{PV} \times 100$$

Table 19-1 illustrates that a positive variance indicates something desirable (that is, you're either under budget or ahead of schedule) and a negative variance indicates something undesirable (you're either over budget or behind schedule).

| Table 19-1 | Interpretations of Cost and Schedule Variances | | |
| --- | --- | --- | --- |
| *Variance* | *Negative* | *Zero* | *Positive* |
| Cost | Over budget | On budget | Under budget |
| Schedule | Behind schedule | On schedule | Ahead of schedule |

Finally, determine the Estimate at Completion (EAC), your estimate of the total expenditures for completing a WBS element based on the expenditure history to date as follows:

Estimate at Completion (EAC) = AC ÷ EV × total budget

This estimate is simplistic because it assumes that the spending patterns through the end of the project will be the same as they've been up until now. Of course, circumstances may change the expenditure pattern or you may choose to alter the pattern if you've been overspending and want to get back on track.

## Looking at a simple example

These terms and definitions (see the previous section) are easier to understand when you consider an example. Suppose you're planning to conduct a series of telephone interviews. Your interview guide is ready and each phone interview is independent of the others. You state the following in your project plan:

- ✔ Your project will last ten months.
- ✔ You plan to conduct 100 interviews each month.
- ✔ You plan to spend $300 to conduct each interview.
- ✔ Your total project budget is $300,000.

During your first month, you do the following:

- ✔ Conduct 75 interviews
- ✔ Spend a total of $15,000

Because you planned to conduct 100 interviews in the first month and you only conducted 75, you're behind schedule. But, because you planned to spend $300 per interview and you only spent $200 ($15,000 ÷ 75 interviews = $200 per interview), you're under budget. This example gives you a chance to calculate and then interpret the EV information.

1. **Determine the planned value, earned value, and actual costs at the end of the month as follows:**

   Planned Value (PV) = Budgeted amount for the 100 interviews you planned to conduct in the first month

= 100 interviews × $300 per interview = $30,000

Actual Costs (AC) = Actual costs for the first month

= $15,000

Earned Value (EV) = Budgeted amount for the 75 interviews you actually conducted in the first month

= 75 interviews × $300 per interview = $22,500

2. **Determine your cost and schedule performance during the month as follows:**

Cost Variance (CV) = EV − AC

= $22,500 − $15,000 = $7,500

Schedule Variance (SV)       = EV − PV

= $22,500 − $30,000 = −$7,500

3. **The cost variance and schedule variance percentages are as follows:**

CVP = CV ÷ EV × 100

= $7,500 ÷ $22,500 × 100 = 33%

SVP = SV ÷ PV × 100

= −$7,500 ÷ $30,000 × 100 = −25%

The CVP and SVP make sense when you look at the actual numbers for the month. You originally planned to spend $300 per interview, but in the first month you actually spent $200 per interview ($15,000 actual costs ÷ 75 interviews conducted). The actual cost per interview is $100 (or 33 percent) less than your planned per-interview cost ($100 ÷ $300 × 100 = 33%). This means you're 33 percent under budget, just as your CVP indicates.

You originally planned to conduct 100 interviews in the first month, but you only finished 75. You actually conducted 25 percent fewer interviews in the first month than you planned (100 − 75) ÷ 100 × 100 = −25%). This means you're 25% behind schedule, just as the SVP indicates.

If your work continues in the same fashion for the remainder of your project, your total project expenditures at completion will be as follows:

EAC = AC ÷ EV × total budget = $15,000 ÷ $22,500 × $300,000 = $200,000

In other words, if you continue to perform your interviews for $200 each rather than the planned $300 each, you'll spend two-thirds of your total planned budget to complete all 100 interviews.

Although you don't need a formal EVM analysis on a project this simple, in a project with 50 to 100 activities or more, an EVM analysis can help identify general trends in your project's cost and schedule performance. The earlier you identify such trends, the more easily you can counteract — or enjoy — them.

## Determining the reasons for observed variances

Positive or negative values of the cost or schedule variances indicate your project performance isn't going exactly as you planned. After you determine that a variance exists, you want to figure out the reason(s) so you can take corrective actions (if the variance is negative) or be sure you continue what you've been doing (if the variance is positive).

Possible reasons for positive or negative cost variances are as follows:

✔ Your project requires more or less work to complete a task than you originally planned.

✔ The people performing the work are more or less productive than planned.

✔ The actual unit costs of labor or materials are more or less than planned.

✔ Actual organization indirect rates are higher or lower than you originally planned. (See Chapter 7 for a discussion of indirect rates and how they can affect your project expenditures.)

Possible reasons for positive or negative schedule variances are as follows:

✔ Work is running ahead of or behind schedule.

✔ The project requires more or less work than you originally planned.

✔ People performing the work are more or less productive than planned.

## Applying EVM to Your Project: The How-To

If your project is more complex than the previous example (see the earlier section "Looking at a simple example"), you may consider using EVM to help control performance. By providing cost and schedule performance assessments of both the total project and its major parts, EVM allows you to identify the likely problem areas so you can take the most effective corrective actions.

The following example in this section presents a more realistic illustration of how EVM can support insightful analysis of your project's performance.

Suppose the Acme Company has awarded a contract for the production of two specialized and complex corporate brochures to Copies 'R' Us. The contract calls for Copies 'R' Us to produce 500 copies of Brochure A and 1,000 copies of Brochure B. It further states that Copies 'R' Us will produce Brochure A at the rate of 100 per month and Brochure B at the rate of 250 per month. Production of Brochure A is to start on January 1 and production of Brochure B on February 1.

Table 19-2 depicts the project plan.

| Table 19-2 | Plan for Copies 'R' Us to Produce Brochures A and B | | | | |
|---|---|---|---|---|---|
| **Activity** | **Start** | **End** | **Elapsed Time** | **Number of Copies** | **Total Cost** |
| Brochure A | Jan 1 | May 31 | 5 months | 500 | $100,000 |
| Brochure B | Feb 1 | May 31 | 4 months | 1,000 | $100,000 |
| Total | | | | | $200,000 |

A quick glance suggests that Brochure A will cost $200 per copy ($100,000 ÷ 500 copies) and Brochure B will cost $100 per copy ($100,000 ÷ 1,000 copies).

Suppose it's the end of March, and you're three months into the project. Table 19-3 presents what has happened as of March 31.

| Table 19-3 | | Project Status as of March 31 | | |
|---|---|---|---|---|
| **Activity** | **Start** | **Elapsed Time** | **Number of Copies Produced** | **Total Cost** |
| Brochure A | Jan 1 | 3 months | 150 | $45,000 |
| Brochure B | Feb 1 | 2 months | 600 | $30,000 |
| Total | | | | $75,000 |

Your job is to figure out your schedule and cost performance to date and predict the outcome of the project if expenditure patterns stay the same.

1. **Determine your cost and schedule performance for the production of Brochure A through March 31.**

   PV = $200 per brochure × 100 brochures per month × 3 months = $60,000

   EV = $200 per brochure × 150 brochures = $30,000

   Cost variance (CV) = EV − AC

   $$= \$30{,}000 - \$45{,}000 = -\$15{,}000$$

   $$\text{CVP} \quad = CV \div EV \times 100$$

   $$= -\$15{,}000 \div \$30{,}000 \times 100 = -50\%$$

   Schedule variance (SV) = EV − PV

   $$\text{SV} \quad = \$30{,}000 - \$60{,}000 = -\$30{,}000$$

   $$\text{SVP} \quad = SV \div PV \times 100$$

   $$= -\$30{,}000 \div \$60{,}000 = -50\%$$

   Your analysis reveals that production of Brochure A is 50 percent behind schedule and 50 percent over budget.

2. **Determine your cost and schedule performance for the production of Brochure B through March 31.**

   PV = $100 per brochure × 250 brochures per month × 2 months = $50,000

   AC = $30,000

   EV = $100 per brochure × 600 brochures = $60,000

   $$\text{Cost variance (CV)} \quad = EV - AC$$

   $$= \$60{,}000 - \$30{,}000 = \$30{,}000$$

   $$\text{CVP} \quad = CV \div BCWP \times 100$$

   $$= \$30{,}000 \div \$60{,}000 \times 100 = 50\%$$

   Schedule variance (SV) = EV − PV

   $$\text{SV} \quad = \$60{,}000 - \$50{,}000 = \$10{,}000$$

   $$\text{SVP} \quad = SV \div BCWS \times 100$$

   $$= \$10{,}000 \div \$50{,}000 \times 100 = 20\%$$

   Your analysis reveals that production of Brochure B is 20 percent ahead of schedule and 50 percent under budget.

3. **Determine the overall status of your project by adding the individual cost and schedule variances for Brochures A and B.**

   Project Cost Variance = –$15,000 + $30,000 = $15,000

   Project Schedule Variance     = –$30,000 + $10,000 = –$20,000

4. **Determine your project estimate at completion by adding the individual estimates at completion for Brochures A and B.**

   EAC for Brochure A     = AC ÷ EV × Budget for Brochure A

   = $45,000 ÷ $30,000 × $100,000 = $150,000

   EAC for Brochure B     = AC ÷ EV × Budget for Brochure B

   = $30,000 ÷ $60,000 × $100,000 = $50,000

   EAC for the project     = EAC for Brochure A + EAC for Brochure B

   = $150,000 + $50,000 = $200,000

Table 19-4 shows all this information.

| Table 19-4 | Performance Analysis Summary | | | | | |
|---|---|---|---|---|---|---|
| | *PV* | *AC* | *EV* | *CV* | *SV* | *EAC* |
| Brochure A | $60,000 | $45,000 | $30,000 | –$15,000 | –$30,000 | $150,000 |
| Brochure B | $50,000 | $30,000 | $60,000 | $30,000 | $10,000 | $50,000 |
| Total | | | | $15,000 | –$20,000 | $200,000 |

If project production rates and costs remains the same until all the required brochures are produced, then:

✔ **You'll finish on budget.**

✔ **You'll finish five months late.**

Because Brochure A is being produced at only half the anticipated rate, finishing all of them will take twice the time originally planned.

# Calculating Earned Value

The key to a meaningful EVM analysis lies in the accuracy of your estimates of EV. To determine EV, you must estimate

- How much of a task you've completed to date.
- How much of the task's total budget you planned to spend for the amount of work you've achieved.

If you assume a direct relationship between the portion of a task you've completed and the amount of funds you *should have* spent and if you've completed 60 percent of the task, then you should have spent 60 percent of the total task budget.

For tasks with separate components, like printing brochures or conducting telephone surveys, determining how much of a task you've completed is straightforward. However, if your task entails an integrated work- or thought-process with no easily divisible parts (such as designing the brochure), the best you can do is to make an educated guess.

Figure 19-2 illustrates the following three approaches to estimate EV in different situations. The milestone method and 50/50 method allow you to approximate EV without estimating the portion of a task that you've completed. Choosing which of the three methods to use for your project requires you to weigh the potential for accuracy against the possible misleading conclusions from subjective data.

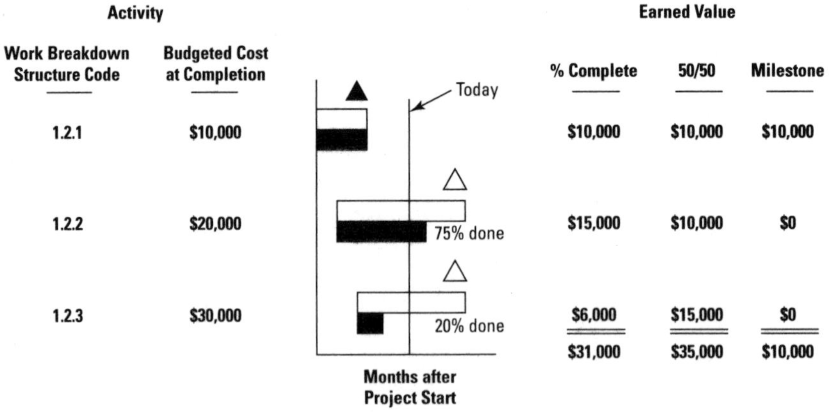

| | Activity | | | | Earned Value | | |
|---|---|---|---|---|---|---|---|
| **Work Breakdown Structure Code** | **Budgeted Cost at Completion** | | | | **% Complete** | **50/50** | **Milestone** |
| 1.2.1 | $10,000 | | Today | | $10,000 | $10,000 | $10,000 |
| 1.2.2 | $20,000 | | 75% done | | $15,000 | $10,000 | $0 |
| 1.2.3 | $30,000 | | 20% done | | $6,000 | $15,000 | $0 |
| | | | | | $31,000 | $35,000 | $10,000 |

Months after Project Start

**Figure 19-2:** Three ways to define earned value.

✔ **Percent-complete method:** EV is the product of the fraction representing activity-completion and the total activity budget.

This method is potentially the most accurate if you correctly determine the fraction of the activity you have completed. However, because that estimate depends on your subjective judgment, this approach is also most vulnerable to errors or purposeful manipulation.

✔ **Milestone method:** EV is zero until you complete the activity, and it's 100 percent of the total activity budget after you complete it.

The milestone method is the most conservative and the least accurate. You expect to spend some money while you're working on the task. However, this method doesn't allow you to declare EV greater than $0 until you've completed the entire activity. Therefore, you'll always appear over budget while you perform the activity.

✔ **50/50 method:** EV is zero before you start the activity, 50 percent of the total activity budget after you start it, and 100 percent of the activity budget after you finish the activity.

The 50/50 method is a closer approximation to reality than the milestone method because you can declare an EV greater than $0 while you perform the task. However, this approximation can inadvertently mask overspending.

Figure 19-2 compares the accuracy of the three different methods for a simple example. Task 1.2 has three subtasks: 1.2.1, 1.2.2, and 1.2.3. For this illustration, assume that you know the following amounts of completed work on each subtask:

✔ Subtask 1.2.1 is complete.

✔ Subtask 1.2.2 is 75 percent complete.

✔ Subtask 1.2.3 is 20 percent complete.

The EV of Task 1.2 is the sum of the EVs for each of the three subtasks in Task 1.2. According to the percent-complete method, the actual EV should be $31,000. (Remember, you can only use this method if you can *accurately* estimate the percentage of the entire task that you've completed.)

Suppose you've completed 30 percent of a task with a $10,000 budget. Arguably, you should have spent about 30 percent of your budget, or $3,000, to complete 30 percent of the work on the task. However, the 50/50 method approximates your EV at $5,000 (50 percent of the total budget for the task). So, if your actual cost for the work was $4,000, you're $1,000 over budget. However, using the 50/50 method to estimate your EV, your expenditures of $4,000 (compared with your approximated EV of $5,000) appear to be $1,000 *under* budget.

When you use either the 50/50 method or the milestone method, observe the following guidelines to improve the accuracy of your EV estimates:

✔ Define your lowest-level activities (see Chapter 4 on Work Breakdown Structures) to be relatively short, usually two weeks or less.

When you determine activity status for your progress assessments, most activities will not have started or will be finished, thereby increasing the accuracy of your EV estimates.

✔ Subdivide activities into components of short duration, determine the EV for each of these components, and add them together to determine the EV for the entire activity. Again, doing this increases the chances that activities either will not have started or will be finished when you do your performance assessment.

# Part VI
# The Part of Tens

The 5th Wave                    By Rich Tennant

"Sorry Cedric, the King cut my budget for additional fools. He said the project already had enough fools on it."

## In this part . . .

*H*aving hundreds of pages of detailed information to guide you through your project's ups and downs is nice. However, when a crisis hits, you may want to reference a few handy tips to head off potential disaster.

Just like every *For Dummies* book, this part gives you tidbits of interesting information to access as needed. I share tips for how to plan a project and how to be a better project manager.

And don't stop now! This part also includes two helpful appendixes. Appendix A lists definitions for a wide range of technical terms you may encounter as you proceed in your project management assignments. In Appendix B, I present the usual order for the planning and control activities that I discuss throughout this book.

# Chapter 20

# Ten Questions to Help You Plan Your Project

*W*hen you begin a project, you always feel the pressure to jump in and start working to meet the aggressive time schedules. You want to be sure it's planned out before you start, but you're not quite sure where to begin, and you're always under pressure to start producing results.

Answer the following questions in this chapter to be sure you've completely identified all the work your project will require.

## What's the Purpose of Your Project?

As soon as you're assigned to your project, get a clear and complete picture of its significance. Determine the following:

✔ What situation(s) led to your project?

✔ Who had the original idea?

✔ Who else hopes to benefit from it?

✔ What would happen if your project weren't done?

An accurate appreciation of your project's purpose can lead to better plans, a greater sense of team-member commitment, and improved performance. See Chapters 2 and 3 for discussions of a project's purpose.

# Whom Do You Need to Involve?

Knowing early whom you need to involve allows you to plan for their participation at the appropriate times. Involving these people in a timely manner ensures their input will be available when it's needed and lets them know that you value and respect their contributions.

As you determine who may play a role in your project's success, categorize them as follows:

- ✔ **Drivers:** People looking for your project's results.
- ✔ **Supporters:** People who can help your project succeed.
- ✔ **Observers:** People interested in your project.

After you have this comprehensive list, decide whom to involve and when and how you want to involve them. (See Chapters 3, 9, and 10 for more information on identifying project audiences.)

# What Results Will You Produce?

Specify all the outcomes you expect your project to produce. Be sure that you describe clearly each product, service, or impact; make the outcomes measurable and include performance targets.

Confirm that your project's drivers (see Chapter 3) believe these outcomes meet their needs and expectations. See Chapter 2 for more discussion about framing your project objectives.

# What Constraints Must You Satisfy?

Identify all information, processes, and guidelines that may restrict your project activities and your performance. Distinguish between the following:

- ✔ **Limitations:** Restrictions that people outside your project team set.
- ✔ **Needs:** Restrictions that you and your project team members establish.

When you know your constraints, then you can plan to minimize their effect on your project. See Chapter 2 for more information on project constraints and ways to overcome them.

# What Assumptions Are You Making?

As soon as you begin thinking about your project, document all assumptions about its key information because each of these assumptions leads to one or more project risks that you may choose to plan for in advance. Continue adding to your list of assumptions as you develop the parts of your plan. Update your plans whenever an assumption changes or you find out its actual value. See Chapter 2 for further details about project assumptions.

# What Work Must Be Done?

Identify all the activities required to complete your project so you can assign responsibilities for them, develop schedules, estimate resource needs, give specific tasks to team members, and track your project during performance. For each activity, specify

- ✔ **The work to be done:** The processes and steps that each activity requires.

- ✔ **Inputs:** All people, facilities, equipment, supplies, raw materials, funds, and information necessary to perform each activity.

- ✔ **Results you expect:** Products, services, or situations that you expect each activity to produce.

- ✔ **Interdependencies:** Activities that you must complete before you can start the next one; activities you can start after you've completed the current one.

- ✔ **Duration:** The actual calendar time to perform each activity.

See Chapter 4 for information on describing project work.

# When Does Each Activity Start and End?

Develop a detailed schedule with clearly defined activities and frequent intermediate milestones. Having this information allows you to give team members precise guidance on when to perform their assignments. This information also supports your ongoing monitoring and control of work in progress. Take the following into account when you create your schedule:

✔ **Duration:** The actual calendar time to perform each individual activity.

✔ **Interdependencies:** What you must finish before you can begin your activity.

✔ **Resource availability:** When you need particular resources and when they're available.

See Chapter 5 for more information on how to develop a project schedule.

# Who Will Perform the Project Work?

Knowing who will perform each task and how much effort they'll have to devote allows you to plan for their availability and more accurately estimate the overall project budget. Specify the following information for all people who need to work on your project:

✔ Identify each person by name, by position description or title, or by the skills and knowledge required to do the assignment.

✔ When more than one person must work on the same activity, describe the specific roles and how these people can coordinate their efforts.

✔ Specify the level of effort each person has to invest.

✔ If a person will work less than full time on an activity, specify exactly when she will work.

Consult with the people who'll perform the project tasks to develop this information. See Chapter 6 for help with estimating personnel requirements.

# What Other Resources Do You Need?

Identify all equipment, facilities, services, supplies, and funds that you need to perform your project work. Specify how much of each resource you'll need and when. See Chapter 7 for more discussion on how to identify nonpersonnel resources.

# What Can Go Wrong?

Identify those parts of your project that may not go according to plan. Decide which risks pose the greatest dangers to your project's success and develop plans to minimize their negative effects. See Chapter 8 for information on how to address project risks.

# Chapter 21

# Ten Tips for Being a Better Project Manager

S uccessful project management depends not just on what you do, but also on how you do it. Your attitudes and behaviors toward people affect how they respond to you. If I could, I'd place a large *Tip* icon on this entire chapter. This chapter can help you successfully win people's support.

## Be a "Why" Person

Look for the reasons behind requests and actions. Understanding *why* helps ensure you respond appropriately to team members, upper managers, and all other project audiences (which increases people's motivation and buy-in.) First find out reasons for yourself, and then share the information with other people. (Check out Chapter 2 to find out more about how you can be a *why* person.)

## Be a "Can-Do" Person

Look at all problems as challenges and find ways to overcome them. Be creative, flexible, and tenacious. Keep working at the problem until you solve it. (Flip to Chapters 2, 4, 5, and 12 for more on how to be a tenacious problem solver.)

# Say What You Mean; Mean What You Say

Communicate clearly. Be specific, letting people know exactly what you mean. Tell them what you want them to know, what you want them to do, what you'll do for them. You may think that being vague gives you more leeway. In reality, being vague just increases the chances for misunderstanding. (Check out Chapter 13 for ways to communicate clearly.)

# View People as Allies, Not Adversaries

Focus on common goals, not individual agendas. Making people feel comfortable encourages brainstorming, creative thinking, and the willingness to try new ideas. But viewing and treating people as adversaries can put them on the defensive and encourage them to become enemies. (Refer to Chapters 3 and 14, where I tell you how to get people on your side.)

# Respect Other People

Focus on people's strengths rather than their weaknesses. Find a quality in each person that you can respect. People work harder and enjoy their work more when they're around others who appreciate them. (See Chapter 14 to find more helpful tidbits on respecting people.)

# Think Big Picture

Keep events in perspective. Understand where you want to go and how your plan will get you there. Recognize the effect of your actions on current and future efforts. Share your vision with other people. (Flip to Chapters 2 and 14 for ways you can keep your project elements in perspective.)

# Think Detail

Be thorough. If you don't think your project's issues through, who will? The more clearly you describe your intended results, the more easily people can recognize the associated benefits. And the more clearly you define your intended work, the more often people will ask important and insightful questions — *and* believe that they can perform the work successfully. Clarity leads to increased personal motivation and reduced chances of mistakes. (Check out Chapters 2 and 4 for tips on thinking in detail.)

# Assume Cautiously

Take the time to find out the facts; use assumptions only as a last resort. With every assumption comes a risk that you're wrong. The fewer the assumptions, the more confidence you can have in your plan.

# Acknowledge Good Performance

Take a moment to acknowledge good performance. Tell the person, tell the person's boss, tell team members, and tell the person's peers. Recognizing good performance confirms to a person the accuracy and value of his work; your praise tells a person that you appreciate his efforts, which motivates him to work with you and other team members on future projects.

When acknowledging a person's performance, mention the quality of the results he accomplished as well as the effort he invested. Be specific — tell the person exactly what he did or produced that you appreciate. Provide your feedback promptly. (See Chapter 14 for more about acknowledging good performance.)

# Be a Manager and a Leader

Attend to people as well as to information, processes, and systems. Create and share your vision and excitement in addition to a sense of order and efficiency. Encourage people to strive for outstanding results and provide the guidance and support to achieve those results. (See Chapter 14 for more information about management and leadership.)

# Appendix A

# Glossary

**accountability:** Feed back of consequences to people based on their performance.

**activities plan:** A table that lists planned project *activities* with their start and end dates.

**activities report:** A table that lists project *activities* with their planned start and end dates and their actual start and end dates.

**activity:** The work required to move from one *event* to the next in a project.

**activity-in-the-box diagram:** A *network diagram* format in which boxes represent *events* and *activities*.

**activity-on-arrow diagram:** A *network diagram* format in which circles represent *events* and arrows represent *activities*.

**assumption:** A statement about uncertain information that you take as fact as you conceive, plan, and perform a project.

**audience:** A person or group that supports, is affected by, or is interested in a project.

**authority:** The ability to make binding decisions about a project's products, schedule, *resources,* and work packages.

**availability:** The portion of time a person is actually on the job.

**background:** How and why a project was created, by whom, and its organizational and external environmental contexts; the **why** of a project.

**backing in:** The process of identifying *activities* and estimates of *duration* that equal the project's allotted time by starting at the end of a project and working back toward the beginning.

**backward pass:** The process of calculating *latest* allowable *start* and *finish* *dates* for each *activity* by beginning at the end of a project and moving back along each path toward the start of the project.

**bar chart:** See *Gantt chart.*

**baseline:** The plan that guides project *activities* and supports project performance assessments.

**budget:** A detailed, time-phased estimate of the costs to perform a project.

**benefit-cost analysis:** A comparative assessment of a project's anticipated benefits with respect to its estimated costs.

**business-requirements document:** A description of the business needs that a requested product, service, or system must address.

**centralized-organization structure:** An organizational approach in which individual units in an organization handle the specialty work for all projects.

**champion:** A person in a high position in the organization who strongly supports a project; will advocate for the project in disputes, planning meetings, and review sessions; and will take the necessary actions to help ensure the project's successful completion.

**confirmation of purchase order:** A reply from a vendor agreeing to provide a requested item and reconfirming the price and associated costs.

**constraint:** A restriction that limits what your project must achieve, how and when you can do it, and for what cost.

**cost report:** A table listing *activities* with their planned costs and their actual expenditures.

**critical path:** A sequence of *activities* in a project that takes the longest time to complete.

**delegation:** Assigning some or all of your authority to someone else.

**deliverable:** See *event.*

**dependency:** A relationship between *activities* in which one activity must finish before the other can start.

**dependency diagram:** See *network diagram.*

**detailed budget estimate:** An itemization of estimated costs for each project *activity*.

**direct costs:** Expenditures for *resources* used solely for a particular project.

**distribution list:** List of people who receive a written project-communication.

**driver:** A person who has some authority in defining the results of a project; a person for whom you perform the project.

**duration:** The actual calendar time to perform an *activity;* also called *span time*.

**earliest finish date:** The earliest possible date to finish an *activity*.

**earliest start date:** The earliest possible date to start an *activity*.

**Earned Value Management:** An analysis approach based solely on *resource expenditures* to determine whether a project is over or under budget and whether the project is ahead of or behind schedule.

**efficiency:** The proportion of time a person spends solely on project work, not including organizational tasks not related to specific projects.

**event:** A significant occurrence in the life of a project; also called a *milestone*.

**fast tracking:** Performing two or more *activities* at the same time to reduce the overall project time.

**feasibility study:** A formal investigation to determine the likelihood of successfully performing certain work or achieving certain results.

**float:** See *slack time*.

**forward pass:** The process of calculating *earliest start* and *finish* dates for all *activities* by beginning at the start of a project and moving along each path toward the end of the project.

**functional manager:** A person responsible for the business and technical performance of *activities* in a specialized, organizational function (such as finance or engineering).

**functional organization structure:** An organizational approach in which separate units address the same specialty in various *functional* groups.

**Gantt chart:** Named after Henry Gantt, a graph comprised of bars on a timeline that depict when each *activity* starts, is performed, and ends.

**general and administrative costs:** *Expenditures* that help keep an organization operational.

**Human Resources Matrix:** A table depicting the people who work on each lowest-level project *activity* and the total effort each person invests in each activity.

**indirect costs:** *Expenditures* for personnel, materials, equipment, facilities, and services that support projects but aren't tracked by the projects.

**initiator:** The person who had the original idea leading to a project.

**key-events list:** A table that lists planned project *events* and their dates.

**key-events report:** A table that lists project *events* with their planned and actual dates.

**kickoff meeting:** A formal meeting to announce the start of a project.

**known unknown:** Project information which you don't have but someone else does have. See also *unknown unknown*.

**labor report:** A table that lists *activities* with their planned and actual work effort.

**latest finish date:** The latest possible date you can finish an *activity* and still complete the project in the fastest possible time.

**latest start date:** The latest possible date you can start an *activity* and still complete the project in the fastest possible time.

**level of effort:** See *person effort*.

**limitation:** A restriction on a project's results, time frames, *resources,* or approach.

**Linear Responsibility Chart:** A matrix depicting the role each project *audience* plays in each project *activity*.

**Market Requirements Document:** A formal request for a product to be developed or modified.

**matrix organization structure:** An organizational approach where people from different parts of the organization work on project teams for less than or equal to 100 percent of their time.

**micromanagement:** A person's excessive, inappropriate, and unnecessary involvement in a task that he assigns to another person.

**milestone:** See *event.*

**network diagram:** A flowchart illustrating the order of a project's *activities.*

**noncritical path:** A sequence of *activities* whose delays (up to a certain amount) don't affect the length of the overall project.

**objective:** A project's desired outcome or result; comprised of a statement, one or more *performance measures* (or indicators), and *performance targets* (or specifications).

**objective statement:** A brief narrative description of what a project is to achieve.

**observer:** A person interested in the *activities* and results of a project.

**overhead costs:** *Expenditures* for *resources* that are too difficult to subdivide and allocate directly to one *activity.*

**performance measure:** An indicator for assessing achievement of an *objective.*

**performance period:** Time span of monitored project progress.

**performance target:** The value of a *performance measure* that constitutes success.

**person effort:** The actual amount of time a person works on an *activity.* Also called *work effort.*

**Person Loading Chart:** A table that displays a *person's* planned *effort* level each day, week, or month on a specific project *activity.*

**Person Loading Graph:** A graph that displays a *person's* planned *effort* level each day, week, or month on a specific project *activity;* also called a *resource histogram.*

**PERT (program evaluation and review technique):** A *network diagram* analysis that uses three estimates (optimistic, pessimistic, and most likely) to describe the range of an *activity's* span time.

**PERT chart:** A *network diagram* in the *activity-on-the-arrow* format.

**post-project evaluation:** A meeting that reviews a project's experiences, recognizes people's achievements, takes steps to ensure repetition of good practices in future projects, and develops plans to avoid problems of the current performance in future projects.

**power:** The ability to influence the actions of other people.

**precedence diagram:** A *network diagram* in *activity-in-the-box* format.

**primary information source:** The location of original information.

**process:** A routine series of steps to perform a particular function.

**productivity:** The results produced per unit of time on an *activity*.

**program:** Ongoing efforts to accomplish a long-range mission; comprised of a series of *projects*.

**progress Gantt chart:** A *Gantt chart* that depicts *activity* progress by shading in the appropriate portion of the activity's bar.

**project:** A work assignment that has specific outcomes, definite start and end dates, and established *resource* budgets.

**project abstract:** Highlights of key project information. Also called a *project summary* or a *project profile*.

**project activity level:** The hierarchical position in the project *Work Breakdown Structure (WBS)*.

**project charter:** A document issued by upper management that specifies the project manager's authority to spend time and *resources* on project work and to direct project personnel.

**project control:** The process of ensuring that project work goes according to plan and that the desired results are achieved.

**project dashboard:** An information display that depicts key indicators of project performance in a format that resembles an instrument panel on a dashboard.

**project director:** See *project manager*.

**project leader:** See *project manager*.

**project leadership:** The process of creating and sharing the project vision and *strategy*, eliciting people's commitment and support, and sustaining ongoing motivation.

**project management:** The process of guiding a project from the beginning, through the performance, to the closure; includes planning, organizing, and control.

**project manager:** The person ultimately responsible for the successful completion of a project.

**project planning:** Developing a course of action to accomplish specific objectives within established *constraints* and a defined environment.

**project profile:** See *project abstract.*

**project request:** A written request by a group within an organization to have a project performed.

**project summary:** See *project abstract.*

**purchase order:** A formal submission from a *procurement department* to a vendor for an item.

**purchase requisition:** A written, approved request from a *project manager* to the *procurement department* for an item.

**purpose:** A brief statement of a project's *background, scope,* and *strategy.*

**resource:** Personnel, material, or equipment needed to perform an *activity.*

**resource histogram:** See *Person Loading Graph.*

**responsibility:** The commitment to achieve specific project results.

**risk:** The possibility that a project may not achieve a product, schedule, or *resource* target because of an unexpected occurrence.

**risk factor:** A situation that may cause one or more project *risks.*

**risk management:** The process of identifying possible *risks,* assessing their potential effect on the project, and developing and implementing plans for minimizing any negative effects.

**rough order of magnitude (ROM) estimate:** An estimate of costs based on a general sense of the work a project will entail.

**scope:** A high-level description of the work a project will entail; the what of the project.

**Scope Statement:** See *Statement of Work*. Term also refers to a comprehensive description of a project's *objectives* and results, *constraints* and *assumptions*, and work to be done.

**secondary information source:** A report that cites information from another source; see also *primary information source*.

**Skills Roster:** A table that depicts people's skills, knowledge, and interests.

**slack time:** The amount of time that an *activity* can be delayed without affecting the length of the overall project. Also called *float*.

**span time:** See *duration*.

**span time estimate:** A project manager's best sense of an *activity*'s *duration*.

**stakeholder:** A person or group that a project needs or that will be affected by the project.

**Statement of Work (SOW):** Written confirmation of a project's products and the terms and conditions of project work.

**strategy:** An approach to the major work of a project; the **how** of a project.

**supporter:** A person who helps perform a project.

**task:** The second level of detail in a *Work Breakdown Structure;* also called a *level-2 breakout*.

**unknown unknown:** Project information that you don't have because it doesn't exist yet. See also *known unknown*.

**weighted labor rate:** A combination of a person's hourly salary and associated *indirect costs*.

**Work Breakdown Structure (WBS):** An organized, hierarchical representation of all work in a project.

**Work Breakdown Structure dictionary:** A compilation of key descriptive information about all lowest-level work in a *Work Breakdown Structure*.

**work effort:** See *person effort*.

**work-order agreement:** Written description of work to be done by people or groups within an organization in support of a project.

# Appendix B

# Combining the Techniques into Smooth Flowing Processes

- - - - - - - - - - - - - - - - - - - - - - - - - - - - - - - - - - - - - - - - -

*Y*ou'll use the tools and techniques in this book many times during your project — as you hammer out your initial plan, monitor work in progress and its results, and continue to tweak the details as necessary. Even though you can't avoid surprises or changes as your project unfolds, you can provide logical order for your project's planning and its control activities. This sense of order discourages bad surprises (and their faithful companions — change and redirection). In this appendix, I illustrate this order.

## *Preparing Your Project Plan*

Figure B-1 depicts the steps in project planning and the parts of the plan that you produce along the way.

When you receive a project assignment, you can take the following steps:

1. **Clarify the reasons for the project and the desired outcomes.**

   Figure B-1 illustrates the two important activities you need to do:

   - Identify the audiences who will have a say in your project.

   - Get all info from the audiences and written sources about expectations.

   Perform these two activities interactively because the initial statement of your assignment may suggest additional audiences. Those audiences, in turn, may raise more issues to address. The outcomes from these activities are a Statement of Work (SOW) and an Audience List. (See Chapter 2 for preparing a SOW and Chapter 3 for putting an Audience List together.)

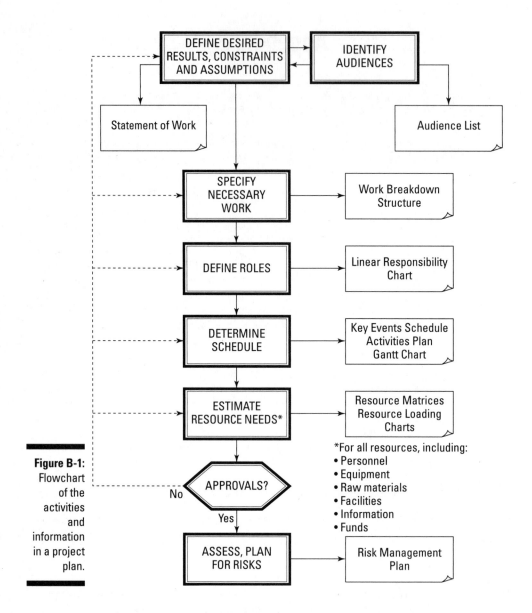

**Figure B-1:**
Flowchart
of the
activities
and
information
in a project
plan.

2. **After you know all the results your project is to achieve, identify the work required to produce them.**

Record this information in a Work Breakdown Structure (WBS). See Chapter 4 for information on how to prepare a WBS.

3. **Consider the WBS and the Audience List together to decide on each audience's roles and responsibilities for each project activity.**

   Display this information in a Linear Responsibility Chart. (See Chapter 10 for a discussion on preparing a Linear Responsibility Chart.)

4. **Create and analyze a network diagram of the activities from the WBS to develop a schedule that your project drivers require and that your project supporters believe is possible.**

   Display your final schedule in a Key-Events List, an Activities Plan, or a Gantt chart. (See Chapter 5 for how to prepare and display a project schedule.)

5. **Estimate your resource needs, which you display in a Resource Matrix, Resource Loading Chart, and a project budget.** See Chapters 6 and 7 for preparing and displaying project resource needs.

6. **Identify, analyze, and plan for any significant project risks.** See Chapter 8 for suggestions on dealing with project risks.

Continue working on each step in this initial process until all project drivers and supporters agree with and support your results.

# Controlling Your Project during Performance

Figure B-2 illustrates the steps you routinely perform to monitor and control your project throughout its performance.

To monitor and control your project, follow these steps:

1. **At the start of each performance period, reconfirm that the necessary people and resources are available and scheduled in accordance with your current project plan.**

2. **At the end of each period:**

   • **Gather activity start and end dates, milestone dates, resources expenditures, and the results of quality assessments.**

   • **Compare the actual results with planned results, identify any issues or problems, and take any necessary corrective actions.**

3. **Report your progress for the period to your project audiences.** See Chapters 12 and 13 for information on tracking, assessing, and reporting project performance.

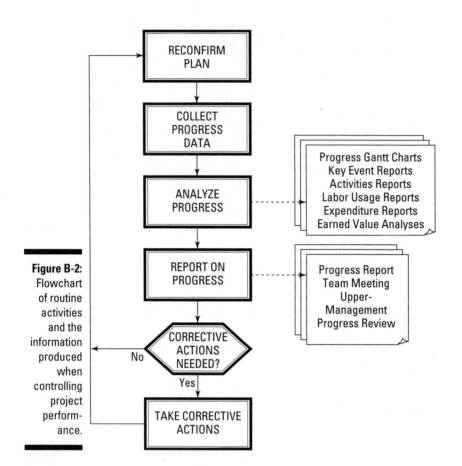

**Figure B-2:**
Flowchart of routine activities and the information produced when controlling project perform-ance.

# Index

## • F •

• *T* •